The United States in World War II

Uncovering the Past: Documentary Readers in American History
Series Editors: Steven Lawson and Nancy Hewitt

The books in this series introduce students in American history courses to two important dimensions of historical analysis. They enable students to engage actively in historical interpretation, and they further students' understanding of the interplay between social and political forces in historical developments.

Consisting of primary sources and an introductory essay, these readers are aimed at the major courses in the American history curriculum, as outlined further below. Each book in the series will be approximately 225–250 pages, including a 25–30 page introduction addressing key issues and questions about the subject under consideration, a discussion of sources and methodology, and a bibliography of suggested secondary readings.

Published

Paul G. E. Clemens
The Colonial Era: A Documentary Reader

Sean Patrick Adams
The Early American Republic: A Documentary Reader

Stanley Harrold
The Civil War and Reconstruction: A Documentary Reader

Steven Mintz
African American Voices: A Documentary Reader, 1619–1877

Robert P. Ingalls and David K. Johnson
The United States Since 1945: A Documentary Reader

Camilla Townsend
American Indian History: A Documentary Reader

Steven Mintz
Mexican American Voices: A Documentary Reader

Brian Ward
The 1960s: A Documentary Reader

Nancy Rosenbloom
Women in American History Since 1880: A Documentary Reader

Jeremi Suri
American Foreign Relations Since 1898: A Documentary Reader

Carol Faulkner
Women in American History to 1880: A Documentary Reader

David Welky
America Between the Wars, 1919–1941: A Documentary Reader

William A. Link and Susannah J. Link
The Gilded Age and Progressive Era: A Documentary Reader

G. Kurt Piehler
The United States in World War II: A Documentary Reader

The United States in World War II

A Documentary Reader

Edited by G. Kurt Piehler

A John Wiley & Sons, Ltd., Publication

This edition first published 2013
Editorial material and organization © 2013 Blackwell Publishing Ltd

Blackwell Publishing was acquired by John Wiley & Sons in February 2007. Blackwell's publishing
program has been merged with Wiley's global Scientific, Technical, and Medical business to form
Wiley-Blackwell.

Registered Office
John Wiley & Sons, Ltd., The Atrium, Southern Gate, Chichester, West Sussex, PO19 8SQ, UK

Editorial Offices
350 Main Street, Malden, MA 02148-5020, USA
9600 Garsington Road, Oxford, OX4 2DQ, UK
The Atrium, Southern Gate, Chichester, West Sussex, PO19 8SQ, UK

For details of our global editorial offices, for customer services, and for information about
how to apply for permission to reuse the copyright material in this book please see our website
at www.wiley.com/wiley-blackwell.

The right of G. Kurt Piehler to be identified as the author of the editorial material in this work has
been asserted in accordance with the UK Copyright, Designs and Patents Act 1988.

Library of Congress Cataloging-in-Publication Data

The United States in World War II : a documentary reader / edited by G. Kurt Piehler.
     p.   cm. – (Uncovering the past : documentary readers in American history)
   Includes bibliographical references and index.
   ISBN 978-1-4443-3120-2 (pbk. : alk. paper) – ISBN 978-1-4443-3119-6 (hardcover)
 1. World War, 1939–1945–United States–Sources.   2. World War, 1939–1945–Participation,
American–Sources.   3. World War, 1939–1945–Personal narratives, American.   I. Piehler, G. Kurt.
   D769.A2U65 2013
   940.53′73–dc23

                                        2012016531

A catalogue record for this book is available from the British Library.

Cover image: *United We Win*, poster, 1943. Photograph by Alexander Liberman.
National Archives and Records Administration, NWDNS 44-PA-370.
Cover design by Simon Levy

Set in 10/12.5pt Sabon by SPi Publisher Services, Pondicherry, India
Printed and bound in Singapore by Markono Print Media Pte Ltd

1   2013

Contents

List of Illustrations

Series Editors' Preface

Primary sources have become an essential component in the teaching of history to undergraduates. They engage students in the process of historical interpretation and analysis and help them understand that facts do not speak for themselves. Rather, students see how historians construct narratives that recreate the past. Most students assume that the pursuit of knowledge is a solitary endeavor; yet historians constantly interact with their peers, building upon previous research and arguing among themselves over the interpretation of documents and their larger meaning. The documentary readers in this series highlight the value of this collaborative creative process and encourage students to participate in it.

Each book in the series introduces students in American history courses to two important dimensions of historical analysis. They enable students to engage actively in historical interpretation, and they further students' understanding of the interplay among social, cultural, economic, and political forces in historical developments. In pursuit of these goals, the documents in each text embrace a broad range of sources, including such items as illustrations of material artifacts, letters and diaries, sermons, maps, photographs, song lyrics, selections from fiction and memoirs, legal statutes, court decisions, presidential orders, speeches, and political cartoons.

Each volume in the series is edited by a specialist in the field who is concerned with undergraduate teaching. The goal is not to offer a comprehensive selection of material but to provide items that reflect major themes and debates; that illustrate significant social, cultural, political, and economic dimensions of an era or subject; and that inform, intrigue, and inspire undergraduate students. The editor of each volume has written an introduction that discusses the central questions that have occupied historians in this field

xii Series Editors' Preface

and the ways historians have used primary sources to answer them. In addition, each introductory essay contains an explanation of the kinds of materials available to investigate a particular subject, the methods by which scholars analyze them, and the considerations that go into interpreting them. Each source selection is introduced by a short headnote that gives students the necessary information and a context for understanding the document. Also, each section of the volume includes questions to guide student reading and stimulate classroom discussion.

Today we remember and celebrate World War II as the "Good War" fought by the "greatest generation." The United States, Great Britain, the Soviet Union, and France defeated the forces of fascism and military aggression represented by Germany, Italy, and Japan. Yet G. Kurt Piehler's *The United States in World War II: A Documentary Reader* provides a more complicated picture of the war. This compilation, which includes public speeches, newspaper editorials, diary entries, personal letters, and government reports, shows that Americans were initially reluctant to enter the conflict in Europe. President Franklin D. Roosevelt maneuvered the nation toward war by shaping public opinion in support of the Allies in ways that were provocative and not always truthful. After the attack on Pearl Harbor, however, the nation rallied in support of the war, but the road to victory was difficult and the outcome far from certain. Military and diplomatic advisors often disagreed about the best strategy to pursue, and issues such as when to start a "second front" in Europe against Germany divided the Allies. The monumental decision to drop atomic bombs on Japan to end the war, while applauded at the time, in retrospect poses moral and political questions about the necessity and consequences of deploying what General Dwight D. Eisenhower called "that awful thing." The atomic bomb may have ended one war, but it drove a wedge between the United States and the Soviet Union that launched a frightening Cold War of potential nuclear destruction for the next four and one-half decades. The Holocaust, the genocidal slaughter of millions of Jews and other innocent civilians perpetrated by the Nazis, also raises nagging questions. Could the United States have done more to rescue Holocaust victims before entering the war and subsequently shape its military tactics to disrupt the slaughter? The dropping of atomic bombs and the timid response to the Holocaust, as well as air raids on civilians by both sides, painfully illustrate that morality was not simple.

Not only did World War II have a profound impact on world affairs, but it also transformed the United States at home. African Americans and women benefited in particular. The wartime ideology of democracy against fascism encouraged blacks to demand their civil rights at a time when racial discrimination still flourished in the United States. In addition, the manpower shortage in defense industries provided African Americans, women, and other minorities with unprecedented employment opportunities, which in turn created new expectations for the postwar period that would be difficult to reverse. The war also ended the Great Depression of the 1930s, and increased the power of labor unions, which brought new economic gains to working people and raised their hopes for the future. However, confronted by sweeping change many Americans sought to reverse the advances made by blacks, women, and organized labor, waging a political and social counterassault that contained but did not eradicate these improvements.

In this volume G. Kurt Piehler offers an informative introductory essay that presents challenging themes on many aspects of World War II. He then follows this with a splendid array of documents accompanied by headnotes and questions in each chapter that will encourage students to create history and show that facts do not speak for themselves. Students can analyze the views of politicians, diplomats, generals, ordinary soldiers, clergymen, journalists, women and men, black, white, and Hispanic Americans, as they struggled to fight an epic world war abroad and at home.

Steven F. Lawson and Nancy A. Hewitt,
Series Editors

Source Acknowledgments

The editor and publisher gratefully acknowledge the permission granted to reproduce the copyright material in this book:

1.5   [*Rutgers University*] *Anthologist*, 16 (February 1941): 14–15, 21. Reprinted with permission of Rutgers University

2.1   Jan K. Herman, *Battle Station Sick Bay: Navy Medicine in World War II* (Annapolis: Naval Institute Press, 1997), pp. 25–27. Copyright © Jan K. Herman. Reprinted with the kind permission of the author

2.5a   George C. Marshall, *The Papers of George Catlett Marshall, Volume 3: "The Right Man for the Job," December 7, 1941–May 31, 1943*, ed. Larry I. Bland and Sharon Ritenour Stevens (Baltimore: Johns Hopkins University Press, 1991), p. 276. © 1991 The Johns Hopkins University Press. Reprinted with permission of The Johns Hopkins University Press

3.1   Alvin Kernan, *Crossing the Line: A Bluejacket's World War II Odyssey* (Annapolis: Naval Institute Press, 1994), pp. 44–46. Copyright © Alvin Kernan

3.2   John Hersey, "The Battle of the River," *Life*, November 23, 1942, pp. 111–115. Copyright © 1942 The Picture Collection Inc. All rights reserved

3.4   John Ciardi, *Saipan: The War Diary of John Ciardi* (Fayetteville: University of Arkansas Press, 1988), pp. 58–61. Copyright © 1988. Reprinted with the permission of The Permissions Company, Inc., on behalf of the University of Arkansas Press, www.uapress.com

3.5 Sam Smith, interview with G. Kurt Piehler and Cynthia Tinker, February 13, 2004, Center for the Study of War and Society, University of Tennessee, Knoxville, Tennessee. Reprinted with permission of Center for the Study of War and Society, University of Tennessee

4.1 George C. Marshall, *The Papers of George Catlett Marshall*, Volume 3: *"The Right Man for the Job," December 7, 1941–May 31, 1943*, ed. Larry I. Bland and Sharon Ritenour Stevens (Baltimore: Johns Hopkins University Press, 1991), pp. 454–455. © 1991 The Johns Hopkins University Press. Reprinted with permission of The Johns Hopkins University Press

4.3 Dwight David Eisenhower, *The Papers of Dwight David Eisenhower, The War Years: III*, ed. Alfred D. Chandler, Stephen E. Ambrose, and others (Baltimore: Johns Hopkins University Press, 1970), pp. 1908, 1915–1918. © The Johns Hopkins Press. Reprinted with permission of The Johns Hopkins University Press

4.5 Letters from Paul Fergot, Paul Fergot Papers, Wisconsin Society of Wisconsin, Madison, Wisconsin. Available online at http://www.wisconsinhistory.org/. Reprinted with permission of Wisconsin Historical Society

4.6 Emiel W. Owens, *Blood on German Snow: An African American Artilleryman in World War II and Beyond* (College Station: Texas A & M University Press, 2006), pp. 60–62, 65–66. Reprinted with permission of Texas A & M University Press

5.4 LEAGUESBORO-ON-THE-AIR No. 24. Black Market. Folder 40, Box 21, League of Women Voters of New Jersey Records, MC-1082, Special Collections and University Archives, Rutgers University Libraries, New Brunswick, New Jersey. Reprinted with permission of League of Women Voters of New Jersey and Rutgers University, New Brunswick, New Jersey

5.5 Summary of Meeting on Care of Mothers and Children of the Newark Defense Council. File, Newark Defense Council (Unpublished Manuscript), New Jersey Room, Newark Public Library, Newark, New Jersey

5.6 "Wartime Influence on Juvenile Delinquency" and "Delinquency in New York State" from Christian Commission for Camp and Defense Communities, "Church Letter on War Communities," No. 2 (December 1942), pp, 2–14, File 13, Box 5, RG 18, Federal Council of Churches Records, Presbyterian Historical Society, Philadelphia, Pennsylvania. Reprinted with permission of Presbyterian Historical Society

6.1   Extracts from Donald M. Nelson, *Arsenal of Democracy: The Story of American War Production* (New York: Harcourt, Brace, 1946), pp. 185–186, 246–251. Reprinted by permission of Houghton Mifflin Harcourt Publishing Company

6.2   Interview with Lee Wilson by Nadine Wilmot, June 22, 2006, pp. 19–20, 28–29, Regional Oral History Office, Bancroft Library, University of California, Berkeley, California. Also available online at http://bancroft.berkeley.edu/ROHO/projects/rosie/. Reprinted with permission of The Bancroft Library, University of California, Berkeley

6.4   Flyer Distributed by Montgomery Ward, January 11, 1943, Folder 6, Box 25, and Sewell Avery and Appeasement Folder 2, Box 26, Montgomery Ward Collection, American Heritage Center, University of Wyoming, Laramie, Wyoming. Reprinted with permission

6.5   Guards removing Sewell Avery in a chair from the Montgomery Ward building, April 28, 1944, Chicago, Illinois. © Bettmann/CORBIS

6.6   "Law and Responsibility," Editorial, *Washington Post*, April 28, 1944, p. 8. Reprinted with permission

6.7   Collection 54: Janice C. Christensen, US Women and World War II Letter Writing Project. Created and compiled by Judy Barrett Litoff. Bryant University Library, Smithfield, Rhode Island. Reprinted with permission

6.8   Dae D. Baird, Jr. Papers (09.0169), Institute on World War II and the Human Experience, Department of History, Florida State University, Tallahassee, Florida

7.1   John Haynes Holmes, "The Case of Jehovah's Witnesses," *The Christian Century*, July 17, 1940, pp. 896–898. Copyright © 1940 by the Christian Century. Reprinted with permission as an excerpted version

7.3   File: Negro Service, Box 209, Papers of American Jewish Welfare Board, Army Navy Division (I-180), Memo from Frederick Wells to Dr. Harry A. Wann, dated February 13, 1942 12:30 A.M., American Jewish Historical Society, Center for Jewish History, New York City. Reprinted with kind permission

7.4   Excerpt from *Journey to Washington* by Senator Daniel K. Inouye with Lawrence Elliott. Copyright © 1967 by Prentice Hall Inc.; copyright renewed 1995 by Senator Daniel K. Inouye. All rights reserved. Reprinted with permission of Simon & Schuster Inc.

7.5   John Modell (ed.), *The Kikuchi Diary: Chronicles from an American Concentration Camp: The Tanforan Journals of Charles Kikuchi*

(Urbana: University of Illinois Press, 1973), pp. 56–57, 81–83. Copyright © 1973 by the Board of Trustees of the University of Illinois. Used with permission of the University of Illinois

7.6   Jacques E. Levy, *Cesar Chavez: Autobiography of La Causa* (Minneapolis: University of Minnesota Press, 1975), pp. 81–85. Reprinted with permission of University of Minnesota Press

8.1   Ferdinand M. Isserman, *Sentenced to Death: The Jews in Nazi Germany* (St. Louis: The Modern View Publishing Co., 1933), pp. 3–4, 25–27. Reprinted with permission of Ferdinand Isserman, Jr.

8.3   Jack Sutters (ed.), *American Friends Service Committee, Philadelphia, Volume 2, Part 1, 1932–1939*, in *Archives of the Holocaust*, ed. Henry Friedlander and Sybil Milton (New York: Garland, 1990), pp. 482–483. Reprinted with permission of Taylor & Francis Group LLC

8.4   Breckinridge Long, *The War Diary of Breckinridge Long: Selections from the Years 1939–1944*, ed. Fred L. Israel (Lincoln: University of Nebraska Press, 1966), pp. 128, 161, 282, 283, 307, 336–337. Reprinted by permission of the University of Nebraska Press. Copyright © 1966 by the University of Nebraska Press. Copyright renewed © 1944 by the University of Nebraska Press

8.6   "11 Allies Condemn Nazi War on Jews," *New York Times*, December 18, 1942, pp. 1, 10. Reprinted with permission of PARS International

8.7   Henry Morgenthau, "Personal Report to the President," in *The Abandonment of the Jews: America and the Holocaust 1941–1945*, ed. David S. Wyman, Vol. 8 (New York: Garland Publishing, 1990), pp. 194–202. Reprinted with permission of Taylor & Francis LLC

8.9   David Max Eichhorn, *The GI's Rabbi: World War II Letters of David Max Eichhorn*, ed. Greg Palmer and Mark S. Zaid (Lawrence: University Press of Kansas, 2004), pp. 188–190. Reprinted with permission of University Press of Kansas

8.10   Unpublished letter from photocopy of original letter, Simon Chilewich, personal collection of editor. Reprinted with kind permission of Sandy Chilewich

9.7   Diary entries, Friday and Saturday, August 10 and 11, 1945, Henry Stimson Diary, Manuscripts and Archives, Yale University Library, New Haven, Connecticut. (Also available on microfilm.) Reprinted with permission of Yale University Library, Manuscripts and Archives

9.8   "Wailing Shall Be in All the Streets," from *Armageddon In Retrospect and Other New and Unpublished Writings on War and Peace* by Kurt

Vonnegut, copyright © 2008 by the Kurt Vonnegut, Jr. Trust. Used by permission of G. P. Putnam's Sons, a division of Penguin Group (USA) Inc. and Random House UK

10.1   Henry R. Luce, "The American Century," *Life*, February 17, 1941, pp. 64–65. Copyright © 1941 The Picture Collection Inc. Used with permission. All rights reserved

10.3   Langston Hughes, "My America," *Journal of Educational Sociology*, 16 (February 1943): 334–336. Reprinted with permission of David Higham Associates Limited

11.1   Jack J. Toffey IV, *Jack Toffey's War: A Son's Memoir* (New York: Fordham University Press, 2008), pp. 214–215, 225–227, 229–230. Reprinted with permission of Fordham University Press

11.3a   "Wistful Vista II," *Harvard Crimson*, June 21, 1946, http://www.thecrimson.com/article.aspx?ref=469700. Reprinted with permission

11.3b   "The Counsellor and the Dean," *Harvard Crimson*, March 12, 1947, http://www.thecrimson.com/article.aspx?ref=471121. Reprinted with permission

11.4   Eli Ginzberg et al., *Breakdown and Recovery* (New York: Columbia University Press, 1959), pp. 115–117. Copyright © 1959 Columbia University Press. Reprinted with permission of the publisher

11.5   Mira Ryczke Kimmelman, *Life Beyond the Holocaust: Memories and Realities* (Knoxville: University of Tennessee Press, 2005), pp. 71, 73–75, 79. Reprinted with permission

12.1   Archibald MacLeish, "Memorials Are For Remembrance," *The Architectural Forum*, September 1944, pp. 111–112, 170. Courtesy of the Estate of Archibald MacLeish and Houghton Mifflin Harcourt

12.4   Tom Brokaw, National WWII Memorial Dedication, American Battle Monuments Commission, Washington, DC. Text available online at http://www.wwiimemorial.com/. Reprinted with kind permission of the author

12.5   Geoffrey Wheatcroft, "Munich Shouldn't be Such a Dirty Word," *Washington Post*, September 28, 2008. Copyright © Geoffrey Wheatcroft, 2008. Reprinted with kind permission of the author

Every effort has been made to trace copyright holders and to obtain their permission for the use of copyright material. The publisher apologizes for any errors or omissions in the above list and would be grateful if notified of any corrections that should be incorporated in future reprints or editions of this book.

Introduction

World War II has a powerful grip on the American imagination. Hailed by many as the "good war," it is often remembered as a conflict that united the American people behind the common purpose of defeating Nazi Germany, Fascist Italy, and Imperial Japan. It is a struggle that required over 15 million men and women to serve in uniform on battle fronts around the world.

In their classic study of the experience of the American soldier in World War II published by Princeton University Press in 1949, Samuel Stouffer and his colleagues wrote:

> Probably the strongest group code, except for the condemnation of expressions of flagrant disloyalty, was the taboo against any talk of a flag-waving variety. Accounts of many informal observers indicate that this code was universal among American combat troops, and widespread throughout the Army. The core of the attitude among combat men seemed to be that any talk that did not subordinate idealistic values and patriotism to the harsher realities of the combat situation was hypocritical, and a person who expressed such ideas a hypocrite. The usual term by which disapproval of idealistic exhortation was invoked was "bullshit," which conveyed a scornful expression of the superiority of the combat man's hard-earned, tough-minded point of view.[1]

[1] Samuel Stouffer et al., *The American Soldier: Combat and Its Aftermath*, 2 vols. (Princeton: Princeton University Press, 1949), 2: 150.

The United States in World War II: A Documentary Reader, First Edition.
Edited by G. Kurt Piehler. Editorial material and organization © 2013 Blackwell Publishing Ltd.
Published 2013 by Blackwell Publishing Ltd.

This outlook reflected the views of a generation that came of age during the 1920s and 1930s weaned on conflicting memories of World War I. Although America had played an important role in defeating Germany and saving France, the war had not been the "war to end all wars," nor had it "made the world safe for democracy." The generation that served in World War II was more overtly skeptical than their parents and they grumbled more. Infantrymen, especially, resented the short, brutish life they endured in order to get the job done.

With the passage of time, we have come to enshrine those who fought in World War II as part of the "greatest generation" that fought in the "good war." Or as World War II veteran and novelist Kurt Vonnegut observed, the United States "fought on the side of right and the Germans and Japanese on the side of wrong." But American participation cannot be told as a simple morality tale; reading the scores of public speeches, newspaper editorials, diary entries, personal letters, and countless other historical documents left by this generation will show there is much ambiguity, and a number of paradoxes, that surround this conflict – beginning with a consideration of how the United States entered World War II in the first place.

The worldwide depression of the 1930s destabilized the economies and governments of a number of countries, and allowed politicians with extreme views to seize power in Italy, Japan, Germany, and Spain. These leaders often gained a following with policies that implied war-like aims or direct aggression toward neighboring countries. In the 1930s, there existed little support for Americans to enter another foreign war, even though many were sympathetic to the plight of the victims of Japanese militarism, German Nazism, and Italian fascism. Secretary of State Henry Stimson denounced Japanese actions in Manchuria in 1932, but threatened neither military nor economic actions to reverse them. Within months of Hitler assuming the German Chancellorship in 1933, several Jewish groups, led by the Jewish War Veterans, organized public protests against his regime's anti-Semitic measures and started a boycott of German goods. African American leaders and newspapers denounced the Italian invasion of Ethiopia in 1935. Many American communists and other leftists in 1936 went to Spain to fight in defense of the Republican government against the forces of the fascist Francisco Franco and those sent by Germany and Italy. But the dominant impulse of American leaders was isolationism and the desire to avoid another European conflict. The US Congress passed a series of neutrality laws that sought to ensure Americans did not drift into another war. When war broke out in Europe in 1939, the United States officially declared neutrality.

Americans have understandably focused their attention on the role played by the United States in this conflict. But the United States did not fight alone; in fact, eventually achieving victory required the United States draw on the other members of the war-time alliance termed by President Franklin D. Roosevelt in 1942 the "United Nations." It would be the Soviet Union, not the United States, that fought the bulk of the German Army in Europe. It would be the British Royal Navy and the Royal Canadian Navy that bore the brunt of the Battle of the Atlantic. In the war in Asia, the bulk of the Japanese Army would fight against Chinese forces.

Of course, America's allies in this conflict did not always possess the purest motives. Although the Soviet Union and communist parties around the world had called for a common front to oppose the rise of fascism in the 1930s, Joseph Stalin, in August 1939, signed a Non-Aggression Pact with Nazi Germany. But this truce between two nations ruled by ruthless dictators proved to be fleeting, and in June 1941, Hitler invaded the Soviet Union and almost succeeded in capturing Moscow before the year ended. Many Americans, especially conservative isolationists, saw little ideological difference between the two regimes. If anything, Hitler seemed less threatening since he favored capitalist interests, and a number of American firms continued to do business as usual in Nazi Germany. In contrast, Stalin led the only communist nation in the world and embraced an ideology that officially espoused Karl Marx's call for workers to revolt against their capitalist overlords. Moreover, the Soviet Union had abolished capitalism and established state ownership of the means of production. Even more alarming to many Americans, Stalin embarked on a campaign to promote atheism within Russia in the 1930s.

Great Britain and the United States shared a common language and deeply rooted democratic traditions. But not all Americans saw Britain as an ally worth aiding or defending. For many non-interventionists, the Atlantic and Pacific Oceans still protected America from a direct invasion and they questioned whether American national security would be threatened if the Nazis conquered all of Europe. Others wondered why the United States should embrace a nation that ruled an empire and suppressed the aspirations of colonial peoples for independence, most notably in India. Furthermore, many Irish Americans still had vivid memories of the plight of their grandparents and parents fleeing British oppression of their homeland.

However, while hostilities among the European powers began in 1939, the road to war for the United States was not inevitable. In fact, if it were not for the controversial polices pursued by FDR after the fall of France in June 1940, the United States might conceivably have avoided entering another world war. Roosevelt took bold action, even if at times he wavered on whether he saw America's entrance in the war as inevitable. Militarily, Roosevelt convinced Congress to enact peace-time conscription and vote vast sums for rearmament. Not only did Roosevelt seek to ready America for war, but he responded favorably to Great Britain's calls for assistance. Initially, FDR offered Britain 50 of what he termed overage destroyers in return for the right to place American military bases in British possessions in the Western Hemisphere. After winning re-election in 1940, Roosevelt proposed loaning war material and munitions to Britain and argued that American national security depended on ensuring the survival of this island nation. Lend-Lease did pass Congress in 1941 and aid began to flow to Britain; after the Soviet Union entered the war, it would be extended to this nation as well.

The Roosevelt Administration took a number of provocative actions against Nazi Germany. Despite legal prohibitions forbidding Americans to serve in the armed forces of foreign powers, the federal government permitted Americans to serve with the British Royal Air Force and the Royal Canadian Air Force without losing their citizenship. Rhetorically, Roosevelt attacked Germany as a threat to Western civilization and even declared that if the Nazis were victorious, they would destroy all religious faiths. In his State of the Union Address to Congress in January 1941, he stressed the need to preserve the Four Freedoms: freedom of speech, freedom of religion, freedom from want, and freedom from fear. To ensure Britain received vitally needed supplies, American naval vessels would convoy merchant ships part of the way across the Atlantic. Although still officially neutral, the American Navy began to cooperate with the Royal Navy and the Royal Canadian Navy in locating German submarines. By autumn 1941, the US Navy would be engaged in undeclared naval war with German naval forces and, in turn, American naval and merchant ships would be attacked. But America's formal entry into World War II stemmed not from events in the North Atlantic but, rather, from those in Asia.

The United States had fought Germany once before, in 1917. During World War I, the United States had been allies with Japan and had played a key role in opening up Japanese society to the wider world. While tensions had existed between the two countries, most notably over American restrictions on Japanese immigration to the United States, the prospect of war remained distant. Moreover, after the devastating earthquake that destroyed much of Tokyo in 1923, Americans had opened up their purses to aid the victims of this natural disaster, which killed over 100,000 people in the Japanese capital.

In retrospect, the Japanese seizure of Manchuria in 1931 would set the two nations on the road to war. After coming to office, Franklin Roosevelt continued his predecessor's policy of non-recognition of the Japanese occupation of Manchuria. After full-scale war broke out between China and Japan in 1937, Roosevelt condemned Japanese actions in China in oblique terms. During a speech focusing on international affairs given in Chicago in

October, FDR invoked the analogy of doctors quarantining an infectious patient, and asked whether it was time for the international community to take similar action against aggressor nations. Couched only in generalities, FDR's speech managed to alarm those who wanted to avoid engaging in a foreign war at all costs. There were voices of protest against Japanese actions, and supporters of China organized a campaign to boycott Japanese goods and donate to charitable organizations aiding war victims.

In 1940, relations with Japan worsened after it formally aligned itself with Germany and Italy under the Tripartite Pact to form the Axis Alliance. The Japanese government's occupation of French Indochina with military forces further increased tensions with the United States. To protest these actions, the United States in 1941 placed embargoes on oil and steel shipments to Japan, while at the same time encouraging negotiations. In contrast to the war in Europe, where the Roosevelt Administration abandoned any hope of negotiating with Germany after 1939, there were efforts to find a peaceful settlement in Asia and to use economic sanctions to pressure Japan to back down. At the same time, the differences between the two nations were wide. Japan wanted both to retain its conquests in East Asia and an end to economic sanctions by the United States. For its part, the United States wanted Japan to withdraw from China and to end its alliance with Nazi Germany. Japanese leaders, facing an impending shortage of petroleum and unwilling to make major concessions to the United States, opted for war. On December 7–8, they attacked not just the United States at Pearl Harbor, but also British and Dutch colonies throughout Asia.

Pearl Harbor galvanized American public opinion behind the war. The next day (December 8), the United States declared war on Japan. Three days after that, Germany honored its commitments under the Axis Pact and declared war on the United States. Engaged in a global war of unprecedented scale, the United States and the allies that fought under the banner of the United Nations faced a daunting task. Nazi Germany controlled most of continental Europe and German troops could see the spires of the Kremlin outside of Moscow. In North Africa, German forces had the potential to overrun British forces in Egypt and advance into Palestine, threatening the nascent Jewish homeland. In the Pacific, within a matter of months, Japanese forces had captured the Dutch East Indies and a number of British colonies, including Burma, Malaysia, and Hong Kong. After destroying much of the American fleet at Pearl Harbor and capturing Singapore, the Japanese dominated the seas in East Asia and the Pacific, threatening to cut links to Australia and New Zealand.

The documents in this volume should dispel the notion that victory in World War II was easy. Until 1940, Americans had traditionally maintained a small standing army in peace-time, and when Pearl Harbor was attacked the armed forces were still mobilizing. To achieve victory, the military trained millions of civilians to fill the ranks of the Army, Navy, Army Air Force, Marines, and Coast Guard. All of the services, but especially the Army, struggled to categorize, clothe, feed, outfit, and train those who entered the ranks from farms and cities, those with professional degrees, and those who were functionally illiterate. Mistakes were made. For instance, Army Air Force aviators went through a sophisticated training cycle that could last up to two years. Men who formed such elite divisions as the 82nd Airborne received outstanding training. In contrast, infantry replacements might have only a few weeks of basic training before ending up in combat.

There were disagreements over how to achieve victory among FDR's own military advisors. Even before the United States entered the war, Roosevelt agreed with Britain to pursue a Germany first strategy. In 1942, many of FDR's military advisors, especially Admiral Ernest King, began to doubt the wisdom of concentrating on Europe and sought to devote more resources to the Pacific. Roosevelt insisted on adhering to a Europe first strategy and firmly exercised his prerogatives as commander in chief to make the final decision on this crucial matter. Moreover, Roosevelt and the US Army Chief of Staff George Marshall agreed with Stalin that it remained imperative for the Western Allies to open a second front to ensure the survival of the Soviet Union. This second front would not come until 1944, for a variety of reasons. Initially, America lacked men and material to execute such an invasion, most notably enough landing craft, and the British were resistant to bearing the majority role in such an assault. Instead, they wanted to take an indirect approach and favored securing North Africa and later invading Italy. As a result, the US Army began the land war against Germany and Italy not in Europe, but in North Africa. Moreover, the first Army units landing in Casablanca, Oran, and Algiers in November 1942 fought the pro-Nazi forces of Vichy France before meeting the German armies under Erwin Rommel. By May 1943, American and British forces had succeeded in defeating and capturing all German forces in North Africa. Further delaying the opening of the second front would be the decision to invade Sicily and, at the urging of Churchill, to attack the Italian mainland. The landing of American forces at Salerno on September 9, 1943, led to the collapse of Mussolini's fascist government, but nothing could be done to prevent German forces from moving down the boot of Italy to confront Allied forces. Not until June 4, 1944, would the Allies liberate Rome, and German resistance in Italy lasted until the very end of the war. Italy did not prove to be the "soft underbelly" of Europe that Churchill had predicted.

Churchill and British leaders wanted to delay opening the European front again by urging a campaign through the Balkans. This time Roosevelt firmly insisted that it was time to invade France. To lead this major amphibious assault and the land campaign that followed, American general Dwight D. Eisenhower was appointed as Supreme Commander of the Allied Expeditionary Force. His principal subordinates would be British, with Field Marshal Bernard Law Montgomery serving as ground commander, Sir Bertram Ramsay as naval commander, and Air Chief Marshal Sir Arthur Tedder coordinating the air effort.

On June 6, 1944, American, British, and Canadian forces, with smaller contingents from other Allied countries, stormed ashore in Normandy, France. Allied air superiority combined with the failure of German forces to mount an effective counteroffensive allowed the invading force to consolidate a beachhead. Two months of hard fighting followed before the Allies finally broke out of the dense hedgerow country that made up much of the Normandy Peninsula. German forces, while fighting tenaciously, by late July 1944 collapsed under the weight of the Allied offensive, and on August 25, Paris was liberated. In the halcyon days of late summer and early fall, many GIs expressed optimism that the war in Europe would be over by Christmas. But as Allied forces drew closer to the German border, resistance stiffened. For American forces, the largest battle of the war, the Battle of the Bulge, came in December 1944 as Hitler launched his last major offensive in the Ardennes forest. Total victory would not come until May 8, 1945, when Germany finally collapsed under the onslaught of both Soviet forces and those of the Western Allies.

In the Pacific, the Japanese and American forces struggled for naval dominance. In May 1942, Japanese forces sought to deliver a knockout blow to American defenses in the Pacific by capturing the strategically located island of Midway. Outnumbered, American forces not only halted the invasion, but American naval aviators managed to sink four Japanese aircraft carriers in the span of 30 minutes, decisively shifting the balance of power. After Midway, the United States would go on the offensive and begin the long struggle to destroy virtually the entire Japanese fleet, finally achieved at the Battle of Leyte Gulf in October 1944.

American strategy in the war against Japan also called for providing supplies to China through an airlift over the Himalayas and the reopening of a land route – the Burma Road – to supply this ally. The United States never committed a substantial number of land forces to the Asian mainland. Instead, the US Navy launched a series of successful amphibious invasions with the Marine Corps and, often joined by Army troops, captured a number of key strategic islands in the Central Pacific, with the goal of eventually attacking the Japanese home islands by air and land invasion. After successfully launching a campaign against Japanese forces in New Guinea, General Douglas MacArthur fulfilled his vow to return to the Philippines in 1944 and retake it from the enemy. By April 1945 with the invasion of Okinawa, US forces were able to directly attack one of the outer home islands.

Americans sacrificed their lives in defense of freedom, and more than 292,100 men and women in the armed forces were killed in this conflict; more died in World War II than in World War I, Korea, Vietnam, and the Persian Gulf Wars combined. But the toll was far worse for other countries. In sharp contrast, more than 24 million Russian combatants and civilians died. British military losses were slightly fewer at 271,311, but over 60,000 civilians were killed by German bombing. It is estimated that China lost over 1 million soldiers and as many as 10 million civilians. Would Americans have remembered World War II as the "good war" if it had endured these horrendous losses? Or faced the humiliation of surrender or occupation like Poland, the Netherlands, Belgium, France, and countless other countries in Europe and Asia?

In retrospect it appears obvious why Americans fought in World War II: to defeat Nazi Germany and Imperial Japan. But during the war itself many worried about the lack of ideological motivation of the average GI. General Marshall enlisted social scientists to ask why they fought and was dismayed at how little they knew about the goals of the war and their relative lack of hatred of the enemy. Once engaged in combat, most GIs stressed the importance of comradeship and the need not to let their buddies down. Prayer and religious beliefs sustained many GIs, although there was a fair share of atheists in foxholes. To indoctrinate and motivate new recruits, Marshall even enlisted the Hollywood director Frank Capra to make a series of films explaining to soldiers in training camps why they fought.

Most who fought were draftees, not volunteers. In fact, after the United States entered the war, the Roosevelt Administration eventually prevented those of draft age from volunteering because too many men wanted to avoid the infantry in favor of the Navy and Army Air Force. The burden of combat was not shared equally. A modern army fighting a global war depended upon mechanized transportation, and sophisticated weaponry required scores of soldiers to serve behind the lines. In an era without modern computer technology, many soldiers fought their war over the typewriter in order to move, feed, and keep track of those in service. Although the Army Air Force and US Navy routinely rotated aviators out of combat zones to serve as instructors, most infantrymen fought until they were killed, seriously wounded, or the war ended.

American success on the battlefield can certainly be traced to the bravery and determination of the American GI to see the job done. At the same time, American combatants generally had an advantage in the abundance of food, weapons, and munitions when in battle. In World War II, Germany still relied heavily on horse-drawn carriages for supplying and transporting infantry-men, while the United States and the British used trucks and jeeps. Americans, though, did not always have the best weapons: the American Sherman Tank was thinly armored, possessed modest armaments, and when hit by an enemy shell turned into a death trap because of its gasoline-powered engine. But while the German Panzers were tank-for-tank superior, the United States made up for the Sherman's shortcomings with greater numbers. The Germans by the end of the war managed to send aloft fighter jets, but they were no match for waves of British and American fighters. An American artilleryman, especially by 1944, often had a bottomless supply of artillery shells to fire.

The advantages the American GI had in terms of supplies and equipment were due to the unprecedented mobilization of the American economy in support of the war effort. Moreover, as the "Arsenal of Democracy," American factories and farms not only produced enough for US forces, but met many of the needs of the other Allies of the United Nations, especially Great Britain and the Soviet Union. A war-time economy not only increased the role of the federal government in managing the distribution of goods and services, but it quickly led to a full-employment economy that encouraged women to work outside the household to meet the burgeoning need for workers.

American productive capacity in World War II was remarkable, although not unique. One of the strengths of the Grand Alliance was the ability of Great Britain, the Soviet Union, and the United States to out-produce the Axis in all manner of war material. For instance, Britain in the desperate year of 1940, facing the possibility of a Nazi invasion and the onslaught of German bombers during the Battle of Britain, would still manage to produce 15,049 aircraft, and the United States, while only beginning to mobilize for war, turned out 12,804, while Germany finished 10,247 and Japan, 4,467. By 1944 the German production of planes peaked at 39,807 and the Japanese at 28,180, but they were dwarfed by the United States, which completed 96,318, with the Soviets contributing another 40,300 and the British 26,461. In terms of ship construction, the United States over the course of the war was able to build over 8,000 major vessels (warships and merchant ships), and the British completed slightly over 1,000. In contrast, Japan produced fewer than 600 and Germany never built enough surface warships to threaten Allied naval dominance in the Atlantic.[2]

[2] Richard Overy, *Why the Allies Won* (New York: Norton, 1995), p. 331.

Those who stayed on the home front, especially those working in defense factories, also contributed to victory. To become the arsenal of democracy required a massive expansion of the role of the federal government in every aspect of life. Businesses were told what they could produce, how much raw materials they could receive, and how much they could charge consumers for their products. Often their best employees were conscripted into the military. Wage increases were limited and workers lost the right to strike. For the first time, average American wage earners paid income taxes and were encouraged to make voluntary purchases of war bonds. A full-employment economy and the growing number of working mothers forced communities and employers to consider how to find adequate daycare facilities. Housing was in short supply and in major industrial centers, defense workers often lived in crowded, substandard housing. Americans would endure rationing of a number of food items, including meat, butter, and coffee. Gasoline would be rationed, and in early 1942, Detroit stopped making passenger automobiles for the duration of the war. In Great Britain, by comparison, rationing did not end until 1952.

Despite the hardships, life on the home front differed dramatically from the lives of those who served overseas and even from those of most other countries at war. In contrast to the other major belligerents – the Soviet Union, Great Britain, France, Germany, Japan, India – the continental United States never came under direct enemy attack by enemy bombers or faced invading armies. Moreover, even with rationing and the enormous resources devoted to defense production, Americans consumed more goods and services in 1944 than they did in 1940. These factors, combined with the relatively low casualties of this conflict, explain why so many Americans during the war and afterward saw it as a "good war."

But it was not a good war for all. Mobs attacked Jehovah's Witnesses because of their refusal to salute the American flag. After Pearl Harbor, Japanese Americans living on the West Coast were deprived of their civil liberties without trial and forced to enter internment camps run by the federal government. Racism still remained endemic in American society; the United States fought with a segregated military, and African Americans continued to be denied the right to vote through much of the South. Nonetheless, the demands for labor and the quest for freedom spurred a massive migration of African Americans from the South to the North and West in search of better-paying jobs and a better life.

There were expressions of hope. Despite the racism that permeated American society, many minority groups still remained hopeful of the potential promise of America. When given the chance to enter combat, many African Americans and Japanese Americans embraced the opportunity to serve their country. There were visions of a new world order, enunciated by the Republican presidential candidate Wendell Willkie, who envisioned an end to racial discrimination at home. Moreover, while African Americans endured discrimination in the North and West, they could exercise the right to vote.

Americans would confront one of the ugliest forms of racism when they liberated the Nazi death camps in 1945. By late 1942, Allied leaders were well aware of Nazi persecution of European Jewry, and on several occasions they issued public warnings demanding German leaders halt these atrocities or face war crimes trials after the war. But not until American troops started liberating Ohrdruf, Bergen-Belsen, Dachau, and other concentration camps in the closing months of the war did they witness the full extent of German atrocities. The stench of death from emaciated corpses greeted them in these camps, and soldiers' emotions ranged from rage and pity to sadness and helplessness. They were stunned by the testimony of the survivors they encountered, and many liberators took years to cope with the shock of what they witnessed. Many simply would not talk about it for decades. Over time, the Holocaust had a profound impact on the American memory of World War II. It played a role in ensuring a significant revisionist movement never emerged after 1945, and Americans over time came to understand that World War II was a necessary war. It also helped to discredit the respectability of racism within American society and remained particularly troubling to many white southern liberals. Could genocide be the ultimate outcome of racism carried to its logical extent?

Sadly, the crimes committed during the Holocaust reflected a much deeper ambiguity that surrounds World War II: the troubling decline in protections accorded to civilians. During the nineteenth and early twentieth centuries, statesmen, military leaders, and the nascent peace movement sought to codify and expand international law to protect civilians and keep them out of harm's way. During World War II many of these inhibitions vanished. In the 1930s Axis Powers initiated aerial attacks on civilians in Guernica in Spain and the Japanese in Nanking, China. As the war dragged on, the inhibitions about making civilians legitimate targets dissipated among British and American leaders.

The morality and the effectiveness of aerial bombing campaigns had been the subject of debate even before the war ended. Some of the documents included in this volume do not offer the last word on this topic, although they certainly suggest some of the complexity regarding the use of air power. Moreover, the debate over the use of the atomic bomb in 1945 has been oversimplified and often depicted as a stark choice between a costly land invasion that would kill over 100,000 GIs or the destruction of two Japanese cities and the killing of much of their civilian population through a nuclear attack. Although the historical record suggests that dropping the bomb did play a role in forcing Japan's surrender, the reader of this volume will need to consider what other factors may have played an equally important role: the Soviet entry into the war and the decision to modify the surrender offered to Japan. Unlike Germany, Japan did not surrender unconditionally but was allowed by the Allied victors to maintain the emperor on the throne.

In contrast to 1918, America, after achieving victory over Germany and Japan, did not retreat inward. Instead, World War II led to a profound evaluation by Americans of the place of the United States in the world. After World War I, many voices sought to return to traditional isolationism; now, the creation of a new international organization to replace the League of Nations enjoyed unprecedented support. The United States also established through the Bretton Woods agreement new international institutions, the World Bank and the International Monetary Fund, to stabilize the international order.

There remained conflicting visions for the postwar future. African Americans wanted a postwar society to be more just and there existed widespread support for the "Double V" campaign for victory against the forces of fascism overseas and an end to discrimination at home. Henry Luce, one of the nation's leading publishers, saw America assuming the role of a great power as a result of the war. Former Republican presidential candidate Wendell Willkie insisted that the United States must align itself with the cause of freedom and those colonial peoples seeking independence. A former member of Woodrow Wilson's war cabinet, Franklin D. Roosevelt supported the creation of a new international organization, the United Nations, to secure world peace in the postwar era, but he was also a firm practitioner of power politics.

However, the memory of World War II changed over time. In the years immediately following V-J Day, America initially showed little interest in building statues and other traditional war memorials. Not until the 1970s would the federal government build a memorial to victims of the Holocaust. A national World War II memorial would not be dedicated until the early 2000s.

For many Americans one of the great lessons of World War II was to stand up to totalitarian regimes and stop aggression wherever in the globe it occurred. During the Cold War many Americans perceived the Soviet Union as cut from the same cloth as Nazi Germany. Cold War warriors insisted that the United States must fight expansion anywhere in the world, even if it meant sending Americans to defend peasant villages in Korea and later Vietnam. Others wonder if the lessons of history were so simple, and whether it always remained a stark choice between appeasing totalitarians or going to war.

This volume seeks to provide a cross-section of documents that illustrate the history of World War II. It includes such widely read and circulated texts as the Atlantic Charter, Franklin D. Roosevelt's address to Congress after the Japanese attack on Pearl Harbor, and the opening preamble of the Charter for the United Nations. It also contains once top-secret memoranda and minutes of meetings that plotted American strategy against the enemy. The voices of citizen soldiers and war workers are represented through excerpts from memoirs, diaries, oral histories, and correspondence. To gain a flavor for the times, this work includes a radio script, the lyrics of a popular song, and images of such commonplace items as a ration book.

The World War II generation left us scores of documents, but there are gaps. GIs serving at home and around the globe wrote millions of letters, and unfortunately most of them have been lost, especially the ones written to them. Most GIs were constantly on the move and often had little choice but to destroy correspondence they received. In an era when political leaders, such as Henry Stimson, still relied on correspondence and kept extensive diaries, we have insights into the great decisions made by public servants. But FDR, the only president to win election to four terms, and even create a presidential library to preserve his Administration's records, has left us little written documentation that unveils his innermost thoughts.

One major caveat should be observed in reading the documents: the specter of censorship and self-censorship. Servicemen and servicewomen had their letters censored by their commanders to ensure that military secrets would not fall into the hands of the enemy. The military remained particularly sensitive that troop and ship movements would not be revealed in correspondence. Self-censorship often led GIs, and also journalists covering the war, to say little about the brutal and destructive world of combat so as not to worry loved ones at home. Moreover, Gerald Linderman and other historians seeking to understand the social history of the American GI have emphasized the chasm that existed between officers and enlisted men: officers censoring the mail no doubt inhibited what enlisted men wrote in their letters. The same problem applies to journalistic accounts written during the war. Overseas reporters with the armed forces had to submit their articles to military censors who often broadly interpreted their mandate to restrict the flow of information. Furthermore, the same standard was applied to photographs, with military censors placing strict restrictions on what could be viewed by the American public.

In this volume, every effort has been made to render the documents as they were written and published. As a result, grammatical errors, misspellings, or other mistakes are left to stand. In many cases the documents had to be abridged, but portions dropped have been indicated with ellipses (i.e., ...). Of course, the transcription of a handwritten letter or diary, while improving legibility, does lose some of the intimacy.

No short collection of documents can do full justice to the World War II experiences. If this volume is successful it will spark interest to further explore the history of the conflict. The bibliography offers one place to begin to learn more. There exist several institutions with outstanding collections of material related to this conflict and they have placed some of their gems on their websites. Among the most important are the US National Archives in Washington, DC, the Library of Congress, the presidential libraries of Franklin D. Roosevelt, Harry S. Truman, and Dwight D. Eisenhower, the US Army Heritage and Education Center in Carlisle, Pennsylvania, and the Institute on World War II and the Human Experience at Florida State University. The Rutgers Oral History Archives has placed online over 500 life-course interviews with World War II veterans.

Every community has a unique story to tell in this conflict. Many hosted military bases that have long since been put to other uses or reverted back to a state of nature. Others were home to important factories that made armaments crucial to victory. Colleges and universities played an especially important role in the war effort, providing their expertise to improve radar, develop more effective weapons, find substitutes for material that were in short supply, and develop medicines to improve the health of overseas combatants. Many campuses hosted military training units and offered their professors as instructors to meet the need for more engineers, physicians, and Japanese speakers. It is hoped this text will encourage readers to discover the history of their own communities in World War II.

Chapter 1   The Controversial War

1 Henry Stimson, Diplomatic Note, 1932

Historians traditionally consider World War II as beginning when Nazi Germany invaded Poland on September 1, 1939. But Japan's first act of aggression against China occurred in 1931 with the invasion of Manchuria. Although not a member of the League of Nations and still adhering to a formal policy of isolationism, the United States protested this invasion. President Herbert Hoover's Secretary of State Henry L. Stimson determined that the United States would exert diplomatic pressure on Japan to encourage it to withdraw from Manchuria. Neither Hoover nor Stimson was willing to take military action to protect China or to impose economic sanctions against Japan, but they issued the following protest and also lent their support to the League of Nations to resolve the conflict.

The Secretary of State to the Ambassador of Japan (Forbes)
Washington, January 7, 1932—Noon

7. Please deliver to the Foreign Office on behalf of your Government as soon as possible the following note:

"With the recent military operations about Chinchow, the last remaining administrative authority of the Government of the Chinese Republic in

The United States in World War II: A Documentary Reader, First Edition.
Edited by G. Kurt Piehler. Editorial material and organization © 2013 Blackwell Publishing Ltd.
Published 2013 by Blackwell Publishing Ltd.

South Manchuria, as it existed prior to September 18th, 1931, has been destroyed. The American Government continues confident that the work of the neutral commission recently authorized by the Council of the League of Nations will facilitate an ultimate solution of the difficulties now existing between China and Japan. But in view of the present situation and of its own rights and obligations therein, the American Government deems it to be its duty to notify both the Imperial Japanese Government and the Government of the Chinese Republic that it cannot admit the legality of any situation *de facto* nor does it intend to recognize any treaty or agreement entered into between those Governments, or agents thereof, which may impair the treaty rights of the United States or its citizens in China, including those which relate to the sovereignty, the independence, or the territorial and administrative integrity of the Republic of China, or to the international policy relative to China, commonly known as the open door policy; and that it does not intend to recognize any situation, treaty or agreement which may be brought about by means contrary to the covenants and obligations of the Pact of Paris of August 27, 1928, to which Treaty both China and Japan, as well as the United States, are parties."

State that an identical note is being sent to the Chinese government.

STIMSON

Source: US Department of State, *Foreign Relations of the United States, Japan: 1931–1941, Volume 1* (Washington, DC: US Government Printing Office, 1943), p. 76.

2   William E. Dodd, Letter to Franklin D. Roosevelt, 1934

Adolf Hitler took power as Chancellor of Germany just a few weeks before Franklin D. Roosevelt assumed the presidency. The United States, gripped by the Great Depression, turned inward and Roosevelt responded to public opinion by devoting his energies to implementing a series of reforms under the banner of the New Deal. But Roosevelt, a committed internationalist, continued to follow foreign events, especially those in Germany. Fluent in German, FDR had even attended a German Volksschule *one summer as a young boy when his parents were traveling in Europe. In this letter, Ambassador William Dodd provides a bleak picture of the future of Germany and expresses his misgivings as Hitler assumed full dictatorial powers on the death of President Paul von Hindenburg. The letter mentions Joseph Goebbels, the Minister of Propaganda, and Hjalmar Schacht, who was head of the German central*

bank. In response to this letter, FDR wrote on August 25, 1934,
"It confirms my fear that the drift in Germany, and perhaps in other
countries in Europe, is definitely downward and that something must
break within the next six months or a year." He also told Dodd of his
efforts to meet with Perkins when he arrived at his home in Hyde Park,
New York, and observed, "I too am downhearted about Europe but I
watch for any ray of hope or opening to give me an opportunity to lend
a helping hand. There is nothing in sight at present."

Berlin, August 15, 1934

Dear Mr. President:

According to your suggestion of May 3rd when you gave me a few minutes of your time, I am summarizing the situation in Europe, with especial reference to Germany:

1. On October 17, I had a long interview with the Chancellor, in the presence of the Foreign Minister. When I reminded them of your attitude about crossing borders in a military way, Hitler asserted most positively that he would not allow a German advance across the border even if border enemies had made trouble. I named the French, Austrian and Polish fronts, and he said war might be started by violent S.A. [*Sturmabteilung*] men contrary to his command. That would be the only way.

Now what has happened since? More men are trained, uniformed and armed (perhaps not heavy guns) than in 1914, at least a million and a half; and the funeral all the Ambassadors and Ministers attended at Tannenberg August 7 was one grand military display, contrary to von Hindenburg's known request. Every diplomat with whom I spoke regarded the whole thing as a challenge under cover. And we have plenty of evidence that up to 10 o'clock July 25 the Vienna <u>Putsch</u> against Austria was boasted of here and being put over the radio as a great German performance. Only when defeat became known was the tone changed and the radio speaker removed for his post, Habicht of Munich. So, I am sure war was just around the corner, 30,000 Austro-German Nazis waiting near Munich for the signal to march upon Vienna. These men had been maintained for a year on the Austrian border at the expense of the German people. So, it seems to me that war and not peace is the objective, and the Hitler enthusiasts think they can beat Italy and France in a month – nor is high-power aircraft wanting, the Wrights having sold them machines last April.

2. Last March, in another interview, the Chancellor almost swore to me, without witnesses, that he would never again allow German propaganda in the United States. On March 12 or 13, he issued an order that no man must be arrested and held in restraint more than 24 hours without a warrant. This was supposed to be in response to my representations about the harm done in the United States by violent treatment of the Jews here. I explained to you how, on the assumption that these promises would be kept, I managed to prevent a Hitler mock-trial in Chicago and otherwise persuaded American Jews to restrain themselves. But on the 12ᵗʰ of May I read excerpt on the boat from a speech of Goebbels which declared that "Jews were the syphilis of all European peoples." Of course this aroused all the animosities of the preceding winter, and I was put in the position of having been humbugged, as indeed I was. All the personal protests which I made late in May were without effect, except that the Foreign Office people expressed great sorrow.

I have reviewed these points because I think we can not depend on the promises of the highest authority when we have such facts before us. I am sorry to have to say this of a man who proclaims himself the savior of his country and assumes on occasion the powers of President, the legislature and the supreme court. But you know all this side of the matter: June 30 and July 25!

3. One other point: Germany is ceasing as fast as possible the purchase of all raw stuffs from the United States, in some cases in direct violation of treaty obligations. She is mixing wood fibre in her cotton and woolen cloth, and is setting up plants for this purpose at great expense. Schacht acknowledged this today in conversation. He said: "We can not sell you anything but hairpins and knitting needles. How can we pay you anything?" He does not believe in the system, but he says it can not be stopped.

So the South is about to lose its market for 2,000,000 bales of cotton a year, and the Middle West is losing the last remnants of its German market for farm products. The New York bankers have been here of late to negotiate some sort of corporation deals between German business firms and American banks. "It is the only way to check German defaults on short-term loans" by American banks, some $300,000,000 the last time I had the figures; but this means other loans to save the cotton market and perhaps loss of all, including the cotton market itself.

Mr. Perkins of the National City Bank has tried his best to find a way out, and he will see you soon after his return. When he left here I was a little hopeful Schacht and Hitler might give some more promises with security. But since July 24, events look worse, not better. I have written Perkins my doubting attitude via British pouch. It all looks bad. I do not see any solution so long as present policy continues here. English and French have made barter arrangements. What Sayre and Peek can do, I cannot see. I am inclined again to look at the League of Nations when Russia is admitted. The "encirclement" may include Holland before long. Perhaps you can see a way out.

Yours sincerely,
William E. Dodd

President Franklin D. Roosevelt,
Hyde Park, New York.

Source: William E. Dodd File, President's Personal File 1043, Franklin D. Roosevelt Library, Hyde Park, New York.

3 US Congress, Excerpt from the Neutrality Act, 1935

In 1934, Republican Senator Gerald Nye of North Dakota convinced his colleagues to empanel a special investigative committee to examine the reasons for American entrance into World War I in April 1917. The Nye Committee required a number of companies and banks to open their records in order to investigate the economic ties they had forged with Great Britain and France prior to America's entry into the war. In its investigations, the committee found American banks had provided a significant number of loans to the Allied governments, and munitions makers such as DuPont had made substantial profits in meeting the need for war material. The findings of the Nye Committee helped galvanize support within Congress and among the public to pass a series of Neutrality Acts in 1935, 1936, 1937, and 1939, which sought to ensure America would remain neutral in the event of another overseas war. The provisions of the Neutrality Act would be imposed on Italy in 1935, but also Republican Spain during the Spanish Civil War in 1936.

Providing for the prohibition of the export of arms, ammunition, and implements of war to belligerent countries; the prohibition of the transportation of arms, ammunition, and implements of war by vessels of the United States for the use of belligerent states; for the registration and licensing of persons engaged in the business of manufacturing, exporting, or importing arms, ammunition, or implements of war; and restricting travel by American citizens on belligerent ships during war.

Resolved by the Senate and House of Representatives of the United States of America in Congress assembled, That upon the outbreak or during the progress of war between, or among, two or more foreign states, the President shall proclaim such fact, and it shall thereafter be unlawful to export arms, ammunition, or implements of war from any place in the United States, or possessions of the United States, to any port of such belligerent states, or to any neutral port for transshipment to, or for the use of, a belligerent country.

The President, by proclamation, shall definitely enumerate the arms, ammunition, or implements of war, the export of which is prohibited by this Act.

The President may, from time to time, by proclamation, extend such embargo upon the export of arms, ammunition, or implements of war to other states as and when they may become involved in such war.

Whoever, in violation of any of the provisions of this section, shall export, or attempt to export, or cause to be exported, arms, ammunition, or implements of war from the United States, or any of its possessions, shall be fined not more than $10,000 or imprisoned not more than five years, or both, and the property, vessel, or vehicle containing the same shall be subject to the provisions of sections 1 to 8, inclusive, title 6, chapter 30, of the Act approved June 15, 1917 (40 Stat. 223–225; U. S. C., title 22, secs. 238–245).

In the case of the forfeiture of any arms, ammunition, or implements of war by reason of a violation of this Act, no public or private sale shall be required; but such arms, ammunition, or implements of war shall be delivered to the Secretary of War for such use or disposal thereof as shall be approved by the President of the United States.

When in the judgment of the President the conditions which have caused him to issue his proclamation have ceased to exist he shall revoke the same and the provisions hereof shall thereupon cease to apply.

Except with respect to prosecutions committed or forfeitures incurred prior to March 1, 1936, this section and all proclamations issued thereunder shall not be effective after February 29, 1936.

SEC. 2. That for the purpose of this Act—

(a)   The term "Board" means the National Munitions Control Board which is hereby established to carry out the provisions of this Act. The Board shall consist of the Secretary of State, who shall be chairman and executive officer of the Board; the Secretary of the Treasury; the Secretary of War; the Secretary of the Navy; and the Secretary of Commerce. Except as otherwise provided in this Act, or by other law, the administration of this Act is vested in the Department of State;

(b)   The term "United States" when used in a geographical sense, includes the several States and Territories, the insular possessions of the United

States (including the Philippine Islands), the Canal Zone, and the District of Columbia;

(c) The term "person" includes a partnership, company, association, or corporation, as well as a natural person.

Within ninety days after the effective date of this Act, or upon first engaging in business, every person who engages in the business of manufacturing, exporting, or importing any of the arms, ammunition, and implements of war referred to in this Act, whether as an exporter, importer, manufacturer, or dealer, shall register with the Secretary of State his name, or business name, principal place of business, and places of business in the United States, and a list of the arms, ammunition, and implements of war which he manufactures, imports, or exports.

Every person required to register under this section shall notify the Secretary of State of any change in the arms, ammunition, and implements of war which he exports, imports, or manufactures; and upon such notification the Secretary of State shall issue to such person an amended certificate of registration, free of charge, which shall remain valid until the date of expiration of the original certificate. Every person required to register under the provisions of this section shall pay a registration fee of $500, and upon receipt of such fee the Secretary of State shall issue a registration certificate valid for five years, which shall be renewable for further periods of five years upon the payment of each renewal of a fee of $500.

It shall be unlawful for any person to export, or attempt to export, from the United States any of the arms, ammunition, or implements of war referred to in this Act to any other country or to import, or attempt to import, to the United States from any other country any of the arms, ammunition, or implements of war referred to in this Act without first having obtained a license therefor.

All persons required to register under this section shall maintain, subject to the inspection of the Board, such permanent records of manufacture for export, importation, and exportation of arms, ammunition, and implements of war as the Board shall prescribe.

Licenses shall be issued to persons who have registered as provided for, except in cases of export or import licenses where exportation of arms, ammunition, or implements of war would be in violation of this Act or any other law of the United States, or of a treaty to which the United States is a party, in which cases such licenses shall not be issued.

The Board shall be called by the Chairman and shall hold at least one meeting a year.

No purchase of arms, ammunition, and implements of war shall be made on behalf of the United States by any officer, executive department, or independent establishment of the Government from any person who shall have failed to register under the provisions of this Act.

The Board shall make an annual report to Congress, copies of which shall be distributed as are other reports transmitted to Congress. Such report shall contain such information and data collected by the Board as may be considered of value in the determination of questions connected with the control of trade in arms, ammunition, and implements of war. It shall include a list of all persons required to register under the provisions of this Act, and full information concerning the licenses issued hereunder.

The Secretary of State shall promulgate such rules and regulations with regard to the enforcement of this section as he may deem necessary to carry out its provisions.

The President is hereby authorized to proclaim upon recommendation of the Board from time to time a list of articles which shall be considered arms, ammunition, and implements of war for the purposes of this section.

This section shall take effect on the ninetieth day after the date of its enactment.

SEC. 3. Whenever the President shall issue the proclamation provided for in section 1 of this Act, thereafter it shall be unlawful for any American vessel to carry any arms, ammunition, or implements of war to any port of the belligerent countries named in such proclamation as being at war, or to any neutral port for transshipment to, or for the use of, a belligerent country.

Whoever, in violation of the provisions of this section, shall take, attempt to take, or shall authorize, hire, or solicit another to take any such vessel carrying such cargo out of port or from the jurisdiction of the United States shall be fined not more than $10,000 or imprisoned not more than five years, or both; and, in addition, such vessel, her tackle, apparel, furniture, equipment, and the arms, ammunition, and implements of war on board shall be forfeited to the United States.

When the President finds the conditions which have caused him to issue his proclamation have ceased to exist, he shall revoke his proclamation, and the provisions of this section shall thereupon cease to apply.

SEC. 4. Whenever, during any war in which the United States is neutral, the President, or any person thereunto authorized by him, shall have cause to believe that any vessel, domestic or foreign, whether requiring clearance or not, is about to carry out of a port of the United States, or its possession, men or fuel, arms, ammunition, implements of war, or other supplies to any warship, tender, or supply ship of a foreign belligerent nation, but the evidence is not deemed sufficient to justify forbidding the departure of the vessel as provided for by section 1, title V, chapter 30, of the Act approved June 15, 1917 (40 Stat.; U. S. C. title 18, sec. 31), and if, in the President's judgment, such action will serve to maintain peace between the United States and foreign nations, or to protect the commercial interests of the United States and its citizens, or to promote the security of the United States, he shall have the power and it shall be his duty to require the owner, master, or person in command thereof, before departing from a port of the United States, or any of its possessions, for a foreign port, to give a bond to the United States, with sufficient sureties, in such amount as he shall deem proper, conditioned that the vessel will not deliver the men, or the cargo, or any part thereof, to any warship, tender, or supply ship of a belligerent nation; and, if the President, or any person thereunto authorized by him, shall find that a vessel, domestic or foreign, in a port of the United States, or one of its possessions, has previously cleared from such port during such war and delivered its cargo or any part thereof to a warship, tender, or supply ship of a belligerent nation, he may prohibit the departure of such vessel during the duration of the war.

SEC. 5. Whenever, during any war in which the United States is neutral, the President shall find that special restrictions placed on the use of the ports and territorial waters of the United States, or of its possessions, by the submarines of a foreign nation will serve to maintain peace between the United States and foreign nations, or to protect the commercial interests of the United States and its citizens, or to promote the security of the United States, and shall make proclamation thereof, it shall thereafter be unlawful for any such submarine to enter a port or the territorial waters of the United States or any of its possessions, or to depart therefrom, except under such conditions and subject to such limitations as the President may prescribe. When, in his judgment, the conditions which have caused him to issue his proclamation have ceased to exist, he shall revoke his proclamation and the provisions of this section shall thereupon cease to apply.

SEC. 6. Whenever, during any war in which the United States is neutral, the President shall find that the maintenance of peace between the United States and foreign nations, or the protection of the lives of citizens of the United States, or the protection of the commercial interests of the United States and its citizens, or the security of the United States requires that the American citizens should refrain from traveling as passengers on the vessels of any belligerent nation, he shall so proclaim, and thereafter no citizen of the United States shall travel on any vessel of any belligerent nation except at his own risk, unless in accordance with such rules and regulations as the

President shall prescribe: *Provided, however,* That the provisions of this section shall not apply to a citizen travelling on the vessel of a belligerent whose voyage was begun in advance of the date of the President's proclamation, and who had no opportunity to discontinue his voyage after that date: *And provided further,* That they shall not apply under ninety days after the date of the President's proclamation to a citizen returning from a foreign country to the United States or to any of its possessions. When, in the President's judgment, the conditions which have cause him to issue his proclamation have ceased to exist, he shall revoke his proclamation and the provisions of this section shall thereupon cease to apply.

SEC. 7. In every case of the violation of any of the provisions of this Act where a specific penalty is not herein provided, such violator or violators, upon conviction, shall be fined not more than $10,000 or imprisoned not more than five years, or both.

SEC. 8. If any of the provisions of this Act, or the application thereof to any person or circumstance, is held invalid, the remainder of the Act, and the application of such provision to other persons or circumstances, shall not be affected thereby.

SEC. 9. The sum of $25,000 is hereby authorized to be appropriated, out of any money in the Treasury not otherwise appropriated, to be expended by the Secretary of State in administering this Act.

Approved, August 31, 1935

Source: Neutrality Act of 1935, Pub. Res. 67, 74 Congress, Ch. 837; 49 Stat. 1081.

4 *Chicago Defender,* "League of Nations Holds Meetings," Editorial, 1936

Benito Mussolini seized power in 1922 and made Italy the first fascist state in Europe. Under his leadership, not only were individual freedoms abridged and parliamentary rule ended, but Italy joined Japan in embarking on overseas conquests in an effort to build a new Roman Empire, beginning with the conquest of Abyssinia (Ethiopia) in 1935. In a continent divided into colonies ruled by the British, French, Portuguese, Spanish, and Belgians, Ethiopia remained one of the few independent African nations. The Ethiopians under Emperor Haile Selassie fought bravely to repel Italian invaders for seven months. Selassie also personally appealed to the League of Nations to impose sanctions against the aggressor nation. The League of Nations did impose sanctions, but these neither applied to petroleum products nor closed off the British-controlled Suez Canal to Italian vessels. President Franklin D. Roosevelt did invoke neutrality legislation freezing arms sales to Italy and prohibiting Americans from traveling aboard Italian passenger ships, but otherwise the United States took no action against Italy. Major American newspapers seldom covered events important to the African American community at home or abroad, but several important black newspapers closely followed events in Ethiopia. Below is an editorial that appeared in the Chicago Defender *in 1936.*

League of Nations Holds Meetings

From Geneva comes the news that the League of Nations has held another meeting which was of i[t]self probably the most important meeting held by the league since that body sold Abyssinia to Italy. It was important from another point of view, it gave the fallen Emperor Haile Selassie an opportunity to define to the members of the league their real character and dishonest purposes.

In no uncertain terms he told them in substance that they were traitors to the very cause they professed to espouse. He reminded them of how they deceitfully gained his confidence and respect, then bartered away his country and rights to the enemies. He placed upon them the responsibility and justly so, for the countless thousands of men and women in Ethiopia who have lost their lives by mustard gas, bombs and dynamite.

He made plain to the league that by reason of their deception he refused all proposals made to him to his own advantage, by the Italian government, only to be betrayed by the League of Nations. His indictment was severe, but entirely justified. No self-respecting government can ever have any regard for the character of the League of Nations as now constituted.

It is no longer an institution formed and predicated upon peace and good will, but rather a dangerous band of old-world conniving politicians whose first and foremost thought is to serve their own selfish interest. Emperor Haile Selassie lost his empire, and with it went the respect for the League of Nations. Its name can be fittingly and appropriately changed from the League of Nations, to the league of murderers, wordbreakers, and dishonest politicians. Ethopia lost, but the league did not win.

Source: "League of Nations Holds Meetings," *Chicago Defender* (National Edition), July 11, 1936, p. 16.

5   Jane Woolsey, "No Mr. Churchill!" and Mandy Butler, "Yes, Mr. Churchill!," *Rutgers Anthologist*, 1941

Until the Japanese attack on Pearl Harbor, Americans profoundly differed over whether the United States should enter the conflict against the Axis Powers. Non-interventionists, often called isolationists and led by Republican Senator Robert A. Taft and Charles Lindbergh, opposed any involvement in the war in Europe and remained sharply critical of the provision of aid to Great Britain and, later, the Soviet Union by the Roosevelt Administration. Other Americans, while still seeking to avoid US involvement in a land war in either Europe or Asia, argued that the United States had to take action to stop Nazi Germany from gaining power. Between September 1, 1939, and December 6, 1941, the Roosevelt Administration sought to rearm America by boosting weapons production, placing the National Guard into federal service, and instituting peace-time conscription that required men to enter the armed services if drafted. After the fall of France in June 1940, FDR provided increasing aid to Great Britain, beginning with the transfer of 50 overage destroyers to the Royal Navy to help it win the Battle of the Atlantic. As Britain started to run out of money by late 1940, Roosevelt in 1941 proposed through "Lend-Lease" to provide the material and supplies needed by the island nation to win the war. Fierce debates broke out on college campuses regarding American policies toward Britain and, later, the Soviet Union. The following are opposing views on the war submitted to the Rutgers University literary magazine in February 1941 by two students from the New Jersey College of Women (Douglass College). At this point Great Britain stood alone, although in June of that year Germany would invade the Soviet Union. It is not clear whether the authors of these two articles belonged to either the America First Committee, opposed to intervention, or the Committee to Defend America By Aiding the Allies.

For the past few months the mad dog of war has been running freely through Europe, while Mars has been drinking toasts of blood to his moustachioed beezle.

The question of whether or not to aid Britain, in one form or another, has been paramount in the mind of every thinking American since the beginning of the conflict and ANTHO feels that a discussion of the problem is apropos at this time.

The choice of Miss Woolsey and Miss Butler as commentators is regarded as particularly significant, for they are both very active members of the committees that seem to represent the most popular and controversial viewpoints. The views expressed are not, however, necessarily those for which the two groups stand. As a matter of fact, at the time this is being written Miss Woolsey's committee has not formulated any definite platform.

These two stands on the question are not the only ones advanced by any manner of means. For instance, another group feels that aid should be advanced to England in the form of materials, but that the line should be drawn where troops are concerned. Still another faction is of the opinion that aid should be given in any form, with war as a definite goal.

ANTHO does not necessarily advocate any of these arguments, but is, rather, the medium through which they may be expressed.

W.F.S.

Jane Woolsey, NJC '42, "No Mr. Churchill! Anti-Democratic Britain Denied Aid by Students Strengthening Democracy at Home Rather Than on Foreign Shores," February 1941

We're sorry, Mr. Churchill, but we are not going to war. "We" are a group of American students on a college campus. As such, we don't pretend to know all the answers or to be perfect prophets. But we see ourselves caught in a swift moving sea of events that threatens to drag us along with the tide and wash us up on European shores. We are fighting that tide for all we are worth. We are against Fascism and everything it means—brutality, viscious [sic] racial hatred, suppression of all democratic rights. We are against Fascism in Germany and everywhere else in the world or where it is rising or where the stage is being set for it.

But we don't believe that the bombs and guns of this war can defeat that Fascism or "make the world safe for democracy." Nor do we believe that this war, regardless of the victor, will establish a permanent peace. We are looking toward a warless world in which real democracy can progress. If we are to bring that goal to fulfillment what course must we take—where are we to turn?

Certainly not to this war. Let's forget the well-worn clichés and high-sounding phrases one hears in relation to Britain in this war and look at the facts.

A few years ago all liberals decried the anti-democratic suppressions by Britain of Indian demands for independence. Today, her anti-democratic suppressions have been intensified, yet today the liberals say that a Britain victorious will bring about a world in which small nations can live in independence and security.

After years of disastrous depression, a Britain caught in the talons of this situation will not be able to make an easy transition from totalitarianism to democracy. The government, the same government of Britain which has instituted totalitarian measures today, the same government we must support in an aid-to-Britain program, might find itself unable or unwilling to restore democracy.

Taking all these factors into consideration, we don't believe Britain can bring our aims—a warless, democratic world—into fruition.

We don't believe in government aid to Britain. We know what war means and we stand opposed to any and all measures which will propel that wartide ahead. We do not believe that a country can gear its economy on a wartime basis and remain neutral. We do not believe that a country can endure wartime psychology and remain neutral. There are those who say that aid to England is our first step in keeping out of war. They say that the more aid we give England that less [sic] chance there is that we shall go to war. It is true that our aid to Britain today is concentrated on materials. Today Britain doesn't need our men—but how about tomorrow? Tomorrow the war may spread to any of the many danger spots in the world, and Britain might then need our men. And who can witness the building up of a conscript army along with a gigantic war machine and dare say that the United States will refuse to send our men over to help Britain win, and this means frustration of our aims.

Then where are we to turn? We are neither cynics, nor defeatists, nor appeasers. We ally ourselves with the people of the world who hate Fascism because it crushes their liberties; whose real interest lies in the extension of democracy *everywhere in the world*.

This war holds no hope for the extension of democracy. We in the United States have seen in the past few months the abridgement of many civil liberties—we know that legislation has been suggested which would remove the right of workers to strike in defense industries. We have seen social problems neglected in the interests of national defense. We who believe in democracy stand ultimately and permanently in opposition to abridgement of civil liberties, to racial discrimination, to curtailment of workers' rights.

Let us devote our energies to fighting the forces *everywhere* which destroy our democratic aims. But our fight lies in the extension of social order, in making democracy a *reality*, not a word reserved for campaign speeches and Memorial Days.

That is our job, Mr. Churchill. That is what we're going to do. Sorry, but we don't intend to fight this war.

Mandy Butler, NJC '41, "Yes, Mr. Churchill! Great Britain is Fighting Our War and Democracy Depends on Our Action: Aid Short of War Advocated Here... "

A year or two ago American undergraduates, no matter how divided they were on other issues, had one universal credo: Joe College to Phi Jake, Republican or Communist were sure of one thing—unconditional peace had to be maintained. And peace for the United States meant no arms to belligerents, certainly no credit, and a very clear policy of neutrality in all foreign dealings.

Today, some of us have begun to question the rigidity of that conception of peace as doctrinaire and unrealistic. Does it mean that America must commit suicide by blind isolationism? Does it further mean selfish blindness, thinking as Americans before we think as men? We refuse to uphold these two implications of unconditional neutrality.

We believe that an America without England, confronted by a dominant, acquisitive Germany and an ascendant Japan is lost—for we will then have to choose between two alternatives: a losing war or peaceful submission—two different ways to commit suicide. We cannot expect South America, so long the "bad child" of the Western Hemisphere, to starve happily with us—it is far more likely that she will "cooperate" with Germany. We may then march into Mexico, etc., in an imperialism for self-preservation, or to bow the knee to economic and probably political damnation. In either case we face long years of the defensive, long years of military preparedness, long years of military rule—in short, a perfect breeding ground for Fascism. And those decades can destroy much too easily the whole philosophy of democracy. Too many children will be schooled in that time, too many groups suppressed, and too much power will reside in undemocratic controls. I am afraid it would be far too late for a magical "abracadabra" to call forth the democracy—we once knew—if the threat should ever die of itself (as the isolationists fondly hope it will). As Lewis Mumford says, "Nor may one still hope that time will by itself alter the present situation—men must act."

On the other hand, an independent England means the high water mark of Nazi advance has been reached. More, it means the possibility of economic survival. Certainly it means that a war for self-preservation is forestalled. Since British victory in repelling invasion means this to America, our committee strongly endorses all necessary aid to Britain. In our estimation, however, that aid could not include an expeditionary force in this, the Battle of Britain, for reasons of military expediency if nothing else. For why should Britain want to house, clothe, and feed men she does not need; her home defense seems more than adequate. We are not only against sending troops at this time; we think such a move would be the height of folly and wastefulness.

To sum up, Britain, while her sole aim in the present war is simply and obviously to repel invasion, she is incidentally doing our fighting and our dying for us. Under such circumstances, only the most tight-fisted, near-sighted nation could refuse to send her material aid. When a powerful outlaw is loose in a town or in a world, men band together to stop violence and cruelty; they do not go singly into the night to seek him out.

So far, I believe I have stated fairly accurately the committee's stand. What further stands it takes will depend, of course, on majority opinion when the occasion arises. I have, however, stated the cold, practical reasons for their attitude—the motive of American self-preservation. But there is another motive. For, to quote again, "A person who is only an American is only half a man; indeed only half an American." What we must isolate is not our own democracy, but Fascism. Our committee has expressed this belief in the following statement: "We are convinced that the English people and their government, with all forces fighting aggression, are devoting mind and body to a course in which we as Americans are equally concerned—that of preserving the culture which has for its dominant idea the dignity of individual man. With them, we reject the philosophy of herd-man, of concentration camps and idolatry of the leader. With them, we desire to reinstate a world order in which men were free to pursue in peace and without fear their many goals. With them, we know that Fascism holds out to common man not economic security, but marginal subsistence; not freedom of thought or act, but intellectual and physical slavery; not peace, but a sword."

War is a terrible word. I never thought I would have to use it in any way but an antagonistic sense. But that was when a shrill-voiced, impotent clown goosestepped up and down in Germany; today an all-powerful conqueror surveys *his* Europe. I have no illusions about our Allies; Britain has besmudged too many pages in my history texts; Greece is far from perfection; Chiang Kai-Shek is an unknown quantity, no better in any way, I think, than Winston Churchill. After the war the same Parliament will still be doing business in its muddling way; we have not guarantee of sudden and complete social democracy. But to turn away because there is no Utopia in their victory is an absolutist attitude as unreal as a rainbow in the present very real situation.

It is far from an easy choice for our generation. We were absolutists in an easy time; now we are called upon to desert that absolute. More than anything else, I hope and believe that youth has still the power to face a real challenge with a practical solution, not one of impractical wishful thinking.

We have walked in a dream for too long a time; it is time to awake, no matter how cold the morning.

Source: [*Rutgers University*] *Anthologist*, 16 (February 1941): 14–15, 21.

6 Franklin D. Roosevelt and Winston Churchill, "The Atlantic Charter," 1941

Before 1940 US presidents seldom left the shores of the United States. In fact, the first president to even leave US territory was Theodore Roosevelt in a visit to Panama. In the summer of 1941, FDR, in an elaborate ruse, secretly boarded the American naval cruiser Augusta to rendezvous with British Prime Minister Winston Churchill off the shores of Newfoundland in the North Atlantic. This meeting allowed Roosevelt and Churchill to meet face to face for the first time, and provided an opportunity for their senior advisors and military staffs to get to know one another. By August 1941, the United States was not only committed to providing aid to both Great Britain and the Soviet Union, but increasingly used American naval power in the North Atlantic to meet the threat of German submarines. Even before Pearl Harbor the US Navy fought an undeclared naval war to keep the sea lanes. The Atlantic Charter served as the public statement issued after the meeting of Roosevelt and Churchill; it should not be read as a binding agreement and in many ways glossed over disagreements between the two men. For instance, Churchill remained a fierce imperialist and defended Britain's right to retain its empire while Roosevelt believed in decolonization. In reading the Atlantic Charter, consider not only the ideals Roosevelt sought to take Americans into the war, but also the ambiguity of the document.

... The President of the United States of America and the Prime Minister, Mr. Churchill, representing His Majesty's Government in the United Kingdom, being met together, deem it right to make known certain common principles in the national policies of their respective countries on which they base their hopes for a better future for the world.

First, their countries seek no aggrandizement, territorial or other;

Second, they desire to see no territorial changes that do not accord with the freely expressed wishes of the peoples concerned;

Third, they respect the right of all peoples to choose the form of government under which they will live; and they wish to see sovereign rights and self government restored to those who have been forcibly deprived of them;

Fourth, they will endeavor, with due respect for their existing obligations, to further the enjoyment by all States, great or small, victor or vanquished, of access, on equal terms, to the trade and to the raw materials of the world which are needed for their economic prosperity;

Fifth, they desire to bring about the fullest collaboration between all nations in the economic field with the object of securing, for all, improved labor standards, economic advancement, and social security;

Sixth, after the final destruction of the Nazi tyranny, they hope to see established a peace which will afford to all Nations the means of dwelling in safety within their own boundaries, and which will afford assurance that all the men in all lands may live out their lives in freedom from fear and want;

Seventh, such a peace should enable all men to traverse the high seas and oceans without hindrance;

Eighth, they believe that all of the Nations of the world, for realistic as well as spiritual reasons, must come to the abandonment of the use of force. Since no future peace can be maintained if land, sea or air armaments continue to be employed by Nations which threaten, or may threaten, aggression outside of their frontiers, they believe, pending the establishment of a wider and permanent system of general security, that the disarmament of such Nations is essential. They will likewise aid and encourage all other practicable measures which will lighten for peace-loving peoples the crushing burden of armaments.

Franklin D. Roosevelt
Winston S. Churchill

Source: Franklin D. Roosevelt Library, Hyde Park, New York.

7 US Congress, Excerpt from Hearings, *Propaganda in Motion Pictures*, 1941

During the 1930s most American corporations wanted to maintain normal business relations with Nazi Germany. Americans had substantial investments in Germany, especially in the burgeoning automobile industry, and both Ford Motor Company and General Motors had major German subsidiaries. Hollywood had equally large interests in retaining access to the German film market and most studios continued to do business in Germany. Warner Brothers remained an important exception to this pattern and liquidated business interests in Germany shortly after the Nazis came to power. Moreover, Warner Brothers made a number of pathbreaking films both to alert the American public of fascism and to spur support for

*preparedness. The following is an excerpt from a Congressional hearing held
in late 1941 in which critics such as Republican Senator Gerald Nye of
North Dakota argued Hollywood filmmakers were putting out propaganda
designed to encourage America's entrance into the war. Harry Warner, a
Russian Jew who along with his brothers formed Warner Brothers, had
immigrated with his parents at a young age.*

Testimony of Senator Gerald P. Nye, September 9, 1941

... I entertain no desire for moving-picture censorship. That is quite as unde-
sirable as press censorship. I entertain no sympathy toward any idea which
would have the Government take over the movies or have the Government
dictate what should be run in the pictures.

I do hope, however, that the industry will more largely recognize the
obligation it owes our country and its people, and that in times of peace for
our country, that the industry will entertain that American courage which
will boldly resist any effort by administration agents of our Government to
dictate what kind of picture it shall or shall not make. ...

Mr. Chairman, I am sure that you and members of your committee are
quite aware of the determined effort that has been put forth to convey to
the public that the investigation asked is the result of a desire to serve the
un-American, narrow cause of anti-Semitism. ...

I bitterly resent, Mr. Chairman, this effort to misrepresent our purpose
and to prejudice the public mind and your mind by dragging this racial issue
to the front. I will not consent to its being used to cover the tracks of
those who have been pushing our country on the way to war with their
propaganda intended to inflame the American mind with hatred for one
foreign cause and magnified respect and glorification for another foreign
cause, until we shall come to feel that wars elsewhere in the world are really
after all our wars.

Those primarily responsible for the propaganda pictures are born abroad.
They came to our land and took citizenship here entertaining violent animosities toward certain causes abroad. Quite natural is their feeling and
desire to aid those who are at war against the causes which so naturally
antagonize them. If they lose sight of what some Americans might call the
first interests of America in times like these, I can excuse them. But their
prejudices by no means necessitate our closing our eyes to these interests
and refraining from any undertaking to correct their error. ...

If the anti-Semitic issue is now raised for the moment, it is raised by those
of the Jewish faith ... not by me, not by this committee ...

Propaganda for war is not a new experience for Americans. Eighteen years after the last war it was impossible to lift the lid and study intimately the propaganda that was practiced upon us during those years when we were maintaining a position of neutrality while all of Europe was at war. True, the motion picture and the radio were not then so prominently in evidence as agencies for propaganda as they are now. Both institutions were then rather in a state of still being born. Nevertheless, we know that propaganda in abundance was flooded upon us. We know now that from the lips of Lord Northcliffe himself came the knowledge that Great Britain expended $165,000,000 for propaganda in the United States to get us into Britain's war. We know something about how these millions were spent, how newspapers were paid for favor by the furnishing of newsprint how expensive news sheets were printed and distributed to the press, how writers and American journals paid for services to write the United States into Britain's war then.

Now, I do not charge that these things are being repeated today, I do know what foreign money is being spent for propaganda here in our land. We shall know some day no doubt after it is too late to have any influence upon our thinking at the present time.

Being without any information to bear out such a thought I would not now even insinuate that foreign money is being expended to accomplish propaganda purposes over our radio networks or through the films. I only know that what is coming from the moving-picture studios in the way of pictures, portrays a lot of glory for war, magnifies many times the glory of certain peoples engaged in that war. I only know it makes double black the portrayal of other causes involved in Europe's war, fanning American hates toward those certain causes. These pictures that we are seeing these days are not revealing the sons of mothers writhing in agony in trench, in mud, on barbed wire, amid scenes of battle, or sons of mothers living legless or lungless or brainless or sightless; sons in hospitals. These alleged propaganda picture are not showing us the disemboweled sons of fathers and mothers, lying upon fields of battle—the sons of English, or Greek, or German, or Polish, or Russian parents. We see them instead marching in bright uniforms, in the parade of eloquent and powerful machines, or in the field firing at distant targets. ...

Testimony of Harry M. Warner, President of Warner Bros. Pictures, Inc.

I have read in the public press the accusations made against the motion-picture industry, by Senator Gerald Nye and others. I have also read the testimony of Senators Nye and Bennett C. Clark and others before your committee. After measuring my words, and speaking with full sincerity, I want the record to show immediately that I deny, with all the strength I have, these reckless and unfounded charges. ...

At various points in the charges, Warner Bros. and I have been mentioned specifically. The charges against my company and myself are untrue. The charges are either based on a lack of information or concocted from pure fancy. Yet the gossip has been widely disseminated.

I am opposed to nazi-ism. I abhor and detest every principle and practice of the Nazi movement. To me, nazi-ism typifies the very opposite of the kind of life every decent man, woman, and child wants to live. I believe nazi-ism is a world revolution whose ultimate objective is to destroy our democracy, wipe out all religion, and enslave our people—just as Germany has destroyed and enslaved Poland, Belgium, Holland, France, and all the other countries. I am ready to give myself and all my personal resources to aid in the defeat of the Nazi menace to the American people. ...

Shortly after Hitler came to power in Germany I became convinced that Hitlerism was an evil force designed to destroy free people, whether they were Catholics, Protestants, or Jews. I claim no credit as a prophet. Many appraised the Nazis in their true role, from the very day of Hitler's rise to power.

I have always been in accord with President Roosevelt's foreign policy. In September 1939, when the Second World War began, I believed, and I believe today, that the world struggle for freedom was in its final stage. I said publicly then, and I say today, that the freedom which this country fought England to obtain, we may have to fight with England to retain.

I am unequivocally in favor of giving England and her allies all supplies which our country can spare. I also support the President's doctrine of freedom of the seas, as recently explained to the public by him.

Frankly, I am not certain whether or not this country should enter the war in its own defense at the present time. The President knows the world situation and our country's problems better than any other man. I would follow his recommendation concerning a declaration of war.

If Hitler should be the victor abroad, the United States would be faced with a Nazi-dominated world. I believe—and I am sure that the subcommittee shares my feeling—that this would be a catastrophe for our country. I want to avoid such a catastrophe, as I know you do.

I have given my views to you frankly and honestly. They reduce themselves to my previous statement: I am opposed to nazi-ism. I abhor and detest every principle and practice of the Nazi movement. I am not alone in feeling this. I am sure that the overwhelming majority of our people and our Congress share the same views.

While I am opposed to nazi-ism, I deny that the pictures produced by my company are "propaganda," as has been alleged. Senator Nye has said that our picture *Sergeant York* is designed to create war hysteria. Senator Clark has added *Confessions of a Nazi Spy* to the isolationist blacklist. John T. Flynn, in turn, has added *Underground*. These witnesses have not seen these pictures, so I cannot imagine how they can judge them. On the other hand, millions of average citizens have paid to see these pictures. They have enjoyed wide popularity and have been profitable to our company. In short, these pictures have been judged by the public and the judgment has been favorable.

Sergeant York is a factual portrait of the life of one of the great heroes of the last war. If that is propaganda, we plead guilty. *Confessions of a Nazi Spy* is a factual portrayal of a Nazi spy ring that actually operated in New York City. If that is propaganda, we plead guilty.

So it is with each and every one of our pictures dealing with the world situation or with the national defense. These pictures were carefully prepared on the basis of factual happenings and they were not twisted to serve any ulterior purpose.

In truth, the only sin of which Warner Bros. is guilty is that of accurately recording on the screen the world as it is or as it has been. Unfortunately, we cannot change the facts in the world today …

I have no apology to make to the committee for the fact that for many years Warner Bros. has been attempting to record history in the making. We discovered early in our career that our patrons wanted to see accurate stories of the world in which they lived. I [have] known that I have shown to the satisfaction of the impartial observer that Warner Bros., long before there was a Nazi Germany, had been making pictures on topical subjects. It was only natural, therefore, with the new political movement, however horrible it may be, that we should make some pictures concerning the Nazis. It was equally logical that we should produce motion pictures concerning national defense. …

If Warner Bros. had produced no pictures concerning the Nazi movement, our public would have had good reason to criticize. We would have been living in a dream world. Today 70 percent of the nonfiction books published deal with the Nazi menace. Today 10 percent of the fiction novels are anti Nazi in theme. Today 10 percent of all material submitted to us for consideration is anti-Nazi in character. Today the newspapers and radio devote a good portion of their facilities to describing nazi-ism. Today there is a war involving all hemispheres except our own and touching the lives of all of us. ...

Source: *Propaganda in Motion Pictures: Hearings Before A Subcommittee of the Committee of the Committee on Interstate Commerce, United States Senate, Seventy-Seventh Congress, First Session, On S. Res. 152: A Resolution Authorizing An Investigation of War Propaganda Disseminated By the Motion-Picture Industry And Of Any Monopoly In the Production, Distribution, or Exhibition of Motion Pictures, September 9 to 26, 1941.* Washington, DC: Government Printing Office, 1942, pp. 8, 11, 12, 22–23, 338–339, 343, 346.

8 Cordell Hull Proposal to Japanese Ambassador Nomura and His Reply, 1941

By the fall of 1941, President Roosevelt initiated undeclared naval warfare against German submarines in the Atlantic and sent American troops to occupy Iceland. To many observers, especially opponents of intervention, it appeared only a matter of time before the United States would go to war in Europe. In the case of the Pacific, American and Japanese diplomats were engaged in extensive talks in this same period in an attempt to avert war. In the fall of 1941, Japanese Ambassador to Washington, DC, Kichisaburō Nomura, along with another senior diplomat, Saburō Kurusu, was sent specifically by Tokyo to negotiate with Secretary of State Cordell Hull. Scholars are divided on whether war could have been averted. Negotiations in this period were at a critical juncture, in part because of the US decision to impose an oil and steel embargo on Japan in July 1941, forcing Japan to either seek a peaceful settlement with the United States or go to war to seize the oil necessary for its military and economy. On November 26, 1941, Hull proposed a settlement to Japanese diplomats that would in early December be formally rejected by the Japanese government. As a result of an intelligence breakthrough by American cryptologists, who had been able to break enough of the Japanese diplomatic code, on the evening of December 6, 1941, Franklin Roosevelt and his senior military leaders knew the Japanese had rejected Hull's terms for a settlement. The Japanese representatives, unfortunately, had difficulties decoding the message and consequently would formally deliver their government's reply to Hull after the Japanese Navy began to attack American military and naval bases in Hawaii.

Document Handed by the Secretary of State to the Japanese Ambassador (Nomura) on November 26, 1941

Strictly Confidential
Tentative and Without
Commitment

Washington, November 26, 1941

OUTLINE OF PROPOSED BASIS FOR AGREEMENT BETWEEN THE UNITED STATES AND JAPAN

Section I
Draft Mutual Declaration of Policy

The Government of the United States and the Government of Japan both being solicitous for the peace of the Pacific affirm that their national policies are directed toward lasting and extensive peace throughout the Pacific area, that they have no territorial designs in that area, that they have no intention of threatening other countries or of using military force aggressively against any neighboring nation, and that, accordingly, in their national policies they will actively support and give practical application to the following fundamental principles upon which their relations with each other and with all other governments are based:

(1)   The principle of inviolability of territorial integrity and sovereignty of each and all nations.

(2)   The principle of non-interference in the internal affairs of other countries.

(3)   The principle of equality, including equality of commercial opportunity and treatment.

(4)   The principle of reliance upon international cooperation and conciliation for the prevention and pacific settlement of controversies and for improvement of international conditions by peaceful methods and processes.

The Government of Japan and the Government of the United States have agreed that toward eliminating chronic political instability, preventing recurrent economic collapse, and providing a basis for peace, they will actively support and practically apply the following principles in their economic relations with each other and with other nations and peoples:

(1)   The principle of non-discrimination in international commercial relations.

(2)   The principle of international economic cooperation and abolition of extreme nationalism as expressed in excessive trade restrictions.

(3) The principle of non-discriminatory access by all nations to raw material supplies.

(4) The principle of full protection of the interests of consuming countries and populations as regards the operation of international commodity agreements.

(5) The principle of establishment of such institutions and arrangements of international finance as may lend aid to the essential enterprises and the continuous development of all countries and may permit payments through processes of trade consonant with the welfare of all countries.

Section II
*Steps To Be Taken by the Government of the United States
and by the Government of Japan.*
   The Government of the United States and the Government of Japan propose to take steps as follows:

1. The Government of the United States and the Government of Japan will endeavor to conclude a multilateral non-aggression pact among the British Empire, China, Japan, the Netherlands, the Soviet Union, Thailand and the United States.

2. Both Governments will endeavor to conclude among the American, British, Chinese, Japanese, the Netherland and Thai Governments an agreement whereunder each of the Governments would pledge itself to respect the territorial integrity of French Indochina and, in the event that there should develop a threat to the territorial integrity of Indochina, to enter into immediate consultation with a view to taking such measures as may be deemed necessary and advisable to meet the threat in question. Such agreement would provide also that each of the Governments party to the agreement would not seek or accept preferential treatment in its trade or economic relations with Indochina and would use its influence to obtain for each of the signatories equality of treatment in trade and commerce with French Indochina.

3. The Government of Japan will withdraw all military, naval, air and police forces from China and from Indochina.

4. The Government of the United States and the Government of Japan will not support—militarily, politically, economically—any government or regime in China other than the National Government of the Republic of China with capital temporarily at Chungking.

5. Both Governments will give up all extraterritorial rights in China ...

6. The Government of the United States and the Government of Japan will enter into negotiations for the conclusion between the United States and

Japan of a trade agreement, based upon reciprocal most-favored-nation treatment and reduction of trade barriers by both countries, including an undertaking by the United States to bind raw silk on the free list.

7. The Government of the United States and the Government of Japan will, respectively, remove the freezing restrictions on Japanese funds in the United States and on American funds in Japan.

8. Both Governments will agree upon a plan for the stabilization of the dollar-yen rate, with the allocation of funds adequate for this purpose, half to be supplied by Japan and half by the United States.

9. Both Governments will agree that no agreement which either has concluded with any third power or powers shall be interpreted by it in such a way as to conflict with the fundamental purpose of this agreement, the establishment and preservation of peace throughout the Pacific area.

10. Both Governments will use their influence to cause other governments to adhere to and give practical application to the basic political and economic principles set forth in this agreement.

Memorandum Handed by the Japanese Ambassador (Nomura) to the Secretary State at 2:20 P.M. on December 7, 1941

1. The Government of Japan, prompted by a genuine desire to come to an amicable understanding with the Government of the United States in order that the two countries by their joint efforts may secure the peace of the Pacific Area and thereby contribute toward the realization of world peace, has continued negotiations with the utmost sincerity since April last with the Government of the United States regarding the adjustment and advancement of Japanese-American relations and the stabilization of the Pacific Area.

The Japanese Government has the honor to state frankly its views concerning the claims the American Government has persistently maintained as well as the measures the United States and Great Britain have taken toward Japan during these eight months.

2. It is the immutable policy of the Japanese Government to insure the stability of East Asia and to promote world peace and thereby to enable all nations to find each its proper place in the world.

Ever since China Affair broke out owing to the failure on the part of China to comprehend Japan's true intentions, the Japanese Government has striven for the restoration of peace and has consistently exerted its best efforts to prevent the extension of war-like disturbances. It was also to that end that in September last year Japan concluded the Tripartite Pact with Germany and Italy.

However, both the United States and Great Britain have resorted to every possible measure to assist the Chungking régime so as to obstruct the establishment of a general peace between Japan and China, interfering with Japan's constructive endeavours toward the stabilization of East Asia. Exerting pressure on the Netherlands East Indies, or menacing French Indo-China, they have attempted to frustrate Japan's aspirations to the ideal of common prosperity in cooperation with these regions. Furthermore, when Japan in accordance with its protocol with France took measures of joint defense of French Indo-China, both American and British Governments, wilfully misinterpreting it as a threat to their own possessions, and inducing the Netherlands Government to follow suit, they enforced the assets freezing order, thus severing economic relations with Japan. While manifesting thus an obviously hostile attitude, these countries have strengthened their military preparations perfecting an encirclement of Japan, and have brought about a situation which endangers the very existence of the Empire. ...

... As for the China question which constituted an important subject of the negotiation, the Japanese Government showed a most conciliatory attitude. As for the principle of non-discrimination in international commerce, advocated by the American Government, the Japanese Government expressed its desire to see the said principle applied throughout the world, and declared that along with the actual practice of this principle in the world, the Japanese Government would endeavour to apply the same in the Pacific Area including China, and made it clear that Japan had no intention of excluding from China economic activities of third powers pursued on an equitable basis. Furthermore, as regards the question of withdrawing troops from French Indo-China, the Japanese Government even volunteered, as mentioned above, to carry out an immediate evacuation of troops from Southern French Indo-China as a measure of easing the situation. ...

... The American proposal contained a stipulation which states—"Both Governments will agree that no agreement, which either has concluded with any third power or powers, shall be interpreted by it in such a way as to conflict with the fundamental purpose of this agreement, the establishment and preservation of peace throughout the Pacific area." It is presumed that the above provision has been proposed with a view to restrain Japan from fulfilling its obligations under the Tripartite Pact when the United States participates in the War in Europe, and, as such, it cannot be accepted by the Japanese Government.

The American Government, obsessed with its own views and opinion, may be said to be scheming for the extension of the war. While it seeks, on the one hand, to secure its rear by stabilizing the Pacific Area, it is engaged, on the other hand, in aiding Great Britain and preparing to attack, in the name of self-defense, Germany and Italy, two Powers that are striving to establish a new order in Europe. Such a policy is totally at variance with the many principles upon which the American Government proposes to found the stability of the Pacific Area through peaceful means. ...

... It is impossible not to reach the conclusion that the American Government desires to maintain and strengthen, in coalition with Great Britain and other Powers, its dominant position it has hitherto occupied not only in China but in other areas of East Asia. It is a fact of history that the countries of East Asia for the past hundred years or more have been compelled to observe the *status quo* under the Anglo-American policy of imperialistic exploitation and to sacrifice themselves to the prosperity of the two nations. The Japanese Government cannot tolerate the perpetuation of such a situation since it directly runs counter to Japan's fundamental policy to enable all nations to enjoy each its proper place in the world. ...

... The attitude of the American Government in demanding Japan not to support militarily, politically or economically any régime other than the régime at Chungking, disregarding thereby the existence of the Nanking Government, shatters the very basis of the present negotiation. This demand of the American Government falling as it does, in line with its above-mentioned refusal to cease from aiding the Chungking régime, demonstrates clearly the intention of the American Government to obstruct the restoration of normal relations between Japan and China and the return of peace to East Asia.

... In brief, the American proposal contains certain acceptable items such as those concerning commerce, including the conclusion of a trade agreement, mutual removal of the freezing restrictions, and stabilization of yen and dollar exchange, or the abolition of extra-territorial rights in China. On the other hand, however, the proposal in question ignores Japan's sacrifices in four years of the China Affair, menaces the Empire's existence itself and disparages its honour and prestige. Therefore, viewed in its entirety, the Japanese Government regrets that it cannot accept the proposal as a basis of negotiation. ...

... Obviously it is in the intention of the American Government to conspire with Great Britain and other countries to obstruct Japan's efforts toward the establishment of peace through the creation of a new order in East Asia, and especially to preserve Anglo-American rights and interests in keeping Japan and China at war. This intention has been revealed clearly during the course of the present negotiation. Thus, the earnest hope of the Japanese Government to adjust Japanese-American relations and to preserve and promote the peace of the Pacific through cooperation with the American Government has finally been lost.

The Japanese Government regrets to have to notify hererby the American Government that in view of the attitude of the American Government it cannot but consider that it is impossible to reach an agreement through further negotiations.

[Washington,] December 7, 1941

Source: US Department of State, *Papers Relating to the Foreign Relations of the United States, Japan: 1931–1941*, Volume II. Washington, DC: Government Printing Office, 1943, pp. 768–770, 787–792.

Study Questions

1   Compare the rhetoric used by Secretary of State Henry Stimson with the intent of Congress in passing the Neutrality Act of 1935.
2   What was the US ambassador to Germany's assessment of Adolf Hitler in 1934? Why was the ambassador so pessimistic?
3   What were the arguments made by those favoring intervention in the war in Europe? What were the arguments against?
4   Why did non-interventionists fear the power of Hollywood films? How did the film executives respond to critics who accused them of disseminating propaganda?
5   What did the United States demand of Japan on the eve of the attack on Pearl Harbor? How realistic was the proposal put forth by Secretary of State Cordell Hull? Was war inevitable given American demands?

Chapter 2   Pearl Harbor and Meeting the Fight

1 Ruth A. Erickson, Recollections of Attack on Pearl Harbor, 1997

Japanese naval forces delivered a devastating blow against American naval and air bases on the Territory of Hawaii on December 7, 1941. Not only did Japanese naval aviators sink eight battleships, three cruisers, and several smaller vessels, they also destroyed nearby Army Air Force bases and planes. The commanders of American forces on Pearl Harbor had received a warning in November that negotiations with the Japanese were at a crossroads and that if they broke down, war would be imminent. However, few expected that Japan had the capability of striking American forces at Pearl Harbor, and the Army and Navy commanders on the island took only limited precautions to secure it from direct enemy attack. In fact, the most widely held belief among the senior commanders centered around possible sabotage by the island's large Japanese American community, and they took such measures as locking up ammunition and placing the airplanes on airfields so they could be guarded more easily. A Navy nurse, Ruth Erickson, describes her reactions to the attack and her efforts, along with those of other medical personnel, to cope with the wounded who poured into her facility.

The United States in World War II: A Documentary Reader, First Edition.
Edited by G. Kurt Piehler. Editorial material and organization © 2013 Blackwell Publishing Ltd.
Published 2013 by Blackwell Publishing Ltd.

US Navy Nurse Ruth A. Erickson, Oral History Interview

Suddenly we heard planes roaring overhead and said, "The fly boys are really busy at Ford Island this morning." The island was directly across the channel from the hospital. We didn't think too much about it since the reserves were often there for weekend training.

We no sooner got those words out than we started to hear noises that were foreign to us. I leaped out of my chair and dashed to the nearest window in the corridor. Right then there was a plane flying directly over the top of our quarters, a one-story structure. The rising sun under the wing of the plane denoted the enemy. One could almost see [the pilot's] features around his goggles. He was obviously saving his ammunition for the ships. Just down the row, all the ships were sitting there—the *California*, the *Arizona*, the *Oklahoma*, and others.

My heart was racing, the telephone was ringing, the chief nurse, Gertrude Arnest, was saying, "Girls, get into your uniforms at once. This is the real thing!"

I was in my room by that time changing into uniform. It was getting dusky, almost like evening. Smoke was rising from burning ships.

I dashed across the street through a shrapnel shower, got into the lanai and just stood still for a second, as were a couple of doctors. I felt like I was frozen to the ground, but it was only a split second. I ran to the orthopedic dressing room but it was locked. A corpsman ran to the OD's [officer of the day] desk for the keys. It seemed like an eternity before he returned and the room was opened.

We drew water into every container we could find and set up the instrument boiler. Fortunately we still had electricity and water. Dr. [Comdr. Clyde W.] Brunson, the chief of medicine, was making sick call when the bombing started. When he was finished, he was to play golf ... a thought never to be uttered again.

The first patient came into our dressing room at 8:25 A.M. with a large opening in his abdomen and bleeding profusely. They immediately started a transfusion. I can still see the tremor of Dr. Brunson's hand as he picked up the needle. Everyone was terrified. The patient died within the hour.

Then the burned patients streamed in. The USS *Nevada* had managed some steam and attempted to get out of the channel. They were unable to make it and went aground on Hospital Point right near the hospital. There was heavy oil on the water and the men dove off the ship and swam through these waters to Hospital Point, not too great a distance, but when one is burned ... How they ever managed, I'll never know.

The tropical dress at that time was white T-shirts and shorts. The burns began where the pants ended. Bared arms and faces were plentiful.

Personnel retrieved a supply of new flit guns [insecticide sprayers] from stock. We filled these with tannic acid to spray burned bodies. Then we gave these gravely injured patients sedatives for their intense pain.

We eased orthopedic patients out of their beds with no time for linen changes, as an unending stream of burn patients continued until mid-afternoon. A doctor, who several days before had had renal surgery and was still convalescing, got out of his bed and began to assist the other doctors.

A Japanese plane that had been shot down crashed right next to the tennis court. It sheared off a corner of the laboratory and a number of laboratory animals—rats and guinea pigs—were destroyed.

About twelve noon the galley personnel came around with sandwiches and cold drinks; we ate on the run. About two o'clock the chief nurse was making rounds to check on all the units and arrange relief schedules. I was relieved around four P.M. and went to the nurses' quarters where everything was intact. I freshened up, had something to eat, and went back on duty at eight P.M. I was scheduled to report to a surgical unit.

By now it was dark and we worked with flashlights. The maintenance people, and anyone else who could manage a hammer and nails, were putting up black drapes on black paper to seal the crevices against any light that might stream to the outside.

About ten or eleven o'clock, there were planes overhead. I really hadn't felt frightened until this particular time. My knees were knocking together and the patients were calling, "Nurse, nurse!" The other nurse and I went to them, held their hands a few moments, and then went on to others. The noise ended very quickly and the word got around that these were our own planes.

I worked until midnight on that ward and then was directed to go down to the basement level to the main hospital building. Here the dependents— the women and children, the families of the doctors, and other staff officers— were placed for the night. There were ample blankets and pillows. We lay body by body along the walls of the basement. The children were frightened and the adults tense. It was not a very restful night for anyone.

Source: Jan K. Herman, *Battle Station Sick Bay: Navy Medicine in World War II* (Annapolis: Naval Institute Press, 1997), pp. 25–27.

2 Eleanor Roosevelt, Script for Radio Program, 1941

Although relations between the United States and Japan had deteriorated in late 1941, the Japanese attack on naval and air bases in Hawaii on the morning of December 7 came as a shock to both the general public

*and the Roosevelt Administration. Even those expecting war did not foresee
a direct assault on a major American naval base located so far from Japanese
home islands. Word of the attack did not reach Washington, DC, until the
afternoon of December 7, and for the rest of the day and into the evening,
scores of military and civilian leaders streamed into the White House to
confer with the president. Although FDR began drafting a speech to be
delivered before Congress asking for a declaration of war, he made no public
speech or statement that day. It would be left to his wife, Eleanor Roosevelt,
to address the nation. The First Lady used part of her regularly scheduled
radio show to speak directly about the perils facing the nation. In her talk,
she refers to her own children. In 1941, all four of her sons were already
serving in the military – one in the Army Air Force, two in the US Navy,
and one in the US Marine Corps. This was a scripted show and the
transcript reproduced below varies slightly from the program that actually
aired on the NBC Radio Network. Like most radio shows of this era, it had
a commercial sponsor and the line between advertising and program content
remained ill defined. The original script, written before the attack on Pearl
Harbor, contained more overt references encouraging individuals to drink
more coffee.*

Eleanor Roosevelt Radio Address, December 7, 1941

W J Z   PAN-AMERICAN COFFEE BUREAU
6:45 – 7:00 P.M.   MRS. FRANKLIN D. ROOSEVELT   PROGRAM #11
                 DECEMBER 7, 1941   SUNDAY

LEON PEARSON: This is Leon Pearson speaking for the Pan-American
                 Coffee Bureau which represents seven Good Neighbor
                 coffee-growing nations, and presenting to you American
                 families your Sunday evening visit with Mrs. Franklin
                 D. Roosevelt. This evening Mrs. Roosevelt has as her
                 guest, Corporal James Cannon, 1229th Reception Center,
                 Fort Dix. But first, Dan Seymour has a word from our
                 sponsors, the Pan-American Coffee Bureau.

DAN SEYMOUR: In this moment of trial, the seven neighbor countries which
                 make up the Pan-American Coffee Bureau, welcome the
                 chance to express their support for their Great Good
                 Neighbor, the United States. The new solidarity which has
                 been effected between the Americas in the last few years
                 stands us all in good stead, in the face of this emergency.
                 This applies not only in a commercial sense – for Uncle

LEON PEARSON:

MRS. ROOSEVELT:

Sam can count on Latin America for essential materials, whether oil or tin or copper or coffee – but also in a political sense. The Americas stand together.

Thank you, Dan Seymour, and now, here's the Pan-American Coffee Bureau's Sunday evening news maker to give us her usual interesting observations on the world we live in ... Mrs. Franklin D. Roosevelt,

Good evening, ladies and gentlemen. I am speaking to you tonight at a very serious moment in our history. The Cabinet is convening, and the leaders in Congress are meeting with the President. The State Department and Army and Navy officials have been with the President all afternoon. In fact the Japanese ambassador was talking to the President at the very time that Japan's airships were bombing our citizens in Hawaii and the Philippines and sinking one of our transports loaded with lumber on its way to Hawaii.

By tomorrow morning, the members of Congress will have a full report and be ready for action. In the meantime we, the people, are already prepared for action. For months now the knowledge that something of this kind might happen has been hanging over our heads and yet it seemed impossible to believe, impossible to drop the everyday things of life and feel that there was only one thing which was important, and that was preparation to meet an enemy, no matter where he struck.

That is all over now and there is no more uncertainty. We know what we have to face and we know that we are ready to face it.

I should like to say just a word to the women in the country tonight. I have a boy at sea on a Destroyer. For all I know he may be on his way to the Pacific. Two of my children are in coast cities on the Pacific. Many of you all over this country have boys in the Services who will not be called upon to go into action. You have friends and families in what has suddenly become [a] danger zone. You can not escape anxiety, you can not escape a clutch of fear at your heart and yet I hope that the certainty of what we have to meet will make you rise above these fears. We must go about our daily business more determined than ever to do the ordinary things as well as we can and when we find a way to do anything more in our communities to help others to build <u>morale</u>, to give a feeling of security we must do it. Whatever is asked of us, I am sure we can accomplish it. We are the free and unconquerable people of the United States of America.

To the young people of the nation I must speak tonight. You are going to have a great opportunity – there will be high moments in which your strength and your ability will be tested. I have faith in you! Just as though I were standing upon a rock and that rock is my faith in my fellow citizens.

Now we will go back to the program which we had arranged for tonight and as I spoke to you a few weeks ago on the subject of Army morale, I suggested one of the best ways to make the boys in our armed forces more contented with their lot was for the people at home to really do their duty in the various activities of home defense. This evening, I wish to discuss army morale again. But this time in an even more concrete and specific way. And that's why I am delighted to have as my guest a young man who is a member of our armed forces ... Corporal James Cannon of Fort Dix. How long have you been in the army, Corporal Cannon[?]

CANNON: I've been in six months, Mrs. Roosevelt.

MRS. ROOSEVELT: You were a selectee?

CANNON: Yes, Mrs. Roosevelt.

MRS. ROOSEVELT: Well, after six months of army life, how do you like it?

CANNON: I want to tell you, honestly, I am proud to be a bad soldier in this grand army of the people.

MRS. ROOSEVELT: I don't believe you're such a bad soldier, not with those stripes on your arm, Corporal Cannon.

CANNON: Honestly, Mrs. Roosevelt, I'm not so hot. Why, my eyes are blood-shot from looking at the red flag ... the one they wave on the rifle range when you miss the target. By the way, Mrs. Roosevelt, you know who had the second highest score in our outfit ... the fellow who used to play a pipe organ in a roller skating rink. He'd never held a rifle in his hands before. But competent instructors have made him a sharpshooter in less than a year. And I'll bet there are men like him in every army post in America.

MRS. ROOSEVELT: Then you feel from your personal observation ... and, after all, Corporal Cannon, you are a trained newspaper

	man ... that the army is making civilians into good soldiers?
CANNON:	Mrs. Roosevelt, in the six months I've been in, I've seen a miracle take place. I've seen ordinary, easy-going guys turned into efficient members of a powerful fighting force. That's what's taking place in every training base in this country.
MRS. ROOSEVELT:	I am sure that is true, Corporal. But let me ask you a rather personal question. Aside from actual military training, do you find you are learning anything which is of value to you as a person, as a citizen?
CANNON:	Mrs. Roosevelt, I'm glad you asked me that question. I think I speak for hundreds of thousands of us in training camps ... everywhere, when I tell you the army has given me a completely new set of values.
MRS. ROOSEVELT:	You certainly are an honest soldier. Can you tell me just how the army has given you this new set of values?
CANNON:	Well, Mrs. Roosevelt, I was born and raised a New Yorker. I used to think America was a sort of suburb of New York. I had the New Yorker's contempt for people who lived beyond the Hudson. Now I soldier with a lot guys from the brambles and the bushes and the whistle stops. And I find they can do a lot of things I can't do. Sure, I can write a f[a]ir piece for a paper or a magazine. I can get wisecracks in a Broadway column. But I've neglected myself physically. I've gone soft. It sounds corny, I suppose, but you know I've learned to respect these guys from the sticks. They aren't wisecrackers ... all of them ... they don't know all the New York fancy talk ... but they're good soldiers and I'm proud to be serving with them. When it comes to a showdown, they'll be out there making the sacrifices to preserve the American way of life.
MRS. ROOSEVELT:	I am sure that there are many boys like you, Corporal who are learning the greatness of America and the greatness of their fellow Americans perhaps for the first time. But surely, Corporal, there are things which you don't like about the army?
CANNON:	I don't like hikes ... my feet tear and blister. I don't like getting up in the dark of the morning. I'm a clumsy chamber-maid. My bed always looks like a hay stack. But these discomforts are small. I've had a lot of laughs in the thirty-two years of my life.

I'm willing to kick back one or two years—so that I can live the rest of my life with dignity. I feel ashamed of the grumbling I've done—the complaining about the little unpleasant things—because at this minute soldiers of our army are proving under fire that they are true and brave and worthy of the trust our democracy places in them.

MRS. ROOSEVELT: Corporal, do you find an interest among the men in the army in the present world situation?

CANNON: I'm on Captain John Parker's Morale staff—attached to the 1229th Reception Centre—Fort Dix. I talk to the guys when they first come into the army. Up to now ... the only things they were interested in was—where they were going to be shipped—and if they were on the list for Kitchen Police. I'm certain all that will change now. When I left camp we were a peace-time army—now we are the army of a country that has been attacked. But all of them had a very definite opinion on the army and the state of the world.

MRS. ROOSEVELT: And what is that opinion?

CANNON: They know they are in the army because we have had no choice here in this country. They realize that all we Americans have lived for and died for will vanish from the earth unless we have a strong army. Their philosophy is: We were minding our business ... and they picked on us ... well, we'll show them.

MRS. ROOSEVELT: I think your answer is a very good one to those who would question the morale of the army. Speaking of morale, what would you suggest to the average civilian, Corporal Cannon, as the best way in which they can be helpful to the man in the service?

CANNON: You'll have to excuse me if I give a pretty strong answer to that question, Mrs. Roosevelt. First, the civilians can cut out those stale jokes and stop that mocking salute too many of them hand a man in uniform. Let them give a soldier the dignity he is entitled to. Tell them to treat a soldier as you would a civilian ... let him go unnoticed. The same fools think it is their privilege to break into a group of soldiers in a restaurant and violate their privacy. Tell them to cut out calling a soldier "Sarge." The same guys call a Pullman porter "George." We're a civilian army ... we're the army of the people ... and we want to be treated that way.

MRS. ROOSEVELT:	I hope that our listeners will take your words to heart, Corporal Cannon. To sum up, then, you think that democracy is working in our new army?
CANNON:	Not only in the army, but right here. Where else in the world would a guy like me be able to talk to the First Lady of the Land?
MRS. ROOSEVELT:	Thank you, Corporal Cannon. I am sure we are training a very gallant army as well as a brave one. And now I see that Mr. Leon Pearson is anxious to ask me some questions.
LEON PEARSON:	Yes, Mrs. Roosevelt, there are some very important questions I would like to ask you. First, of course, is this: Have you any comment to make on the strike Bill which passed the House of Representatives?
MRS. ROOSEVELT:	It was interesting to read the editorials in the *Herald Tribune* and *New York Times* on the bill. I think the wisest suggestion made is that the Senate should limit any legislation of this kind for a period of six months. The Times editorial stressed the fact that certain parts of the bill seemed ill-considered. But I think there is a more important reason than that for limiting the period for any kind of labor legislation which is passed at present. Until legislation is actually on the statute books, we cannot tell what effect it will have in practice, nor can we tell at present what conditions we will be meeting in the months to come. Therefore, like so many other things, it is hard to make a blue print which will meet unknown needs.
LEON PEARSON:	Mrs. Roosevelt, there is another question I'd like to ask.
MRS. ROOSEVELT:	Yes, Mr. Pearson.
LEON PEARSON:	A lot of writers and commentators are criticizing the government for not letting the people know enough about what is actually going on in public affairs. What would your reply be to these critics?
MRS. ROOSEVELT:	Thursday morning, Mr. Pearson, Mr. Walter Lippmann published what to me was a most interesting column on this subject. It was interesting not because of the facts alone, but because in the light of present day happenings, he interpreted some of the difficulties which have faced responsible people in government during the past six months. I think that most of us should take to heart this kind of explanation for many times responsible

people are accused of not telling the people of the country enough or not taking them into their confidence. Yet,
if they did so, it would probably be the greatest show of
weakness than any leader could make. It is always easy
to blurt out all you know, to try to get your burdens
shared by other people. It is far more difficult to take
the best advice you can get and make your own decisions, knowing that you will only be adding to the risks
of the situation if you try to turn the decision over to
others who cannot have the same background and
knowledge.

LEON PEARSON: That is certainly a candid answer to the question,
                     Mrs. Roosevelt.

MRS. ROOSEVELT: I would add one other thought along the same line,
                     Mr. Pearson. It is interesting to note how carefully the
                     Axis Powers sugarcoat any bad news which they have
                     for their people. I hope the people of this nation always
                     are strong enough to accept the bad news and still keep
                     up their courage. That is the one thing about Mr. Winston
                     Churchill's treatment of the British people, for which I
                     have the greatest admiration. He expects them to meet
                     bad news with complete fortitude and the mere fact that
                     he expects it, brings the proper response.

LEON PEARSON: And now, Mrs. Roosevelt, we understand you spent part
                     of this week in New York City. Were you Christmas
                     shopping?

MRS. ROOSEVELT: Yes, I did do some Christmas shopping. And one after-
                     noon I found myself in a crowded elevator in a large
                     department store. Suddenly, a lady near me seemed to
                     have a brain storm and looking at me, she asked, "Are
                     you Mrs. Roosevelt?" "Yes," I said, and she then pro-
                     ceeded with a ... "Do you mean to say you go around
                     without any guards?" I thought there was nobody left in
                     New York City who would be surprised at meeting me
                     almost anywhere at any hour of the day or night, so I
                     was quite shocked to find that I was looked upon as a
                     curiosity when found in broad daylight in the elevator of
                     a large shop!

LEON PEARSON: And Friday, I understand, Mrs. Roosevelt, you graciously
                     received at the White House the charming young ladies
                     who are representing my sponsor, the Pan-American
                     Coffee Bureau, in a Good Will tour of this country.

MRS. ROOSEVELT: It was a great pleasure to meet these young women from Latin-America who are here on a tour of Good Will, and I hope they enjoyed their cups of coffee in the White House.

LEON PEARSON: I am sure they did, Mrs. Roosevelt. And now, speaking of coffee, Dan Seymour, I understand you have a word or two to say on that subject.

DAN SEYMOUR: I certainly have. The seven young ladies who, as guests of the Pan-American Coffee Bureau, have come from their Republics to enjoy a visit with leaders in public and social life in the United States, are delighting everyone with their charm and their beauty. Just as coffee, the delicious product of their homelands, delights more and more of us every day with its glorious flavor, its pleasing aroma.

Next week, at this same time, Mrs. Roosevelt will be with us again to give us more of her interesting views on world affairs. This is Dan Seymour, saying good evening for the Pan-American Coffee Bureau ... and don't forget that goodnight cup of coffee.

Source: Pan American Coffee Bureau, Program #11, December 7, 1941, Speeches and Article File, 1941, Eleanor Roosevelt Papers, Franklin D. Roosevelt Library, Hyde Park, New York.

3 Franklin D. Roosevelt, Address to the Joint Session of Congress, 1941

The attack on Pearl Harbor stunned the nation, even those who were expecting the United States to enter the war against Germany and Japan. Although the United States made no serious efforts to negotiate with Nazi Germany after the invasion of Poland, the Americans and Japanese had attempted to resolve their differences in 1941. The Japanese government had dispatched two diplomats to Washington to negotiate with Secretary of State Cordell Hull over the issues that divided the two nations. Unfortunately, the differences were immense and the Japanese were unwilling to meet American demands to withdraw from China. In turn, the United States, by embargoing oil and iron shipments to Japan, forced the issue and the Japanese government had to decide between compromise or war to seek the raw materials it needed for its economy and military. In the end, Japan opted for war and launched a series of attacks against American, British, and Dutch interests in the Pacific and Asia. Although American intelligence had learned on the night before December 6, 1941, that the Japanese were breaking off negotiations the next day and that the chances of war had increased, the United States had not yet cracked the Japanese naval code. Moreover, the fleet that attacked Pearl Harbor maintained strict radio silence and managed to navigate a considerable distance across the Pacific undetected by the US Navy. FDR's address to the nation is widely regarded as one of the great public addresses in history by a US president and played a crucial role in galvanizing the nation to unite behind the common purpose of fighting Japan. Three days after the attack on Pearl Harbor, Nazi Germany declared war on the United States.

President Franklin D. Roosevelt Address to Joint Session of Congress, December 8, 1941

Mr. Vice President and Mr. Speaker, Members of the Senate and the House of Representatives:

Yesterday, December 7, 1941—a date which will live in infamy—the United States of America was suddenly and deliberately attacked by the naval and air forces of the Empire of Japan.

The United States was at peace with that Nation and, at the solicitation of Japan, was still in conversation with its Government and its Emperor looking toward the maintenance of peace in the Pacific. Indeed, one hour after Japanese air squadrons had commenced bombing in the American island of Oahu, the Japanese Ambassador to the United States and his colleague delivered to our Secretary of State a formal reply to a recent American message. And, while this reply stated that it seemed useless to continue the existing diplomatic negotiations, it contained no threat or hint of war or of armed attack.

It will be recorded that the distance of Hawaii from Japan makes it obvious that the attack was deliberately planned many days or even weeks ago. During the intervening time the Japanese Government has deliberately sought to deceive the United States by false statements and expressions of hope for continued peace.

The attack yesterday on the Hawaiian Island has caused severe damage to American naval and military forces. I regret to tell you that very many American lives have been lost. In addition, American ships have been reported torpedoed on the high seas between San Francisco and Honolulu.

Yesterday the Japanese government also launched an attack against Malaya.

Last night Japanese forces attacked Hong Kong.

Last night Japanese forces attacked Guam.

Last night the Japanese forces attacked the Philippine Islands.

Last night the Japanese attacked Wake Island.

And this morning the Japanese attacked Midway Island.

Japan has, therefore, undertaken a surprise offensive extending throughout the Pacific area. The facts of yesterday and today speak for themselves. The people of the United States have already formed their opinions and well understand the implications to the very life and safety of our nation.

As Commander in Chief of the Army and Navy, I have directed that all measures be taken for our defense.

But always will our whole Nation remember the character of the onslaught against us.

No matter how long it may take us to overcome this premeditated invasion, the American people in their righteous might will win through to absolute victory.

I believe that I interpret the will of the Congress and of the people when I assert that we will not only defend ourselves to the uttermost but will make it very certain that this form of treachery shall never again endanger us.

Hostilities exist. There is no blinking at the fact that our people, our territory, and our interests are in grave danger.

With the confidence in our armed forces—with the unbounding determination of our people—we will gain the inevitable triumph—so help us God.

I ask that the Congress declare that since the unprovoked and dastardly attack by Japan on Sunday, December 7, 1941, a state of war has existed between the United States and the Japanese Empire.

Source: Samuel I. Rosenman (ed.), *The Public Papers and Addresses of Franklin D. Roosevelt, 1941* (New York: Harper & Brothers, 1950), pp. 514–516.

4   William Dyess, Excerpt from *The Eye-witness Account of the Death March from Bataan*, 1944

Throughout the interwar years American military and naval planners debated over the best way to defend the American-held Philippines. Although the Roosevelt Administration had bolstered the defense of the islands earlier in 1940 and 1941, sending in troop reinforcements, deploying a fleet of long-range bombers, and calling back retired General Douglas MacArthur to active service as commander of American and Filipino forces on the territory, it would not be enough to forestall the Japanese invasion on December 10, 1941. Moreover, a day after Pearl Harbor, the Japanese managed to destroy much of America's air power on the island. The destruction of most of the Pacific Fleet at Pearl Harbor meant the US Navy could not come to the relief

*of the besieged forces on the Philippines. By the end of December 1941,
MacArthur abandoned efforts to defend all the Philippines and concentrated
the bulk of his forces on the island fortress of Corregidor, which blocked the
access to Manila and the Bataan Peninsula. For several months, American
and Filipino forces fought valiantly despite lacking food, medicine, and
ammunition. In March 1942, President Roosevelt ordered MacArthur to
leave the Philippines for Australia; one month later, General Jonathan
Wainwright, MacArthur's successor, surrendered to superior Japanese forces.
Lt. Colonel William E. Dyess, an army aviator, arrived in the Philippines on
the eve of war and was eventually taken prisoner when American forces
surrendered on the Bataan in April 1942. He survived not only the Bataan
Death March, which he describes in detail in his memoir, but also three
brutal prison camps before escaping with the aid of Filipino guerillas on the
island of Mindanao. Upon his return to the United States Dyess wrote this
memoir, based on interviews with the* Chicago Tribune, *and resumed his
career. Dyess would not survive the war; he was killed in December 1944
when the P-38 he piloted crashed in California.*

We disembarked at Manila on November 20 [1941] and were relieved to
learn there still was no war. At Nichols field we were gratified to find preparations proceeding at a furious pace. It was obvious at once that we were
facing a colossal task, and with each day's developments the international
situation grew more explosive.

On November 26 the United States warned Japan to get out of the Axis
and out of China and to cease all aggression. Tokio responded bluntly that
it could not comply.

A few days later, Japan massed troops on Thailand's borders in the face of
warnings by President Roosevelt. The government shut off shipments of
American oil to Japan and froze Japanese credits in the United States.
Simultaneously, we began speeding troops and material to the Philippines.
How anything short of war could have been expected I do not know.

The story I am about to tell covers the twenty months between our arrival
in the Philippines and my return to the United States. In the telling I hope I
can picture with lasting realism the selfless courage of those thousands—
those few thousands—of American and Filipino fighting men who held the
Philippines against the fury of the Japanese for four long months.

I want to picture in stark detail the barbaric cruelties inflicted upon the
survivors in a succession of Japan prison camps; the horrors of hunger and
thirst, of sickness and neglect, and of a daily existence in which the sight and
stench of death were ever present.

But even more terrible than the prison camp sufferings was the barbaric Death March from Bataan, an 85-mile trek from Mariveles, Bataan province, to San Fernando, Pampanga, under the merciless tropical sun. It began on April 10, 1942, the day after our surrender. The wanton murder, by beheadal, of an American army captain as the march was getting under way symbolized the horrors that were to come.

In the days that followed I saw the Japs plunge bayonets into malaria-stricken American and Filipino soldiers who were struggling to keep their feet as they were herded down the dusty roads that led to hell. I saw an American colonel flogged until his face was unrecognizable.

I saw laughing and yelling Jap soldiers lean from speeding trucks to smash their rifle butts against the heads of the straggling prisoners.

I saw Jap soldiers roll unconscious American and Filipino prisoners of war into the path of the Japanese army trucks which ran over them.

I saw and experienced for the first time the infamous Japanese sun cure, which can break a strong man. Thousands of American and Filipino war prisoners, mostly bareheaded, were forced at noonday, when the tropical sun was at the zenith, to sit in its direct rays until the sturdiest of us thought we must give up and until hundreds of our sick and weakened comrades did give up to delirium and death.

And it was on this march of death that most of us went practically without food for six days, others for twelve days, and all of us without water except for a few sips dipped from vile carabao wallows.

Source: Lt. Col. Wm. E. Dyess, *The Dyess Story: The Eye-witness Account of the Death March from Bataan and the Narrative of Experiences in Japanese Prison Camps and of Eventual Escape* (New York: G. P. Putman's Sons, 1944), pp. 24–25.

5 General George Marshall to Admiral Ernest King, Memorandum, and Franklin D. Roosevelt to Harry L. Hopkins, General Marshall, and Admiral King, Memorandum, 1942

Even before the United States entered the war, the Roosevelt Administration had stressed that Germany remained the greater threat to American national interests. The major setbacks delivered by Japanese forces led Roosevelt and his military advisors to reconsider this Germany first strategy. Moreover, in late spring 1942, the US Navy under the leadership of Admiral Ernest King sought to shift the focus of American resources to the Pacific. FDR remained adamant that America should concentrate forces against Germany before attacking Japan. In deciding in favor of a Germany first strategy, FDR was partly responding to calls by Soviet leader Joseph Stalin to open a second front in Europe to relieve German pressure on his country. Roosevelt and his Army Chief of Staff George Marshall were eager to confront the German Army and launch an invasion of France. But Winston Churchill and British leaders were cool on the idea of Sledgehammer, and the cross-Channel invasion did not materialize until June 1944. However, FDR did successfully push his British allies and his military leaders to land American forces in North Africa in November 1942 to confront the forces of Vichy France, which were aligned with Germany, before meeting and eventually fighting German forces led by General Erwin Rommel.

[George Marshall] Memorandum for Admiral [Ernest] King, July 15, 1942, Secret

The President in his conversation with me this morning referred to the proposal to transfer our major effort to the Pacific as something of a red herring, the purpose for which he thoroughly understood. However, he stated that he thought the record should be altered so that it would not appear in later years that we had proposed what amounted to the abandonment of the British. I think he refers to our joint memorandum to him on the subject, though I have not had time to look into the matter. If this last assumption is correct his idea evidently is that we should alter that memorandum insofar as may be necessary to present our views in such a fashion that it will not appear that we are proposing such abandonment. I did not think we were, with at least the Magnet force of ground troops going in there and a considerable air complement.

I am sending this to you now so that you will have an opportunity to consider the matter before we talk it over.

Source: George C. Marshall, *The Papers of George Catlett Marshall*, Volume 3: *"The Right Man for the Job," December 7, 1941–May 31, 1943*, ed. Larry I. Bland and Sharon Ritenour Stevens (Baltimore: Johns Hopkins University Press), p. 276.

MEMORANDUM FOR HON. HARRY L. HOPKINS, GENERAL MARSHALL, ADMIRAL KING, July 16, 1942

SUBJECT: INSTRUCTIONS FOR LONDON CONFERENCE – JULY, 1942

1. You will proceed immediately to London as my personal representatives for the purpose of consultation with appropriate British authorities on the conduct of the war.

2. The military and naval strategic changes have been so great since Mr. Churchill's visit to Washington that it becomes necessary to reach immediate agreement on joint operational plans between the British and ourselves along two lines:
    (a) Definite plans for the balance of 1942.
    (b) Tentative plans for the year 1943 which, of course, will be subject to change in the light of occurrences in 1942, but which should be initiated at this time in all cases involving preparation in 1942 for operations in 1943.
3. (a) The common aim of the United Nations must be the defeat of the Axis Powers. There cannot be compromise on this point.
    (b) We should concentrate our efforts and avoid dispersion.
    (c) Absolute coordinated use of British and American forces is essential.
    (d) All available U.S. and British forces should be brought into action as quickly as they can be profitably used.
    (e) It is of the highest importance that U.S. ground forces be brought into action against the enemy in 1942.
4. British and American material promises to Russia must be carried out in good faith. If the Persian route of delivery is used, preference must be given to combat material. This aid must continue as long as delivery is possible and Russia must be encouraged to continue resistance. Only complete collapse, which seems unthinkable, should alter this determination on our part.
5. In regard to 1942, you will carefully investigate the possibility of executing SLEDGEHAMMER. Such an operation would definitely sustain Russia this year. It might be the turning point which would save Russia this year. SLEDGEHAMMER is of such grave importance that every reason calls for accomplishment of it. You should strongly urge immediate all-out preparations for it, that it be pushed with utmost vigor, and that it be executed whether or not Russian collapse becomes imminent. In the event of Russian collapse becomes probable SLEDGEHAMMER becomes not merely advisable but imperative. The principle objective of SLEDGEHAMMER is the positive diversion of German Air Forces from the Russian Front.
6. Only if you are completely convinced that Sledgehammer is impossible of execution with reasonable chances of serving its intended purpose, inform me.
7. If SLEDGEHAMMER is finally and definitely out of the picture, I want you to consider the world situation as it exists at that time, and determine upon another place for U.S. Troops to fight in 1942.

It is my present view of the world picture that:

(a)   If Russia contains a large German force against her, ROUNDUP becomes possible in 1943, and plans for ROUNDUP should be immediately considered and preparations made for it.

(b)   If Russia collapses and German air and ground forces are released, ROUNDUP may be impossible of fulfillment in 1943.

8.   The Middle East should be held as strongly as possible whether Russia collapses or not. I want you to take into consideration the effect of losing the Middle East. Such loss means in series:

(1)   Loss of Egypt and the Suez Canal.

(2)   Loss of Syria.

(3)   Loss of Mosul oil wells.

(4)   Loss of the Persian Gulf through attacks from the north and west, together with access to all Persian Gulf oil.

(5)   Joining hands between Germany and Japan and the probable loss of the Indian Ocean.

(6)   The very important probability of German occupation of Tunis, Algiers, Morocco, Dakar and the cutting of the ferry route through Freetown and Liberia.

(7)   Serious danger to all shipping in the South Atlantic and serious danger to Brazil and the whole of the East Coast of South America. I include in the above possibilities the use by the Germans of Spain, Portugal and their territories.

(8)   You will determine the best methods of holding the Middle East. These methods include definitely either or both of the following:

(a)   Sending aid and ground forces to the Persian Gulf, to Syria and to Egypt.

(b)   A new operation in Morocco and Algiers intended to drive in against the backdoor of Rommel's armies. The attitude of French Colonial troops is still in doubt.

9.   I am opposed to an American all-out effort in the Pacific against Japan with the view to her defeat as quickly as possible. It is of the utmost importance that we appreciate that defeat of Japan does not defeat Germany and that American concentration against Japan this year or in 1943 increases the chance of complete German domination of Europe and Africa. On the other hand, it is obvious that defeat of Germany, or the holding of Germany in 1942 or in 1943 means probable, eventual defeat of Germany in the European and African theatres and in the Near East. Defeat of Germany means the defeat of Japan, probably without firing a shot or losing a life.

10. Please remember three cardinal principles – speed of decision on plans, unity of plans, attack combined with defense but not defense alone. This affects the immediate objective of U.S. ground forces fighting against Germans in 1942.

11. I hope for total agreement within one week of your arrival.

COMMANDER-IN-CHIEF

Source: Box 4, Safe File, Franklin D. Roosevelt Library, Hyde Park, New York. Available online at http://www.fdrlibrary.marist.edu/.

Study Questions

1   What emotions did Ruth A. Erickson remember feeling during the attack on Pearl Harbor and in its immediate aftermath?

2   Compare and contrast the messages Eleanor and Franklin Roosevelt offered to the nation in their separate radio addresses. What do each leave unsaid? Which one offered more comfort to the nation?

3   What happened to the American troops who surrendered to the Japanese in the Philippines?

4   What factors led Roosevelt to insist on a Germany first strategy in 1942? What did FDR fear by delaying the opening of a second front against Germany?

Chapter 3   The Pacific War

1 Alvin Kernan, Excerpt from *Crossing the Line: A Bluejacket's World Odyssey*, 1994

Alvin Kernan joined the Navy before Pearl Harbor to escape the limited economic opportunities on offer in his hometown in rural Wyoming. Kernan, who went on to a distinguished career as a literary scholar, was in 1942 a young sailor serving aboard the aircraft carrier Enterprise. *In this excerpt from his memoir, he describes the grim living conditions and claustrophic character of a naval vessel at war as men waited for the battle of Midway to begin. Even before confronting the Japanese, death stalked the* Enterprise *and Kernan describes how quickly a simple error could turn to tragedy.*

Wartime cruising had settled down to a routine in which boredom and tiredness ate away at life at sea. Stripped of paint and linoleum, rusting everywhere, constantly hot from cruising near the equator, with few air blowers open below deck, shuddering with high-speed maneuvers in a way that knocked over anything set on a shelf or table, the ships and life aboard them began to get to us. Fresh food lasted only a few days after we had been in port; we had only salt water to wash and shave in, with the irritation of

The United States in World War II: A Documentary Reader, First Edition.
Edited by G. Kurt Piehler. Editorial material and organization © 2013 Blackwell Publishing Ltd.
Published 2013 by Blackwell Publishing Ltd.

sandy saltwater soap; there was no entertainment of any kind, only work and sleep. Men began to get irritable.

Dungarees and blue work shirts, the standard uniform of the day, were never ironed, only washed and dried together in a great bag that had to be rummaged through to find those with your name stenciled on them. Put on clean and dry, they were soaking wet from the heat in a few minutes. White hats were dyed an anemic purple, and white socks were forbidden in order to avoid the flashes of white on the flight deck that would betray the presence of the ship to a snooper aircraft. Heat rash tormented everyone, particularly around the waist where several layers of clothing twisted and pulled inside the belt. A story circulated that when the heat rash—a quarter of an inch high and several inches wide, red and angry—girdled your waist, you died. No one believed it, but everyone kept a careful eye on the progress of the rash around his middle.

No one died, but every free moment was spent somewhere where the cooling breeze could blow over the rash and the sun could dry it out. Lacking any movies and music to entertain us, we gambled. It became the only relief from the tedium of what now was becoming not weeks but months at sea without even seeing land in the distance. I was a more enthusiastic than skillful poker player, but I loved the game, as I did the bridge, and even though I regularly lost my money in games in one small compartment or another about the ship, the first glimpse of the five cards in draw poker or the hole card in stud poker were the high moments, ironically, of days that were routinely filled with the real adventure of accidents and frequent death.

Death lived on an aircraft carrier operating in wartime conditions. One day a plane would crash taking off, and the lucky pilot lost no more than an eye on his telescopic sight mounted in front of him. The next day a plane landing on deck would drop a wheel strut into the catwalk and run screeching up it for a hundred feet. A mangled crewman would be carried away. A thoughtless step backward on the flight and hanger decks where the planes were turning up led to decapitation and gory dismemberment by propeller. Planes went out on patrol and were never heard of again. Death took many forms, but I think I first really came to know him on a day when I was standing on the flight deck and a Dauntless dive-bomber flew across the ship to drop a message about something seen on a patrol.

Once ships had put to sea, strict radio silence was maintained except for certain high-frequency VHF short-range transmissions used to direct the CAP (Combat Air Patrol) of fighters, close by the ship. Beanbags trailing long red streamers were used for message drops in order to preserve radio silence. As the dive-bomber came across the ship at about 120 knots, with the starboard wing sharply down to give the radioman an open field to throw the message bag on the flight deck, the down wing caught, ever so slightly, just a tick, the railing on the catwalk at the very edge of the ship. Just a flicker, but it was enough. In an instant the plane was in the water off the starboard side, broken in half between the radiomen and the pilot, neither of whom, knocked out by the crash, head hanging limply forward, moved. Then in an instant both pieces were gone, the water unruffled, and the ship sailed on. The quickness with which active life, so much energy and skill in the banking plane, disappeared as if it had never been stunned me.

It was the instantaneous contrast of something and nothing that caught my attention, and like some eighteen-year-old ancient mariner, I went around for days trying to tell people what had *really* happened, how astounding it was. The response was polite; death was a grave matter to everyone and never lightly dismissed. But no one, quite rightly, wanted to philosophize or make too much of what was common and likely to be the end of all us, much sooner than later.

Source: Alvin Kernan, *Crossing the Line: A Bluejacket's World War II Odyssey* (Annapolis: Naval Institute Press, 1994), pp. 44–46.

2 John Hersey, Excerpt from "The Battle of Rivers," *Life*, 1942

The finest of war-time journalists in World War II were not content to summarize press releases issued by headquarters staff but sought to observe the war first-hand. John Hersey ranks along with Ernie Pyle, Donald Whitehead, and William Shirer as among the great journalists of this conflict. In this article, which appeared in 1942, Hersey recounts his experience accompanying a US Marine patrol during the Guadalcanal campaign. Guadalcanal represented a decisive turning point in the war, marking the first time the United States went on the offensive as it attacked and held this Japanese-controlled island.

Captain Charles Alfred Rigaud, standing there in the drizzle about to lead his heavy machine-gun company forward, looked like anything except a killer who took no prisoners. He had a boy's face. There were large, dark circles of weariness and worry under his eyes. His mustache was not quite convincing.

We stood on a high grassy ridge above a 300-ft. cliff. In the valley below was a little stream, which ran into the Matanikau River. Captain Rigaud's mission was to clear the valley of snipers, push to the river, and force a crossing.

The crossing was supposed to be made easy by the fact that Whaling's force was working around behind the Japs on the other side of the river, so that the enemy would be trapped. But Whaling had run into trouble and been delayed. Therefore Captain Rigaud's mission was doomed before it started—but he had no way of knowing.

I asked Captain Rigaud if I could go along with him. "You may go if you want to," he said, as if any one who would want to was crazy. My valor was certainly of ignorance: if I had had any understanding of what Company H might meet, I never would have gone along.

This was a company of veterans. They had been in every battle so far, and except perhaps for Edson's Raiders had been in all the toughest spots. The company had already lost 22 dead. They were tired. In the last war, men seldom stayed in the front lines more than two weeks. These men had been on Guadal[canal] two months. They were veterans, sure of themselves but surfeited with fighting.

We went down into the valley in single file. My position in line was immediately behind Captain Rigaud. About half the company was ahead of us, about half behind. The company's proper weapons were heavy machine guns, which the men carried broken down. Quite a few of the men carried ammunition boxes in both hands—a terrible load in such country. Some had rifles. Captain Rigaud and some of his platoon had Browning automatic rifles.

"Keep five paces apart!"

After we had forded the stream once, the jungle suddenly became stiflingly thick. This was enemy territory in earnest. Our column moved in absolute silence. Captain Rigaud whispered to the man in front of him and to me that we should pass the word along for men to keep five paces apart, so as not to give snipers bunched targets. The message hissed forward and backward along the line in a whisper. "Keep five paces ... keep five paces ... keep five paces ..."

It is impossible to describe the creepy sensation of walking through that empty-looking but crowded-seeming jungle. Parakeets and cockatoos screeched from nowhere. There was one bird with an altogether unmusical call which sounded exactly like a man whistling shrilly through his fingers three times—and then another, far off in Jap territory, would answer.

As we sneaked forward, the feeling of tenseness steadily increased. The next word to be passed back from the head of the line came slowly, in whispers, for it was a long message: "Keep sharp lookout to right and to left ... keep sharp lookout to right and to left ... keep sharp lookout to right and to left ..."

As if we had to be told! After this word, another kind of message came back along the line: the tiny clicks of bullets being slipped into the chamber of weapons.

It was probably because I was a bad soldier, and looked at the ground rather than up in the trees, that I stumbled on my first really tangible evidence of the enemy. To the left of the trail, at the foot of a huge tree, I found a green headnet. It was small, and was made like some little minnow net. I picked it up, touched Captain Rigaud on the arm, and showed it to him.

Without changing his expression, he nodded, and shaped the soundless word "Jap" with his lips. Belatedly, it occurred to me to look up in the tree. There was nothing there.

A little farther along, I noticed a rifle lying in the stream. It had a very short stock and a very long barrel—not like any U.S. type I had seen. Again I touched Captain Rigaud's arm and pointed. He nodded again, and shaped the same word: "Jap."

First shot from a sniper

We were moving very slowly now. It seemed strange to me to be walking erect. I had had visions of men in the jungle slithering along on their bellies, or at least creeping on all fours, like animals. But we didn't even stoop.

Up ahead, suddenly, three or four rifle shots—the high-pitched Jap kind— broke the silence. Almost at once a message came cantering back along the line: "Hold it up ... hold it up ... hold it up ..."

A strange little conversation followed. Several of us were bunched together waiting to move—Captain Rigaud, Peppard, Calder, Brizard. Suddenly one of them whispered: "Jesu, what I'd give for a piece of blueberry pie!"

Another whispered: "Personally I prefer mince."

A third whispered: "Make mine apple with a few raisins in it and lots of cinnamon: you know, Southern style."

The line started moving again without any more shots having been fired and without the passing of an order. Now we knew definitely that there were snipers ahead, and all along the line there were anxious upturned faces.

About a hundred yards farther along, I got a real shock. I had been looking upward along with the rest when suddenly right by my feet to the left of the trail I saw a dead marine. Captain Rigaud glanced back at me. His lips did not shape any word this time, but his bitter young face said, as plainly as if he had shouted: "The Japs are bastards."

We kept on moving, crossing, and recrossing the stream, which got wider and more sluggish. We were apparently nearing the Matanikau. Up ahead, as a matter of fact, some of the men had already crossed the river. There seemed to be no opposition; we had reason to hope that Whaling had already cleaned out whatever had been on the other side, and that our job would be a pushover. Just a sniper or two to hunt down and kill.

The captain and I were about 75 ft. from the river when we found out how wrong our hope was.

The signal was a single shot from a sniper. A couple of seconds after it, snipers all around opened up on us. Machine guns from across the river opened up. But the terrible thing was that Jap mortars over there opened up, too.

The Japs had made their calculations, perfectly. There were only three or four natural crossings of the river. This was one of them. And so they had set their trap. They had machine guns all set up ready to pour stuff into the jungle bottleneck at the stream's junction with the river. They had snipers scattered on both sides of the river. And they had their mortars all set to lob the deadly explosions into the same area. Their plan was to hold their fire and let the enemy get well into the trap before snapping it, and this they had done with too much success.

Had we been infantry, the trap might not have worked. Brave men with rifles and grenades could have wiped out the enemy nests. Captain Rigaud's helplessness was that he could not bring his weapons to bear. Heavy machine guns take some time to be assembled and mounted. In that narrow defile his men, as brave as any, never succeeded in getting more than two guns firing.

The mortar fire was what was terrifying. Beside it, the Japs' sniper fire and even machine-gun fire, with its high, small-sounding report, seemed a mere botheration. But each explosion of mortar fire was a visitation of death.

When the first bolts of this awful thunder began to fall among Rigaud's men, we hit the ground. We were like earthy insects with some great foot being set down in our midst, and we scurried for little crannies—cavities under the roots of huge trees, little gullies, dead logs. Explosions were about ten seconds apart, and all around us, now 50 yd. away, now 20 ft. And all the while snipers and machine gunners wrote in their nasty punctuation. Our own guns answered from time to time with good, deep, rich sound, but not enough.

Individually the marines in that outfit were as brave as any fighters in any army in the world. But when fear began to be epidemic in that closed-in place, no one could resist it. The marines had been deeply enough indoctrinated so that even flight did not wipe out the formulas, and soon the word came whispering back along the line: "Withdraw ... withdraw ... withdraw ..." Then they started moving back, slowly at first, then running wildly.

Captain Rigaud saves the day

It was then that Charles Alfred Rigaud, the boy with tired circles under his eyes, showed himself to be a good officer and grown man. Despite the snipers all around us, despite the machine guns and the mortar fire, he stood right up on his feet and shouted out: "Who in Christ's name gave that order?"

This was enough to freeze the men in their tracks.

Next, by a combination of blistering sarcasm, orders and cajolery, he not only got the men back into position; he got them in a mood to fight again. I am certain that all along, Captain Rigaud was just as terrified as I was (i.e., plenty), for he was eminently human. And yet his rallying those men was as cool a performance as you can imagine.

When he had put them back into position, he immediately made preparations to get them out in an orderly fashion. He could see that the position was untenable; staying there would merely mean losing dozens of men who could live to fight successfully another day. He could not get his weapons into play; obviously Whaling's force had not unsettled the enemy across the river. Therefore he beckoned to a runner, filed out a request for permission to withdraw on his yellow message pad, sent the runner off to the rear C. P. [Command Post], and then set about passing whispered orders for the withdrawal.

Now the heroism of the medical corpsmen and bandsmen showed itself. They went into the worst places and began moving the wounded. I joined them because, I guess, I just thought that was the fastest way to get the hell out of there.

I attached myself to a group who were wounded in a dreadful way. They had no open wounds; they shed no blood; they seemed merely to have been attacked by some mysterious germ of war that made them groan, hold their sides, limp, and stagger. They were shock and blast victims.

There were not enough corpsmen to assist more than the unconscious and leg-wounded men, so they had set these men to helping each other. It was like the blind leading the blind. I commandeered three unhurt privates, and we began to half-carry, half-drag the worst of these strange casualties.

The rain and trampling had made the trail so bad now that a sound of a man walking alone would occasionally fall, and in some steep places would have to crawl on hands and knees, pulling himself by exposed roots and leaning bamboo trunks. We slid, crept, walked, wallowed, waded and staggered, like drunken men. One man kept striking the sides of his befuddled skull with his fists. Another kept his hands over his ears. Several had badly battered legs, and behaved like football players with excruciating Charley horses.

A wounded boy and his sergeant

The worst blast victim, who kept himself conscious only by his guts, was a boy whom I shall call John Smith, though that is not his name. Part of the time we had to carry him, part of the time he could drag his feet along while I supported him. Before we went very far, a corpsman, who saw what pain he was in, injected some morphine in his arm. Smith had a caved-in chest, and one of his legs was blasted almost out of use.

As we struggled along the trail he kept asking us for his sergeant, whose name I shall change to Bill Johnson. "Don't leave Johnson," the wounded boy pleaded.

Gradually I pieced together what had happened. Smith and several of these others had been the crew of one of the machine guns which did get into action. Sergeant Johnson was in command of the gun. While they were approaching-firing, a mortar-grenade went off near them, knocking the crew all over the place. Most of the men took cover. But Johnson crawled back to the gun just in time for another grenade to come much closer yet.

We asked around in the group to see if Johnson was with us, but he was not. "They got him sure," one said.

"He shouldn't have gone back," Smith said, "Why in hell did he have to go back?"

And all the way out of that valley of the shadow, John Smith mumbled about his friend Sergeant Johnson.

The farther we went, the harder the going seemed to be. We all became tired, and the hurt men slowed down considerably. There were some steep places where we had to sit Smith down in the mud, and slide him down 10 ft. to the stream. In other places, uphill, we had to form a chain of hands and work him up very slowly. It was almost dark when we got out of the jungle, and by the time we had negotiated the last steep ridge, it was hard to tell the difference between the wounded men and the bearers. We turned the wounded over to Doc New, the Navy surgeon, who had an emergency dressing station set up on the crest of the last ridge.

While I talked with Captain Rigaud, who had led his men out by a shorter way and beaten us in, corpsmen and bandsmen hurried down for Johnson. It was pitch dark when those heroic boys found him. They were in territory, remember, where snipers had been all around, and where, if they betrayed themselves by the slightest sound, they would have mortar fire pouring down on them. They asked Johnson: "How you feel, Mac?" He said, "I think I can make it." They fashioned a stretcher out of two rifles and a poncho, and started out. Johnson was in bad shape. He was conscious, but that was about all.

The only way they could find their path was to follow, hand over hand, a telephone wire which some wire stringer had carried down into that hot valley. In the darkness they had great difficulty making progress, and had to halt for long rests.

Men who are wounded do not talk rhetorically; famous last words are usually edited after the fact. Johnson's sentences to Sgt. Lewis W. Isaak and Private Clinton Logan Prater were simple requests: "Help me sit up, will you please, oh God my stomach" ... Soon he said very softly: "I wish I could sleep." The wish was fulfilled: he dropped off in an apparent peace. He gave a few short breaths and then just stopped breathing.

I never did find out exactly how many men were killed, and how many wounded in that valley. But I do not know that one less died than would have otherwise, if Doc New hadn't been mighty handy in an emergency. ...

Source: John Hersey, "The Battle of the River," *Life*, November 23, 1942, pp. 111–115.

3 US Army Research Branch, Excerpt from Report No. B-11, "Factors Affecting Morale of Veteran Infantrymen in the Pacific," 1945

The conflict in the Pacific has been described by John Dower as a "war without mercy" and by Gerald Linderman as an "unrestrained war." How common were war-time atrocities in the conflict between the United States and Japan? Social scientists with the US Army sought to answer this question even before the war ended. In reporting their findings, they were surprised that GIs they questioned did not report witnessing more Japanese atrocities. In surveying soldiers on this issue, they sought to address a wider question: what motivated combatants to fight? Although comradeship, or the "brotherhood of arms," has been remembered as the principal reason for sustaining men in combat, there were other factors in play, as this war-time study suggests.

Enemy Atrocities

In view of the atrocity tales which have come out of the Pacific it is perhaps surprising to find that, like their fellow G.I.'s fighting the Germans, only a small proportion of the enlisted men who are veterans of Pacific warfare have personally seen cases of the enemy using dirty or inhuman methods of fighting. It is possibly even more surprising that less than half of these infantry veterans have heard "true cases" from others of dirty or inhuman methods of fighting.

Question: "How about atrocities: Did you personally ever see with your own eyes cases of Japanese (Germans) using methods of fighting or treating prisoners which you would call dirty or inhuman?"

Percentage answering "Yes"

Veterans of Pacific fighting 13
Veterans of European fighting 13

Question: "How about stories you have heard from others? Did you hear any true cases of Japanese (Germans) using methods of fighting or treating prisoners which you would call dirty or inhuman?"

Percentage answering "Yes"

Veterans of Pacific fighting 45
Veterans of European fighting....... 24

Men who witnessed or heard of "true cases," of atrocities were asked to describe them. Some of the stories make a grisly chronicle, among the more lurid being accounts of the cutting off of genitals or the finding of human flesh in Japanese mess kits. Some of the men commented that practices like the killing of prisoners had become so standard on both sides as hardly to be classified as atrocities unless torture is applied. But the most significant finding, still, is probably the fact that less than half of the men had heard of what they believed to be true cases of dirty or inhuman fighting.

Does hatred help?

The foregoing evidence makes it clear that even among troops fighting a treacherous enemy in the Orient, there are many who do not voice impersonal or personal expressions of vindictiveness. It also suggests that a propaganda campaign instituted from the outside to increase hatred would have tough going—particularly, in view of the skepticism half of the veterans show toward atrocity stories originating in their own outfits.

Assuming that hatred develops in the individual soldier, does hatred help?

Earlier studies made of soldiers fighting the Germans shows [sic] that there are a good many soldiers—officers and men—who think hatred of the Germans helps them fight better. A third of the infantrymen in a sample interviewed behind the lines at Cassino in February said that hatred helped a lot, but the majority said it did not help much or did not help at all. A fifth of the veteran officers and a fourth of the veteran enlisted men questioned in regiments poised in England for the invasion of France said that when the fighting got tough in the Mediterranean hatred of the enemy helped a lot.

How about soldiers in the Pacific? In the three divisions surveyed, 44 percent of the officers and 38 percent of the enlisted men said that when the going was tough they were helped a lot by thoughts of hatred of the enemy. However, the testimony is that other attitudes influenced more men than did hatred. For example, 84 percent of the officers and 60 percent of the men said that when the going was tough they were helped a lot by the thought that "I can't let the other men down."

Source: "Factors Affecting Morale of Veteran Infantrymen in the Pacific": Report No. B-11, Research Branch, Morale Services Division, Army Service Forces, War Department, Report #111, Box 992, RG 330, National Archives, College Park, Maryland.

4 John Ciardi, Excerpts from Diary, 1944

Air power allowed the United States and its allies to take the fighting to the enemy's homeland early in the war. In Europe, the Eighth Air Force began attacking German targets on the European continent in 1942. In contrast to the British Royal Air Force, which bombed at night, the United States possessed heavily armored airplanes bristling with machine guns against enemy fighters and relied on daylight precision bombing through much of the war. In his diary, the poet John Ciardi offers an account of the terror and risks posed by bombing missions against Japan from an American base in the recently captured Saipan. Ciardi flew in a B-29, the only long-range bomber in World War II that possessed pressurized cabins, but as he notes, pressurization would fail on many flights and crews had to resort to bottled oxygen.

Dec. 16, '44

Somewhere in the last few days time swallowed and disappeared. It began with one of those sudden chemical anxieties. Chemical because there was no rational part of me in it. We were put up for a mission to Nagoya and suddenly I dreaded it. It made a sleepless night and left me cursing mad in the morning and very glad to get under way. Once I was in the plane and touching the things that had to be done, the anxiety was over. I doubt that it will return. It takes a little for me to get used to going to sleep at night knowing that I may be killed the next day. Ideally, I'd like to be unmoved by it, but I can't quite seem to manage it.

As it was the sleepless night would pass as a psychic premonition if I leaned toward psychic premonitions. We took off at 8:55, were almost over the target at 1500 and landed at 2205. In between we had trouble.

Nagoya is the third largest city of Japan with a population about that of San Francisco. Unlike Tokio, it is comparatively unmodernized and consequently highly inflammable. Also it has a Mitsubishi engine plant. The engine plant was our target.

We took off and test fired our guns while we jockeyed into formation. Immediately two of the four upper turret guns went out of action and I crawled forward to clean them. As always we flew the first few hours of gas off just above sea level then climbed for altitude when we were lighter. That gave me about four hours in which to have the turret opened before we pressurized.

It didn't do any good. The trouble was perfectly advertised in the raised gun covers. The cover cam was not bearing down on the extractor, and therefore not camming the round into the chamber. I had had the covers off the day before to clean them, and though theoretically they are interchangeable from gun to gun, two of them must have been switched and refused to stay latched under pressure. The wry pleasure of knowing it was my own fault was no help at all. The covers could not be changed in mid-air since they had to be worked on from above and outside. I tried uselessly for three hours to wire them down with odd scraps of wire, but they kept popping loose. Finally we had to climb. I sealed the turret for pressurization. Two guns is still a formidable turret, but that wasn't much help to think of either.

We finally crossed the coastline and saw Japan below us—a brown, wrinkled country. Geologically a new drowned coastline, much like the shores of Maine, except that Maine is green and unvolcanic. A hilly country that fell into the sea letting the water into the endless irregular network of valleys.

We had had lead-navigator trouble all the way and finally hit the coast about 80 miles off course. In the imperative name of SNAFU the formation went cruising about Japan for better than an hour looking for the target finally heading into Nagoya straight across the middle of a major air field we were carefully briefed to avoid.

The field was packed full of Frances's. Frances is the new twin-engine Jap fighter about which intelligence knew nothing except that it looked like a Mosquito. I don't know whether Intelligence knows any more about it now, but I know that it has a rate of climb. I watched the first two race down the runway and within seconds watched them climb to 15,000'. They came up on a least a 70° angle. And they kept coming.

No. 4 Engine picked just that moment to swallow a valve and break a rocker arm. The formation was still scouting around for Nagoya like clay pigeons in the teeth of a 100 knot headwind, and with No. 4 giving practically no power we couldn't keep up. By the time Frances's had gotten between us and the formation it was time to clear out. We let our bombs go at a target of last resort, left the No. 4 prop wind-milling to keep from advertising our trouble, and headed out for sea. A few miles out we were clear and had the prop feathered, but still had about 1/3 of the Pacific to limp across. Skipper called O'Hara for an ETA and was told 6 hours. Then he called Campbell to find out how much gas we had and was told 4 hrs. and a half.

There wasn't much to do but sweat it out. As a last resort we could ditch but even if we landed on the water without cracking up, the Pacific is still no place to be in a rubber life raft. We began to lighten the ship. We depressurized and went on oxygen while we broke open the turrets and hauled out the ammunition to toss into the bomb bays. I was laboring at the belts like a stoker and changing walk-around bottles every 3 minutes. When I wasn't changing a bottle it hung from my shirt like an anchor getting in the way of every move. I finally tore it off and risked 20,000 feet without oxygen, but immediately went faint. The wind was whistling cold through the open turret but I sweated like a pig while the ammunition belts fell in coils around my feet until I was almost caught in my own trap. O'Hara, Franklin, and the radio and navigation equipment have to share one small compartment with the turret and the turret fills most of the space to start with. We had a fine half hour of getting in each other's way and I was limp with exhaustion when I finished and called T. J. to help me haul the belts through the turret.

We finally had the ammunition from the upper turret in the bomb bays. The belts in the lower turrets could be fired out and the links and cases would drop out. Doc salvoed the ammunition and our flak suits went with it for good measure. A while later Bob Campbell had the last gas out of the bomb bay tanks and we dropped those. They fell away trailing gasoline vapor and crashing into the radar dome on the way out, putting the radar spinner out of action.

There was nothing left to do but wait and sweat it out. O'Hara plotted a series of shrewd courses that would pick up favorable tail winds, and Skipper fondled the throttle settings to get the last bit of good out of the gas. And the Pacific stayed endlessly below.

Meanwhile the strike report came over. Good hits and large fires. No ships lost to enemy action. But the VHF was full of ship-to-ship distress. One of our crews—Grice's—had picked up some bad flak hits. It hit the water at 1700 and was lost. Some good boys went down in that one. Bob Campbell was a good red-head, and Kaufman had won a lot of my money by being a good gambler. That's a hell of an epitaph, but what good is an epitaph.

We kept getting VHF distress calls from other ships and sending out a few of our own. A second ship ditched at 1910. Later reports (next day) had them accounted for—picked up by a destroyer. Orenstein kept a log of his calls and position reports and probably was largely responsible for the rescue.

Meanwhile the Pacific stayed where it was and we stayed where we were—not in it. And eventually—Saipan. We called the tower for a straight in approach and they called back for us to land at Gardenia—the B-24 strip.

I thought I had really survived something until Joe Shannon (ground crew) came over in disgust. "Know how much gas you got?" I said it wasn't my department. Joe made a good Irish grimace of disgust and said "1400 gals! What's the matter with your engineer?"

A good question.

Pointedly however we're back and that will do till the next time.

Meanwhile the news is all guns and Doc Grow. Doc went on a moonlight requisitioning spree with colossal results. He borrowed a jeep, drove the jeep into a borrowed landing craft, piloted it over to Tinian, and came back with two 15 × 20 tarps, some lumber, 55 lbs of boneless choice merchant marine steak and a smoked ham. We had a steak fry last night that will do for some very long pleasant memories. And we're building a shack on the line with the tarps and lumber—a place to store guns.

Another mission goes over Nagoya tomorrow. Our crew won't be on it.

Source: John Ciardi, *Saipan: The War Diary of John Ciardi* (Fayetteville: University of Arkansas Press, 1988), pp. 58–61.

5 Sam Smith, Oral History Interview Regarding Battle of Iwo Jima, 2004

Native Americans were not segregated by the US armed forces, with one important exception. The US Marines created a special signal unit composed solely of Navajo speakers to send and receive messages in the Pacific. Since few outside of the Navajo reservation in Arizona and New Mexico spoke the Navajo language and foreign scholars had not documented it, it could be used to communicate messages on the battlefield without fear that the enemy might decode them if intercepted. Sam Smith, a Navajo from New Mexico, lied about his age in order to enlist in the US Marines. Like other native speakers, Smith was placed in an all-Navajo signal unit and participated in several island assaults in the Pacific. Below, he recounts his experiences during the assault on Iwo Jima. He also discusses the need to refine the code and to invent names for certain military weapons and terms.

Before Iwo we went back to Maui and again gather all the Navajo Code Talkers at division headquarters where I was. We have a big tent. It's our classroom, that's where we do all the Code Talker brush-up. Also, on these islands, when we go hit the island we send messages to each other and we find problem with some of the things that we're gonna use over and over. So we thought of a idea [*sic*] to have made for each one of them so that the communication be quicker, faster, shorter—and that's what were doing, too, at these, uh, at these rest periods. ...

It grew. And the other divisions I found out were doing the same thing. What we were doing, at one time they flew me and my assistant teacher to Pearl Harbor and we found out that, uh, the other teachers from other divisions, from other islands were flown there too. So we put all our communication papers together and made this one. ...

And then it was uniform, right. Of course we discuss some of them that were made by other divisions that we thought we'd just do away with and just make one, for the certain thing that was made during the battles. So that's how that one is built, made up. The twenty-nine Navajo Marines had just about three pages of code and we build it up to five, six pages doing that. And that was from the experience of what took place on each island that we fought on. So that's—yeah, we rest after Tinian. And then, uh, we never know—I never know where we're gonna go. We all guess where we're going to go. Somebody always say, "We're going over there," and we start believing him and spread the word and some other guy come around, "We're going over there," to another island, so it was all guessin' til the night before attack. We have a briefing aboard ship and I'm usually one of them in there with other officers, captain, lieutenants, sergeant majors, and me a PFC [Private First Class], be in there in briefing to look at the map and they talk about planning. How we're going to do this. Day One, we're gonna go this far, Day Two that far, and so on. But it didn't work on Iwo Jima. We were to take that island in seven days—one week. They had been bombarding that place for one whole month off the battleships. And bombed. They were bombing that for one whole month, just [one] right after another. And here we was gonna take it, really, I thought we were going to take it in seven days. And, uh, we spend like two days on the beach trying to get in. (Laughs) Yeah. That cinder was so hard to climb. Uphill you had to kind of climb sideways to get to the top. It was really bad and there was a lot of bodies on the beach that were being picked up and taken back. The ones that can move get picked up, the other ones get picked up later. So that's how it was on Iwo Jima. And we, after about two weeks—well they raised that flag on day six I think it was. It was a small flag. I don't know whose flag it was, and then the next day it was gone. There was no flag. And a little later on, there was a flag up there on the mountain again. That's the one they had a problem with. Nobody wanted to go up there to put up that flag, so a few volunteered to do that, uh, and one of 'em was a Pima Indian. The last one barely touching the pole is the Pima Indian Ira Hayes. That took some guts to go up there and do that the second time. The first time nobody thought they would do that. They put it up without problems. I understand that big flag, the next one, was from a boat, one of those little boats. I don't remember the boat, but it was a Navy flag.

Source: Sam Smith, interview with G. Kurt Piehler and Cynthia Tinker, February 13, 2004, Center for the Study of War and Society, University of Tennessee, Knoxville, Tennessee.

Study Questions

1   Was the enemy the only danger that American combatants faced?
2   How common were atrocities in the Pacific? How do they compare to those in Europe?
3   Compare and contrast the differences between combat on land, at sea, and in the air.
4   What unique role did the Navajo play in the war against Japan?
5   What motivated and sustained the American GI in battle? What role did hatred of the enemy play in this regard?

Chapter 4   The War in North Africa and Europe

1 George Marshall to Lesley McNair, Memorandum, 1942

Americans did not engage in ground combat against German forces until late 1942 when a joint Anglo-American force landed in French North Africa at Casablanca, Oran, and Algiers as part of Operation Torch. It was an army ill-prepared for war. While quickly overcoming resistance by Vichy French forces, US troops promptly ran into difficulty when they confronted Erwin Rommel's Afrika Korps. The following memo, written by Marshall just a few weeks after the Operation Torch landing on November 4, 1942, underscores the problems the Army faced as it grew from a force of a little over 200,000 active-duty personnel in 1939 to one numbering over 8 million by the end of the war. General Lesley McNair received this memorandum because of his responsibility, as Commander of Army Ground Forces, for ensuring US troops stationed were properly trained. General Brehon Somervell, mentioned in this memorandum, served as Commander of the Army Services Forces with responsibility for overseeing supply and transport. The G-1 is the Assistant Chief of Staff for Personnel and the G-3 is the Assistant Chief of Staff for Organization and Training.

The United States in World War II: A Documentary Reader, First Edition.
Edited by G. Kurt Piehler. Editorial material and organization © 2013 Blackwell Publishing Ltd.
Published 2013 by Blackwell Publishing Ltd.

Memorandum for General McNair, November 28, 1942

Secret

I have just been listening to an account by Major James Y. Adams on the operation at Safi. One or two of the points he made concern me greatly.

I was shocked to learn that replacements joined the regiment for Safi, without ever having fired a rifle; they had been trained on the fantail of the boat. I suppose this is a matter entirely beyond your control. Nevertheless I want to get your reactions to the administrative set-up that produces such a result.

I was concerned over the reactions of troops first under fire considering that this was a division that was assumed to be more dependable and better trained than others that we had in mind for possible assignment to the operation. I am aware that troop commanders have felt that the quality of their men has deteriorated in recent months due to the over-age and poor physical specimen inductions, also due to the frequent emasculation of units in order to furnish cadres. But I did not realize a division such as the Third would have so much uncertainty in its ranks, even considering the difficulties of the debarkation, when stout resistance was not being made.

Another point fixed my attention, and that was the issue of rocket guns to the troops without anybody knowing how to use them or even what they were for. This seems unbelievable.

I have not had an opportunity to talk to Somervell or to G-1 or G-3 about any of these matters, the assignment of replacements, the issue of rocket guns, etc., but I should like to have you present when I do talk to them, with one or two of your staff. I am dictating this memorandum so that you can check up with Major Adams and be prepared for such a discussion.

Source: George C. Marshall, *The Papers of George Catlett Marshall*, Volume 3: *"The Right Man for the Job,"* December 7, 1941–May 31, 1943, ed. Larry I. Bland and Sharon Ritenour Stevens (Baltimore: Johns Hopkins University Press, 1991), pp. 454–455.

2 James R. Forgan to Commanding General, European Theater of Operations, Memorandum, 1945

> *Women were not permitted to enlist in the combat ranks and their service in the Women's Army Corps (WAC), the US Navy's Women Accepted for Voluntary Emergency Service (WAVES), US Marines, and the US Coast Guard Women's Reserve (SPARS), was severely restricted. Some*

servicewomen did become mechanics, link trainer operators, or codebreakers, but generally they assumed traditional roles as secretaries, medical orderlies, and clerks. Although George Marshall was eager to send WAC units overseas and even encouraged an experiment to incorporate women into anti-aircraft batteries around Washington, DC, the Navy remained much more reluctant to deploy women overseas and, except for hospital ships, banned women from serving aboard naval vessels. The Office of Strategic Services (OSS), the predecessor of the Central Intelligence Agency, did allow some women to volunteer for hazardous duty behind enemy lines, and this document is a report written about one especially heroic female agent deployed to France prior to the cross-Channel invasion (D-Day). In this report, an army colonel recommends Virginia Hall for a major decoration for valor in the face of the enemy. Hall had a wooden leg that gave her a limp, which was known to the Gestapo. Moreover, Hall's involvement in the war predated Pearl Harbor: like many men who joined the Royal Air Force and Royal Canadian Air Force prior to Pearl Harbor, she did not wait for America to enter the war to fight the Nazis. In contrast to the Americans, the British were much more willing to use women as intelligence agents behind enemy lines and to put them into anti-aircraft batteries defending home islands from attack. Hall received the Distinguished Service Cross based on this recommendation.

Colonel James R. Forgan to Commanding General, European Theater of Operations, U.S. Army, 5 February 1945

… Miss Virginia Hall, an American civilian in the employ of the Special Operations Branch, Office of Strategic Services, European Theater of Operations, distinguished herself, by extraordinary heroism against an armed enemy from 21 March 1944 to 26 September 1944. …

From August, 1941 to October, 1943, Miss Hall was serving as an agent in the employ of the British Government in Lyon, France, where she did liaison and intelligence work, established safe houses, recruited Resistance personnel, acted as a courier for other agents, and planned and executed prison escapes for members of the underground who had been arrested by the Gestapo.

Throughout this period, in addition to her other activities, Miss Hall was responsible for the care, hiding, and subsequent escape of a great number of Allied airmen and Prisoners of War.

Due to the fact that her activities became known to the authorities, Miss Hall was forced to leave France. She returned to England via Spain, crossing the Pyrenees on foot and spent several weeks in the greatest discomfort and bad conditions of a Spanish internment camp.

Major Gerard Morel, French Army, who was closely allied with Miss Hall during this period, describes her actions as follows:

> "Her energy, enthusiasm, and devotion to the Allied cause were an inspiration to all. In addition, her courage and physical endurance were of the highest order; and, although handicapped as the result of an accident in which she lost a leg, she never, on any occasion, allowed this physical disability to interfere in any way with her work."

Shortly, after her return to England, Miss Hall was employed by the Special Operations Branch, Office of Strategic Services, and volunteered to return to France for the purpose of work in connection with the organization, supply and operations of Resistance Forces.

Despite the fact that she was well known to the Gestapo because of previous activities, Miss Hall returned to France by sea on 21 March 1944. For the first few weeks, she devoted herself to investigating the underground organizations in the Departments of Creuse, Cher, and Nievre. She succeeded in recruiting and training several groups of loyal Frenchmen with the intention of organizing receptions in the area. Her plans did not materialize, however, since she was ordered by London Headquarters to proceed to the Department of Haute Loire where it was felt that her unusual talent for organization would be better utilized.

Upon her arrival in the Haute Loire, Miss Hall established contact with London Headquarters and made arrangements for the dispatch by plane of supplies for the Resistance Forces in the area. With the help of a Jedburgh team, she succeeded in organizing, arming and training three FFI [French Forces of the Interior] battalions which later took part in many engagements with the enemy and in several acts of sabotage. Following are some of the results achieved by these forces:

(1) Bridge blown at Montagnac cutting road Langegne/Le Puy.
(2) Four cuts on railroads Langegne/Brassac.
(3) Freight train derailed in tunnel at Brassac.
(4) Bridge blown on railway between Brionde/Le Puy.
(5) Freight train derailed in tunnel at Menistrel d'Allier.
(6) Tunnel at Selignac rendered impassable by blowing up rails.
(7) Lavante-sur-Loire railway bridge blown.
(8) Railway bridge wrecked at Chamaliere and Locomotive driven into gulf below.
(9) Telephone lines Brieude/Le Puy rendered useless – lines cut, wires rolled up, and telephone posts cut down.

(10)   19 Milicans arrested and valuable documents seized.

(11)   German convoy of 12 Lorries destroyed near St. Paulisu.

(12)   5 German lorries destroyed near Rotournac.

(13)   Due to blowing of bridges, it was possible to ambush German convoy from Le Puy between Chamelix and Pigeyre. The convoy, after a bitter struggle, surrendered at Estiuareilles in the Loire Department. Approximately 500 Germans were taken alive and 150 killed. The Maquis losses were negligible.

In addition to her duties as an organizer, Miss Hall provided radio communication between London Headquarters and the Resistances [sic] Forces in the Haute Loire Department, transmitting and receiving operational and intelligence information. This was the most dangerous type of work as the enemy, whenever two or more direction finders could be tuned in on a transmitter, were able to locate the transmittal point to within a couple of hundred yards. It was frequently necessary for Miss Hall to change her headquarters in order to avoid detection.

Throughout this entire assignment, Miss Hall displayed most outstanding qualities of courage, perseverance, and ingenuity. Working in a region infested with enemy troops, hunted by the Gestapo, she succeeded in organizing, arming, and directing Resistance Forces whose activities proved to be of inestimable value to the Allied Expeditionary Forces in the successful invasion and liberation of France. ...

Source: File: 18494-32, Box 29, Entry 92, RG 226, US National Archives II, College Park, Maryland. I am indebted to John W. Chambers for providing a copy of this document.

3 Dwight Eisenhower, Draft Statement and Memorandum to the Combined Chiefs of Staff, 1944

Commanders along with journalists write the initial history of a battle. The first document below is the message Eisenhower wrote as Commander of the Supreme Headquarters Allied Expeditionary Force (SHAEF) in case the cross-Channel invasion failed. In the days leading up to the D-Day invasion, Eisenhower had to make a nerve-wracking decision whether to attempt a landing on the beaches of Normandy, France, in uncertain weather conditions that threatened to capsize vessels and drown thousands of men. Added to this tension was the need to wait weeks before attempting another landing on the French coast, given the changing tidal conditions. The second document is the initial report sent by Eisenhower to senior American and

British military leaders directing the Anglo-American war effort through the Combined Chiefs of Staff. While noting the success of the landing and subsequent operations against the enemy, Eisenhower makes clear there were setbacks and losses: tanks floundered on the beaches, landing craft were destroyed by mines, and artillery fire took a heavy toll. As Supreme Allied Commander, Eisenhower led a force made up of a number of Allied countries, with Britain and Canada providing the largest contingents after the United States. In this document he refers to British Admiral Bertram Ramsay, who commanded Allied Naval Forces. The British Royal Navy provided the bulk of the capital ships (i.e., battleships and cruisers) needed for the invasion on D-Day, since most of the US Navy was deployed in the Pacific. The naval officers here referred to are Admiral Grayson Kirk of the US Navy, and Admiral Sir Philip Vian, Commodore Cyril E. Douglas-Pennant, and Commodore Geoffrey N. Oliver of the British Royal Navy.

[June 5, 1944]

Our landings in the Cherbourg-Havre area have failed to gain a satisfactory foothold and I have withdrawn the troops. My decision to attack at this time and place was based upon the best information available. The troops, the air and Navy did all that Bravery and devotion to duty could do. If any blame or fault attaches to the attempt it is mine alone. ...

June 8, 1944

To the Combined Chiefs of Staff from Eisenhower ... Accompanied by Admiral Ramsay I made yesterday a complete tour by destroyer of the landing areas beginning on the right. The landings on the Cotentin Peninsula apparently went about as well as could be expected with the 101st Airborne Division carrying out its missions in good style. Information of the 82d Airborne is meager but General [Omar] Bradley informed me that VII Corps has made contact with it. On Beach O[maha] repeat O attacked by the V Corps opposition was unexpectedly heavy due to the presence on the beaches of a full German division which was on maneuvers. Losses have been considerable in this force and landings have been most difficult due to the coverage of beaches by hostile artillery. Moreover, a large portion of DD tanks foundered on their way to the beaches. Due to the rough weather decision was made on the other beaches not repeat not to attempt to swim in the DD tanks. These were unloaded directly on the beaches from the LCT's [Landing Craft Tanks] carrying them. At noon on June 7 General Bradley felt that conditions were improving on O Beach and steps are being taken to replace artillery which was lost in landing due to hostile artillery fire and sinking of landing craft. Because of the configuration of the ground in this particular area spotting for naval gunfire was rather difficult and since trouble came from field works rather than from fixed batteries, both air bombardment and naval gunfire were relatively ineffective in assisting the landing.

On the whole U.S. repeat U.S. Army front the immediate tactical plan has been altered with the purpose now of both corps making an early drive toward Carentan to join up, after which the original conceptions will be pursued.

On the front of the 50th British Division progress was very good although, as at everywhere else, unloading was interfered with by the rough weather. Likewise on the fronts of the 3d British and 3d Canadian Divisions progress was generally satisfactory although rough weather had finally compelled the naval force commander to direct the drying out of the LST [Landing Ship Tank] because Rhino ferries could not work. On this particular front the beaches were flat and hard and it was believed that no damage would result to the LST's.

Throughout the front we lost considerable numbers of the smaller landing craft, both because of rough weather and mines in the touchdown areas. These were Teller mines which blew sizeable holes in the landing craft but large numbers of which can be repaired as soon as maintenance groups can be placed ashore and start to work. The loss of these craft, added to the rough weather slowed up the landing of all supplies and at noon on D plus 1 we were approximately twenty-four hours behind our expected schedule of unloading. The weather improved markedly at noon on D plus 1. If this good weather stretch can be prolonged for a few days we will do much toward catching up.

During the course of the day I talked with General [Bernard] Montgomery and General Bradley and with Admirals Kirk, Vian, Douglas-Pennant and Oliver. All were disappointed in the unfavorable landing conditions and all felt that improvement of the weather would see a corresponding great improvement in our position.

Upon return of Admiral Ramsay and myself to advance headquarters about 10 P.M. we learned that we had apparently captured Bayeux.

Early this morning I am informed that a German counter attack by parts of two Panzer divisions is pushing in on the right of the British sector and has made some progress. However, yesterday afternoon while I was present on those beaches the 7th Armored Division was busy unloading and this early enemy threat should be effectively countered.

On the American beaches the 2d and 90th Divisions were due to begin landing last night and while I have no reports this morning, I believe that the good weather last night should have permitted the landing of considerable reinforcements in those districts.

Due to the fluid nature of the battle it has been extremely difficult to give logical targets to much of our air forces but I am confident that if weather permits our air will intervene effectively in any attempted counter attacks by the enemy.

Source: Dwight David Eisenhower, *The Papers of Dwight David Eisenhower, The War Years: III*, ed. Alfred D. Chandler, Stephen E. Ambrose, and others (Baltimore: Johns Hopkins University Press, 1970), pp. 1908, 1915–1918.

4 Harold E. Mayo, Letter to Robert Cummins, 1944

To meet the spiritual needs of the American GI as well as to improve morale, the armed forces dramatically expanded the number of military chaplains. Their duties included holding religious services for men and women of their faith, and arranging services for those of other faiths. They were expected to visit the sick, comfort the wounded, encourage GIs to write home, and counsel those in distress. Chaplains were prohibited from taking part in combat and were also exempted from many restrictions on fraternization between officers and enlisted personnel. Harold E. Mayo, a Unitarian minister, was a keen observer of the progress of the war in July 1944. He paints an ambiguous portrait of the American GI in his letter to one of the leaders of the Unitarian Church, seeking to dispel any notion that all GIs were virtuous or brave. At the same time, Mayo makes a number of remarks about the chasm that existed between those deployed overseas and the home front, as well as about the value of the Soviets. The letter opens with a pressing matter in his own family: finding funds to pay for his daughter's education.

18 July 1944

Dr. Robert Cummins,
16 Beacon St.,
Boston, Mass.

Dear Bob,

I am writing to ask if you can help me. My daughter Pauline is planning to enter Tufts College this fall. Would you be able to do anything to help get a scholarship for her? She graduated in the first five or six of a class of over two hundred at Keene High School. This year she has been working but with wages in the Keene offices isn't able to save enough. I want to help all I can but it would be of great assistance if some scholarship aid were available. Perhaps you can do nothing but when I think of Tufts and of my Universalist friends I think of you.

Probably you knew that I am overseas. This is my third month and soon I will have [a] fourth away from home. The location is good and work keeps me busy. In addition to my regular duties I am Mess Treasurer for the Officers' Mess which keeps me going all the time. But I am able to do it all and I expect I am here to be busy.

I have been privileged to have many fine contacts with French leaders and have learned much which should help in my interpretation of the whole picture when I get back to a church. The story of [p]olitical interests has been much mixed here, and I have met people on both sides and of every slant on the situation.

Recently I had to entertain five American generals, two American admirals, a French admiral, the five star French general who is the highest ranking officer of the French Republic, and several high ranking British and Brazilian officers. I have made friends of several French refugee families of standing in old France. The whole experience has been most interesting and constructive.

Our men are good. Their morale, on the whole, is excellent. Some feel fed up and weary of it all after too long overseas. Many in an army hospital where I visited recently, feel that after recuperating from serious operations they want to get back to the front lines and see the job through. Morally, the picture is clouded. One is amazed at the number of strong characters who maintain their faith and convictions under trying circumstances. Then again one is saddened by the n[a]ive efforts of the over sophisticated to raise hell without paying the price.

Houses of prostitution are off limits to our personnel and the shore patrol does a good job safeguarding the men. There is a type of syphilus [*sic*] here which defies our boasted drugs and go[es] on its merry way. The natives often doctor vino [wine] with marihuana which drives the lads temporarily insane and, persisted in, has permanent results that are dangerous.

I can't see that men overseas are much more religious or irreligious than at home. They stack up about as usual. Habits assert them one way or the other with normal people. There are plenty of atheists in foxholes and many who are not. Some get religion under fire, some get mad, and others some simply get.

Recently we had four red alerts in one night with German planes coming over. You become so weary that at last you don't care. On the fourth alert I was awakened, listened to the droning of their motors, and then said to myself, let 'em bomb if they want to, and turned over and went to sleep. It sounds crazy but sometimes sleep is more important than anything else.

If our people at home could get the mental background of people in the old world it might be good for our Pollyanna complex. They seem to feel that God doesn't expect or guarantee happiness to his children, that suffering is an inevitable part of life, and that if one is able to do his duty he should be satisfied. They lose everything with poise and start again from scratch thankful to be there and able to start.

Things at the front are not as easy or as certain as the papers and commentators would indicate. They should stay three days on a beach under a hell of accurate fire, before gaining a hundred yards as some of my friends recently were. They would see what the men are up against. The Russian drive is marvelous but those folks have forgotten self and are ready to die. And die by [the] thousands they do.

Oh, well, I'll bring this to a close. God bless you in your work and write sometimes.

As ever, Harold [E. Mayo]

Source: General Correspondence, Jan.–Aug. 1944, b/MS 392/1 (17), UCA-Chaplains, Harvard-Andover Divinity School Library, Cambridge, Massachusetts.

5 Paul Fergot, Letters to Parents and Wife, 1944, 1945

Paul Fergot of Oshkosh, Wisconsin, served with the Fifteenth Air Force in Italy as navigator of a long-range bomber. In his letters to his parents and wife, he is initially optimistic that he would quickly finish his 50 missions and be able to return home. In contrast to ground troops, bomber crews were routinely rotated home if they flew a certain number of missions. In the first letter to his parents, Fergot mentions flying a mission with fighter escorts piloted by members of the all-black Tuskegee airmen. Fergot's early optimism was unwarranted and on October 10, 1944, he was shot down. Initially he was able to escape capture and was sheltered for several weeks by Italian partisans who were fighting the Germans. Fearing harm might come to those who were protecting him, Fergot surrendered to the Nazis. Fortunately, Nazi Germany obeyed its obligations under the Geneva Convention with regard to American and British prisoners of war. This allowed Fergot to receive and send mail to his family, receive Red Cross packages, and also receive packages from home.

Lt. Paul Fergot to Parents, August 21, 1944

Dear Folks,

I suppose you know that I am with the fifteenth air force somewhere in Italy. — Our quota is 50 missions which will probably take around 6 months. It's all pretty much of a milk run here, because of our air superiority and our fighter cover. There is a squadron of colored boys flying P-51s over here that are the last word in fighter pilots. We have no white squadrons that begin to compare with them. (so they Tell me) Flak is about the only thing all that we have to worry about, & that's not so bad. — Some of our targets are Ploesti, Munich, Bucharest, Fredrickhoven, etc.

The living conditions here are excellent. We have fresh eggs every morning — fresh tomatoes real often, some chops & chicken — and its all well prepared. Whenever we don't fly we are free to go & do what we want so long as we meet our schedules. — So I have been to town once or twice. The towns here are pretty bad, about the smelliest places I've seen — makes you appreciate the living standards of America. —

The Yugoslav Partisans have a rest camp near here, and one of the boys from over there was visiting our post yesterday. He has 48 Germans to his credit & is at the rest camp for the second time. He is about 14 years old. Tito's men seem to be one of our best allies.

Well, I haven't gotten a letter from home yet, but sure hope something materializes soon, — I'd like to know what to write about.

Take care of yourselves, & for petes sake don't worry, cause there is absolutely nothing to worry about. Just have faith that I'm coming back: & I'll be there before you realise I've left.

Love
Paul

Lt. Paul Fergot to Wife, August 28, 1944

Dearest,

I'm sorry I didn't get to write to you yesterday, but it just couldn't be helped. — By the way, the mail situation is on the blink again. It's three days since I got a letter & that was sent from nevada on the twelfth [*sic*]. So I still have no idea yet of what you are doing. I do wish I knew. It's so long since I have seen you. I love you Mrs. Fergot!

Did you know your husband is going to get the "purple heart" (of course, you didn't.) But, anyway, he has been recommended for it. So I 'spect he'll get it. The purple heart, you know is for men wounded in combat. —

I know; you want me to explain. Well, you see, it was this way. Returning from one of our missions, we had some trouble with our ship & had to bail out. So I hurt my knee a little when I landed. Sometime I'll tell you all about what a parachute jump is like. I'll tell you right now it's much easier & more fun than you'd believe. Except the landing.

I said in my last letter that I was going to write to both our folks. Well, I haven't, and I won't tonite, but maybe tomorrow. You use your own judgement about who you tell about that bail out. I'm not telling anyone but you. I only have 43 missions left, by the way.

I think I'll go to sleep now; I'm pretty tired. Keep yourself happy, my Darling & Don't worry cause your husband will be home before you know it.

All my Love,
Paul

Letter to Wife, March 19, 1945

My Dearest—It seems ages since I have heard from home. I certainly hope and pray that Everything is ALRIGHT THERE. There is so little to write about here. Just eating-sleeping-Reading-playing cards, etc. It's Beginning to get on my Nerves. I'D give ANYthing to hear from home, but Don't Dare to even Hope for any thing for another couple of months. Honey, I'd like to ask you again, if you feel when you get this that it is practical, to send whatever parcels the Red Cross allows; and if you send a food parcel to include Plenty of chocolate and all things as condensed as possible such as Bisquick-Buckwheat, Pancake Flour-Jams-nuts fruit cake, e.t.c. perhaps some dried fruits. Use your own Judgement about it all, as I hope you are doing about everything at home. You must take care of everything and everybody, Darling. Keep everything going As USUAL AND soon we'll all be together again. Write to Howie & Janet & Gordon & Bill for me and Tell the folks I'll write to them again as soon as I Can. Missing you more than you know, Dearest, I am still your Lover & Husband Paul.

Source: Paul Fergot Papers, Wisconsin Society of Wisconsin, Madison, Wisconsin. Available online at http://www.wisconsinhistory.org/.

6 Emiel W. Owens, Excerpt from *Blood on German Snow: An African American Artilleryman in World War II and Beyond*, 2006

Most African Americans serving in the armed forces faced discrimination, segregation, and reluctance on the part of senior military leaders to place them in combat units. Until 1942, the US Marines did not even accept black

men in the Corps. Prior to Pearl Harbor, the US Navy made all black sailors
stewards whose principal responsibility was to serve meals to officers and act
as their valets. Despite the heroic service of several all-black regiments since
the Civil War, the US Army consigned most black soldiers to service units
transporting supplies, digging graves, laundering clothes, and serving as
cooks. Pressure from civil rights organizations and, even more important, the
growing shortage of combat personnel forced all branches of the military to
open up the combat ranks to African Americans. Emiel W. Owens, the son of
a black Texas sharecropper, began his college education at Prairie View A & M
College (later University) in 1940. Enrolled in the Reserve Officers' Training
Corps (ROTC), Owens had to interrupt his education before receiving his
bachelor's degree when he was drafted in 1943. Serving as a sergeant with
Number 3, Battery B, 777th Field Artillery Battalion, Owens participated in
several major battles, including the battle of Hürtgen Forest. In this excerpt
from his memoir, Blood on German Snow, *he offers a grim account of the*
fighting in the closing months of 1944. After the war, Owens completed his
college education under the GI Bill of Rights and went on to earn a
doctorate in economics from Ohio State University.

The drive through the towns on the edge of the Hurtgen Forest in early
November was supposed to be part of a limited offensive to reach the Roer
River, but it turned out to be a major battle and the bloodiest yet to be
fought on the western front. The German units had been retreating across
Europe and settled here in these formidable defensive positions to make a
final—and trying—effort to inflict heavy casualties on our forces. The
canopy of trees on the fringe of the forest was so dense that the shadows
created by the sun shining through their leaves left intriguing patterns on the
seemingly flat forest floor, now blanketed by the powder of one of Germany's
worst snowstorms in centuries.

Unfortunately, even though we were aware of the crystalline tree branches,
which drooped under the weight of ice, I doubt that any of us could appreciate the beautiful wintry scene, as the cracking sounds of those branches kept
all of us jumpy. After all, we were in our enemy's homeland now, and they
knew every trail and walkway. It was not long until the high artillery shells
exploded, sending thousands of lethal splinters downward and making
movement across towns near the forest even more hazardous. Incoming
enemy artillery shells truck twenty-five to thirty feet in the air, jolting ground
troops with maximum killing capacity. We suffered our first casualty due to
enemy action when a German 150-mm artillery shell exploded in one of our
positions. Lt. James Wright died later that day of wounds suffered in the
attack, which also wounded several other crew members, who were treated
in our makeshift aid station for the firing batteries. Our guns fired 2,834

rounds from this position during the night and throughout the day. That evening, at approximately dusk, our battalion was ordered up for closer support of our infantry division and a tank battalion, which was under a counterattack by the German 1ˢᵗ and 5ᵗʰ Panzer Divisions. We fired all night and were able to repel the attack. By sunrise, 3,284 shells had been fired. In the event of a German breakthrough in our line, alternative firing positions were prepared near Herzogenaurach. Later, a second group of alternate firing positions was established near North Bradenburg.

The next morning, while we were replenishing our ammunition supply, I noticed trucks passing my gun position at a slow pace. The truck drivers appeared to be driving slowly to protect their cargo. At first, I thought they were ammunition trucks returning from the front a few hundred yards ahead of us. The column was more than a mile long, and the trucks were evenly spaced. They continued passing by for such a long time that it seemed the convoy would never end. Then, as one truck came by, I thought I saw a wristwatch-clad arm swing out from under the tarpaulin covering one of the truck beds. I walked a few paces to the road and pulled the end of the tarpaulin up to find that the truck's cargo consisted of dead American soldiers just killed in the forest. The dead soldier with the wristwatch was laid flat on his back—a short lifetime etched on his young face—one that would see no more birthdays, anniversaries, or even the smile on a future grandchild's face. These killings were different from those occurring on the beaches on D-day and in the fighting across France. In those cases, our soldiers died and were buried in friendly territory. The army had, and still has, a policy of not burying our dead sold[i]ers in enemy territory, so they were being hauled out to receive proper burial on hallowed grounds. Ironically, the same trucks we met on the highway just two days ago that were being used to haul German prisoners were now hauling out our dead soldiers killed just a few miles inside the German border.

When the hearses brought in their daily cargo of dead soldiers from the front, colored burial details sought them out by the hundreds. These young American dead were then sprawled out in separate piles, their bloodstained, torn uniforms soaked black with silt from the gumbo muck so that they looked like heaps of abandoned rubble. It had been raining a thin, bitter drizzle that turned the burial fields into quagmires. I discovered later that the burial organization was the 611ᵗʰ Quartermaster Graves Registration Company and the ground the dead soldiers were lying on would become part of their cemetery. One of the trucks was loaded with colored soldiers, who had the job of classifying and burying the dead. At a distance I heard the white company captain tell the soldiers that their cemetery would grow. This type of work was unpleasant, but they were fortunate because they were not the victims. They were still alive and well. I could see that the soldiers getting off the trucks were mesmerized and, in some cases, horrified by the piles of dead bodies lying before them. Some just could not take the first sight of the bodies of men, some still warm, killed in battle. ...

Aside from the stench of death, two months of supporting the bloody, close-quarters fighting in mud, snow, and cold added to the devastation of morale. In time, when the uncollected bodies were finally covered with the snow, parts of at least three U.S. divisions, pushed beyond all human limits, experienced breakdowns of both cohesion and discipline. The struggle to clear the fringe town of the Hurtgen Forest cost our armed forces approximately fifty-five thousand dead and wounded. ...

As early as December 1944, one of our corps commanders had reported to the supreme commander that his army group lacked seventeen thousand riflemen because of the high casualties caused by prolonged combat and constant exposure to the severe winter weather. Since November, we had been fighting in bitter winter weather, dealing with frostbite and trench foot, as challenging, and as dangerous, as battling the enemy. Although our supreme commander ordered the reclassification of as many support personnel as possible to provide relief to weary troops, we soon began to experience a shortfall that continued to grow. A call for troops to repel the latest German counterattack in the Ardennes-Alsace campaign only made the shortage more critical. Quite simply, even the U.S. selective service system could not close the increasing manpower gap.

As a result, Supreme Commander Eisenhower made a momentous decision. Previously, most African American soldiers in the European theater had been assigned to service units. I saw them during our four-day journey across France in isolated outposts along the lonely roads, all the way through Belgium. I saw long lines of African American hands resting on steering wheels as truck convoys thundered past our slow-moving column of guns. But now, Eisenhower was allowing these troops to volunteer for duty as combat unit infantrymen with the understanding that after the necessary training, they would be committed to front-line service. Eventually, twenty-two hundred were organized into fifty-three platoons and assigned to all-white rifle companies in two U.S. Army groups. The shortage of combat soldiers temporarily had forced the army to discard its racist policy of segregating white and colored soldiers. The forces of necessity here most certainly played a role in spurring the civil rights movement in the United States twenty years later. Historical records illustrate the magnitude of the racist army policy: only eleven out of the seventy-seven African American army units in the European theater of operation were assigned to combat duties, even after the policy was implemented.

Source: Emiel W. Owens, *Blood on German Snow: An African American Artilleryman in World War II and Beyond* (College Station: Texas A & M University Press, 2006), pp. 60–62, 65–66.

Study Questions

1   Were all American soldiers properly trained for battle? What were some of the deficiencies, especially early in the war?
2   What role did the French Resistance play in the Allied invasion of France on D-Day? Given what Virginia Hall accomplished as an OSS agent, is there any reason why she should have been disqualified by virtue of gender from serving in the combat arms of the US Army?
3   What problems did Allied forces encounter during D-Day? What were the biggest obstacles that had to be overcome in the view of Dwight Eisenhower?
4   How religious were American GIs in Europe? Did religion sustain all soldiers?
5   How did the tone of Paul Fergot's letters change over time? How do you think imprisonment affected him?
6   How did the Battle of the Bulge temporarily change Army policies regarding segregation?

Chapter 5   Mobilizing the Home Front

1 US Treasury Department, "This Is *My* Fight Too!" Poster, 1942

Much of the cost of World War II was paid with borrowed money. Although the bulk of the financing came from the wealthiest Americans, Secretary of the Treasury Henry Morgenthau, Jr. wanted average Americans to voluntarily participate in the war effort through the purchase of war bonds. Individuals of modest means could purchase bonds priced in denominations as low as $10 and school children were encouraged to purchase stamps. In contrast to World War I, Morgenthau and the Roosevelt Administration wanted to avoid the jingoism that had engulfed the Liberty Bond campaigns of the earlier conflict and the vigilantism that had often forced individuals to buy bonds. Moreover, the bond drive of World War II stressed the pluralistic and cosmopolitan nature of American society, often gearing special appeals to Chinese Americans, Mexican Americans, and other ethnic groups. The following advertisement to purchase war bonds not only appeals to average citizens to purchase bonds, but also affirms the federal government's call for women to join the paid workforce to replace the men who had gone off to war.

Source: "This Is *My* Fight Too: Put At Least 10% Every Payday in War Bonds" (Washington, DC, US Government Printing Office, 1942).

The United States in World War II: A Documentary Reader, First Edition.
Edited by G. Kurt Piehler. Editorial material and organization © 2013 Blackwell Publishing Ltd.
Published 2013 by Blackwell Publishing Ltd.

Figure 5.1   "This Is *My* Fight Too! Put At Least 10% Every Payday in War Bonds." A smiling female factory worker holds war bonds, while a 10% bullseye target motif hangs above the paymaster's window in the background.

Source: UNT Digital Library. http://digital.library.unt.edu/ark:/67531/metadc457/

2 Irving Berlin, "I Paid My Income Tax Today," Song Lyrics, 1942

Until World War II, most Americans did not pay income taxes. By design, advocates of the Sixteenth Amendment (1913) wanted this levy, along with inheritance taxes, to apply only to the wealthiest of Americans, less as a means to raise revenue than as a modest attempt to ensure greater economic equality by placing limits on the wealth controlled by the nation's financial elites. The high cost of World War II required the United States to levy income taxes on working- and middle-class wage earners. Americans bristled at paying the income tax, and to help ease the opposition, the federal government started withholding income tax from individuals' wages. (Prior to the war, individuals paid their taxes as lump sum payments.) To bolster support for the income tax and voluntary compliance, the federal government commissioned Irving Berlin to write a song in praise of this levy. Berlin (1888–1989) was the leading American songwriter of the twentieth century and was responsible for such classics as "God Bless America," "White Christmas," and "There's No

*Business Like Show Business." In the following song, which was widely
played on the nation's radios during the war, Berlin celebrates the fact that the
average citizen is allowed to pay the tax that was once the exclusive preserve
of one of the wealthiest families in America – the Rockefellers.*

Verse:

I said to my Uncle Sam
"Old Man Taxes, here I am."
And he was glad to see me.
Mr. Small Fry, yes indeed,
Lower brackets, that's my speed,
But he was glad to see me

1st CHORUS
I PAID MY INCOME TAX TODAY
I never felt so proud before,
To be right there with the millions more
Who paid their income tax today
I'm squared up with the U.S.A.
You see those bombers in the sky,
Rockefeller helped to build them,
So did I.
I PAID MY INCOME TAX TODAY

2nd CHORUS
I PAID MY INCOME TAX TODAY
A thousand planes to bomb Berlin.
They'll all be paid for, and I chipped in,
That certainly makes me feel okay
Ten thousand more and that ain't hay!
We must pay for this war somehow,
Uncle Sam was worried, but he isn't now
I PAID MY INCOME TAX TODAY.

3rd CHORUS
I PAID MY INCOME TAX TODAY
I never cared what Congress spent.
But now I'll watch over ev'ry cent,
Examine ev'ry bill they pay,
They'll have to let me have my say
I wrote the Treasury to go slow
Careful, Mr. Henry Junior, that's my dough
I PAID MY INCOME TAX TODAY

98 The United States in World War II

Source: Press Release, Treasury Department, Washington, January 26, 1942,
Box 157, Central Files of the Office of the Secretary of the Treasury (Entry 193), RG
56 General Records of the Department of the Treasury, National Archives,
Washington, DC. Also available online at http://www.ocpp.org.

3 US Office of Price Administration, Ration Book Cover, Stamps, Instructions, 1942

*With only a few exceptions, the continental United States was spared from
enemy attack. Americans living in the lower 48 states would never be bombed
by enemy planes, never faced invading armies, and never lived under occupation.
But like virtually all major belligerents, civilians faced restrictions on food,
clothing, and other goods they could purchase, including, meat, sugar, butter,
gasoline, tires, clothing, and shoes. Individuals seeking to purchase these goods
were required to obtain ration books and were allocated stamps based on a
formula of their needs and availability. For instance, those who needed to drive
an automobile in the service of the war effort were granted extra points, whereas
allocations strictly limited the amount of recreational driving. When purchasing
rationed goods, individuals had to pay both with money and with stamps.*

Source: Home Front Coupons, Rare Books, Manuscript and Special Collections
Library, Duke University.

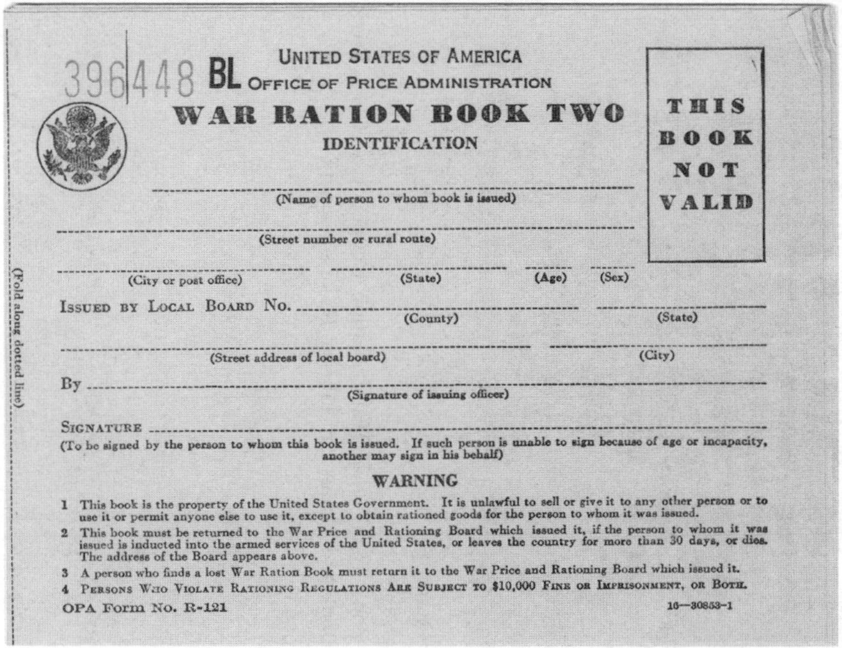

396 448 BL

UNITED STATES OF AMERICA
OFFICE OF PRICE ADMINISTRATION

WAR RATION BOOK TWO

IDENTIFICATION

THIS
BOOK
NOT
VALID

_____
(Name of person to whom book is issued)

_____
(Street number or rural route)

_____ _____ _____ _____
(City or post office)   (State)   (Age)   (Sex)

ISSUED BY LOCAL BOARD NO. _____ _____ _____
                                    (County)   (City)   (State)

_____
(Street address of local board)

By _____
        (Signature of issuing officer)

SIGNATURE _____
(To be signed by the person to whom this book is issued. If such person is unable to sign because of age or incapacity,
another may sign in his behalf)

WARNING

1   This book is the property of the United States Government. It is unlawful to sell or give it to any other person or to
    use it or permit anyone else to use it, except to obtain rationed goods for the person to whom it was issued.

2   This book must be returned to the War Price and Rationing Board which issued it, if the person to whom it was
    issued is inducted into the armed services of the United States, or leaves the country for more than 30 days, or dies.
    The address of the Board appears above.

3   A person who finds a lost War Ration Book must return it to the War Price and Rationing Board which issued it.

4   PERSONS WHO VIOLATE RATIONING REGULATIONS ARE SUBJECT TO $10,000 FINE OR IMPRISONMENT, OR BOTH.

OPA FORM NO. R-121   16-30838-1

(Fold along dotted line)

Figure 5.2a   Ration book cover.

Source: War Ration Book Two, World War II Ration Coupon Collection, David M. Rubenstein Rare Book and Manuscript Library, Duke University.

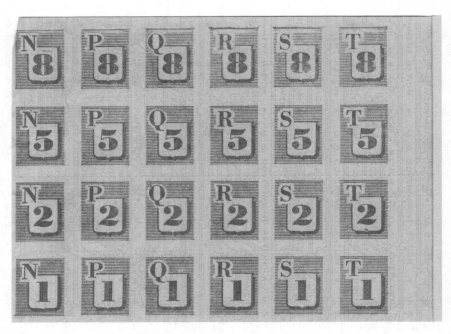

Figure 5.2b   Ration stamps.

Source: War Ration Book Two, World War II Ration Coupon Collection, David M. Rubenstein Rare Book and Manuscript Library, Duke University.

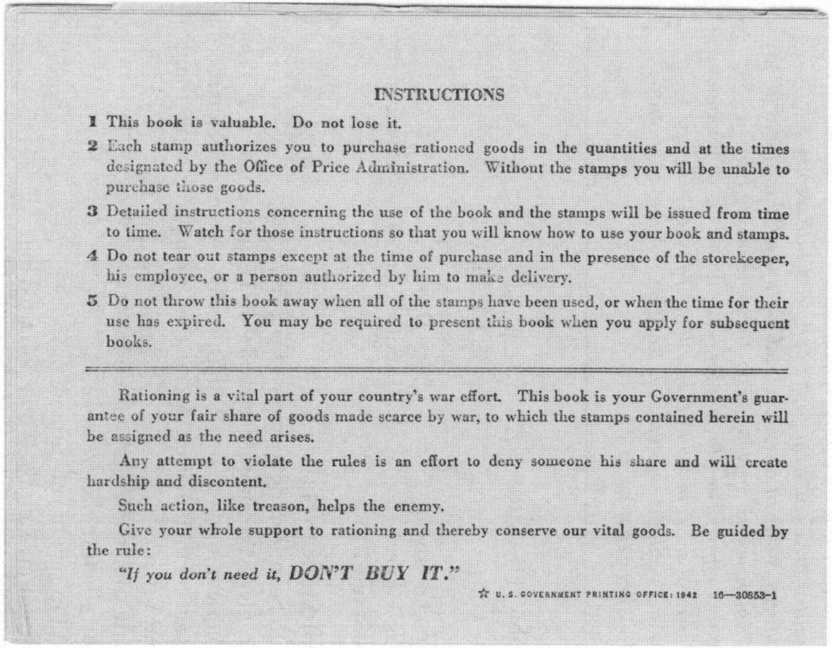

INSTRUCTIONS

1 This book is valuable. Do not lose it.

2 Each stamp authorizes you to purchase rationed goods in the quantities and at the times designated by the Office of Price Administration. Without the stamps you will be unable to purchase those goods.

3 Detailed instructions concerning the use of the book and the stamps will be issued from time to time. Watch for those instructions so that you will know how to use your book and stamps.

4 Do not tear out stamps except at the time of purchase and in the presence of the storekeeper, his employee, or a person authorized by him to make delivery.

5 Do not throw this book away when all of the stamps have been used, or when the time for their use has expired. You may be required to present this book when you apply for subsequent books.

Rationing is a vital part of your country's war effort. This book is your Government's guarantee of your fair share of goods made scarce by war, to which the stamps contained herein will be assigned as the need arises.

Any attempt to violate the rules is an effort to deny someone his share and will create hardship and discontent.

Such action, like treason, helps the enemy.

Give your whole support to rationing and thereby conserve our vital goods. Be guided by the rule:

"*If you don't need it, DON'T BUY IT.*"

☆ U. S. GOVERNMENT PRINTING OFFICE: 1942   16—30858-1

Figure 5.2c   Ration book instructions.

Source: War Ration Book Two, World War II Ration Coupon Collection, David M. Rubenstein Rare Book and Manuscript Library, Duke University.

4 New Jersey League of Women Voters, Leaguesboro-on-the-Air, "Black Market" Radio Script, 1943 or 1944?

Not all Americans were willing to live with the restrictions imposed on them by the federal government. Many Americans flouted rationing and were prepared to pay higher prices on the black market in order to obtain the gasoline, tires, clothing, and foods they desired. Although the government established controls on prices and wages, many businesses defied these restrictions and raised prices or diverted goods to the black market. The Office of Price Administration (OPA) relied heavily on thousands of volunteers to monitor prices at local stores and report discrepancies. The following document is one of a series of radio plays produced and aired by the League of Women Voters of New Jersey focusing on civilian participation in the war effort. The play explores the workings of the black market and the failures of some merchants to adhere to price ceilings. Moreover, it encourages civilians to volunteer for the OPA and to monitor prices charged by local merchants.

LEAGUESBORO-ON-THE-AIR   No. 24
                                     Black Market

CHARACTERS	Mrs. Goodwin	Mrs. Doyle
	Mrs. Paine	Johnny Goodwin Voices
	Dr. Sarah Moore	

MUSIC   THEME SONG
               "Oh beautiful for spacious skies, etc."

NARRATOR   We give you another episode of Leaguesboro, that typical American town that we all know. The women are marketing. Listen to their voices. Aren't they saying the same things in your town?

1st VOICE   I saw some at White's Grocery.

2nd   Hurry before they're gone.

3rd"   Oh I'm sick of substitutes.

4th"   I forgot my stamps. Won't you trust me?

1st"   What does it cost? I don't care if it doesn't take points.

2nd"   Tom wants a steak.

3rd"   Jim says he's sick of soya bean with spinach sauce.

4th"   I've been standing here half an hour.

NARRATOR   Is your voice among them? How big does a pound of butter loom in your life? Step into Doyle's Market with Mrs. Ruth Goodwin, one of Leaguesboro's leading citizens.

(FADE)	SOUND OF CONFUSION
DOYLE	Next! Who's next? Please, please don't handle those grapes, boy! Next!
RUTH	I think I'm next.
DOYLE	O.K. What do you want?
RUTH	Give me one of those cans of crushed pineapple, please.
DOYLE	Here you are, 35 cents, and 12 ration points. What else?
RUTH	But that's a mistake. The ceiling price is 31 cents.
DOYLE	Who said so?
RUTH	The O.P.A. I'm one of the volunteer price assistants.
1st VOICE	Who'd she say she was? P.W.A.?
2nd VOICE	Shh Let's listen.
DOYLE	Well lady, I'm awful busy. Maybe I didn't look at the list this morning. You know they're always changing prices on us.
RUTH	I have the list right here. You see I get a report from the O.P.A. every week, so you can't fool me. You haven't listed all your goods on those shelves. Of course, I don't want to make trouble but —
SOUND	CRASH OF CANS
DOYLE	Doggone those boys! Piling up the cans like that! Say lady, can't you see how busy I am? If you don't want to make trouble, come in when I'm not so rushed, please. Next!
RUTH	All right, I'll be in tomorrow morning, and see that you have your price lists for meats where the customers can see it, and not back there where you have to use a spy-glass.
SOUND	DOOR CLOSES
NARRATOR	As Ruth steps out on the sidewalk, she meets Dr. Sarah Moore.
SARAH	Why Ruth Goodwin, what are you doing here? I didn't know you traded at Doyle's.
RUTH	Hello, Sarah. I don't and I won't. Such manners!
SARAH	I thought you looked pretty red. What's the matter?
RUTH	I'm a Volunteer Price Assistant on my first mission, as it were. I'm afraid I didn't manage too well.
SARAH	That Doyle fellow's all right. I've known him for years. It's hard to make out these days, you know, Ruth. There's a lot of competition, and not all of it honest.
RUTH	Yes, I suppose so. I made a mistake to attack him before a lot of customers in his rush hour. I'll do better tomorrow. I hope. Oh here's Grace Paine. Hello Gracie.
GRACE	Hello girls, don't stop me, I'm in a rush. On my way to Sully's.
SARAH	Who's Sully?
GRACE	Don't you know? The new store, down near the Post Office. We've been trading a lot there lately. Everybody's going there. Why, you

	can get everything. When there's no butter anywhere in town they have it. And they never refuse me meat. I'm getting a steak now.
SARAH	Look here, Grace Paine, that doesn't sound right to me. Maybe they shouldn't have butter these days. Maybe they use the Black Market.
GRACE	Black Market! Wilbur says there's a lot of bosh about that. They want him to go on the Price Panel—naturally enough, he's so important in the town—but I think he'll refuse. He says he doesn't want to sit in judgment on honest storekeepers.
SARAH	Hmmm—the honest ones won't care where he sits.
GRACE	Well, Wilbur has to have a lot of meat. The doctor says he needs more meat at his age. You're a doctor, Sarah, you can see that. Goodbye, I've got to get to Sully's.
SARAH	Goodbye, Grace. Yes, I can see all right. Wilbur could certainly do with a little more warmth. So long, Ruth, better luck with Doyle next time.
MUSIC	TRANSITION
RUTH	Good morning, Mr. Doyle. I've come in to see you again. You remember me? I'm Mrs. Goodwin.
DOYLE	Sure, I remember you. Didn't you give me the raspberry yesterday?
RUTH	I didn't mean to, Mr. Doyle. I'm really not here to make trouble. I'm here to help. You see, if you were disobeying regulations and an inspector found you, you would be called before the Price Panel in short order.
DOYLE	I've heard of that Price Panel, all right. I know some fellers I wish they'd get after, too.
RUTH	Then you know that the Price Panel is made up of conscientious citizens who just want Leaguesboro to obey the rules, keep down prices and keep out of the Black Market.
DOYLE	What do those guys do to you?
RUTH	Well, first you get a warning, and then if you persist in violations you may be called before them and punished with a fine.
DOYLE	Don't I know a feller I wish they'd get after!
RUTH	Then why don't you report him?
DOYLE	It isn't always us storekeepers, Mrs. Goodwin. Sometimes it's the distributors. They make us take a lot of stuff we don't want, to get something we do. And they charge us plenty too.
RUTH	Then report them.
DOYLE	I can't get those birds down on me.
RUTH	But everything is confidential.
DOYLE	O.K. I'll see about it. Now, what's wrong with me today?
RUTH	Let's see. Oh, this is better. You have your list of meats in full view. Yes, and your canned goods and every article on your shelves marked.
DOYLE	Some job, believe me, short-handed as I am.

RUTH	Of course it is, but the customers appreciate it and they'll stand back of you. Just to prove it I'll give you my weekend order.
DOYLE	O.K. Glad to get it.
RUTH	Just a minute, there's a customer coming in. Wait on her first. There's something I want to ask you afterward.
VOICE	A loaf of whole wheat bread, please. And can you give me two pounds of beef for stew?
DOYLE	Sorry, lady, there isn't a bit of beef in the store—not any in town, I guess. They promised us, but nothing came.—How about a nice stewing chicken.
VOICE	Oh, I'm sick of chicken!
	DOOR SLAMS
DOYLE	There you are, Mrs. Goodwin, that's what we're up against. Disappointing customers—new customers, maybe, who go way and don't come back because you can't give them beef when there is no beef.
RUTH	That's just what I wanted to ask you about. How is it, Mr. Doyle, that some storekeepers have the things people want?
DOYLE	What's that?
RUTH	I know of one market in Leaguesboro that can provide anything at any time according to a friend of mine who trades there.
DOYLE	Anything any time! Who is it?
RUTH	Sully over near the Post Office. It's a new store, and they're getting lots of business, I hear.
DOYLE	You're telling me. Don't I know? He has everything, has he? Hmm I'd like to know what he's up to. I've been suspecting that bird for some time.
RUTH	What do you mean? Black Market?
DOYLE	You tell your friends, Mrs. Goodwin, that they'd better know what they're buying these days. When you buy meat you'd better trade at a respectable market.
RUTH	All right. I'll call my friends right away. And you, Mr. Doyle, you might do well to report your suspicions to the Price Panel.
MUSIC	TRANSITION
RUTH	(at telephone) Hill 5-316 —Hello Gracie, is that you? This is Ruth. Did you get your steak all right the other day? ——No. I haven't started trading at Sully's yet. ——You know Grace, you ought to be careful where you trade—you signed one of those O.P.A. pledges, didn't you? ———What I'm getting at is—well, I've heard that Sully's may be a Black Market store—oh dear, no I can't prove, it, but it looks bad—well, I'm only interested in you, Grace, and the good of the town, of course. You wouldn't want Wilbur to have his meat if it was going to—to—to disrupt things, would you? —But we _ought_ to care anyway—

JOHNNY	Mom, oh Mom!
RUTH	Shh Johnny, can't you see I'm telephoning Mrs. Paine?
JOHNNY	Aw, Mrs. Paine! Who care what she says?
RUTH	Shh Johnny, don't be so rude—Well, Grace, I guess I'll have to ring off now. Johnny's just come home. Sorry I bothered you, but you'd better think over what I've told you. Good-bye.
JOHNNY	GEE, Mom, was that really Mrs. Paine? What did she say about Sadie?
RUTH	Why, nothing. What about Sadie?
JOHNNY	Oh, Sadie started bawling in school, and they took her home. She'd oughter be there now. She's an awful cry baby!
RUTH	What was the matter?
JOHNNY	Miss Brown took her home—said she had eaten some hamburger. I didn't know hamburgers made people sick. Gee, did she cry? She always cries like that. Sadie Paine gives me a Pain. D'you get that, Mom?
RUTH	I'm afraid so. Maybe you's [sic] have cried just as hard if you had her pain—I mean ache.
JOHNNY	No sir!
RUTH	Do you know where she got the hamburgers?
JOHNNY	No. The rest of us kids had egg sandwiches or something. This is meatless Tuesday, you know, Mom. Did she feel good with her hamburgers—till a little while later when she started to bawl. Gee, did she cry!
RUTH	Don't say that again, Johnny. I think I'll run over to the Paine's' right away, and see if there is anything I can do to help.
MUSIC	TRANSITION
NARRATOR	When Ruth Goodwin rings the Paines' doorbell, the door is opened by Dr. Sarah Moore.
RUTH	Oh Sarah, I'm glad you're here. How's Sadie?
SARAH	She's all right. Mother Nature took her in hand, and there's mighty little hamburger left in Sadie now.
RUTH	Good. What a relief!
SARAH	But we've got to look into this. There've been three other cases reported.
RUTH	Where did she get the hamburgers?
SARAH	She says she got them at Sully's. Isn't that the store Grace was raving about the other day?
RUTH	The very same. Here she comes.—Hello, Grace —
GRACE	Wilbur's mad as hops! He's gone to see Sully and the Board of Health, and maybe the Price Panel.
RUTH	Good for Wilbur!
GRACE	I suppose that hamburger was made from some old dead horse.

SARAH   Could be. You know, Gracie, this all ties up with what we were talking about with Ruth. The Black Market and consumer responsibility.
TELEPHONE RINGS

GRACE   Hello, hello Wilbur—Yes, Sadie's all right. Sarah's here with her.—
You are—You have—they did —You will—Oh Wilbur, you're wonderful—They did—Well they'd better thank you. Ruth and Sarah are
here and I'll tell them. Good-bye.

GRACE   Do you know what? Wilbur's been to Sully and the Board of Health,
and he's talked with Mr. Morse head of the Price Panel. Mr. Morse
says the're [sic] going to get after that man Sully—seems they had a
complaint about his not keeping to ceiling prices.

RUTH   They did? I'm not surprised.

GRACE   Wilbur's always patriotic like that. He says he owes it to the country
and Sadie to make a row.

SARAH   Splendid

GRACE   And what do you think he's going to do now?

RUTH   Tell us.

GRACE   Well, Wilbur always says the best way to get things done is to do
them yourself—so—

SARAH   So what?

GRACE   So—Wilbur has reconsidered, and he's going to join the Price
Panel.

Source: Folder 40, Box 21, League of Women Voters of New Jersey Records,
MC-1082, Special Collections and University Archives, Rutgers University Libraries,
New Brunswick, New Jersey.

5 Newark, New Jersey, Defense Council, "Summary of Meeting on Care of Mothers and Children," 1942

*Total mobilization of American resources prompted government officials
and businesses to call upon women, even those married with young children,
to enter the workforce. Many women responded to this call, partly motivated
by patriotism, but also spurred on by the opportunity to better provide for
their families financially. As this document indicates, finding adequate child
care remained a significant problem for women and for local communities.
Throughout the war, private organizations and local governments created
a range of ad hoc solutions. This document deals with the efforts of Newark,
New Jersey, to find adequate child care for working mothers. Only late in
1942 did the federal government through the Lanham Act provide funds
to local communities to expand daycare options for working mothers.*

Summary of Meeting on Care of Mothers and Children of the Newark Defense Council. Held at the Newark Department of Health on Thursday, June 18, 1942 at 10:30 A.M.

Dr. Julius Levy, Chairman-Presiding
Present
Miss Charlotte E. Barton (representing Dr. Stanley H. Rolfe)-Newark Board of Ed.
Raymond Gordon-Welfare Federation of Newark.
Mrs. Robert G. Klemm-Burke Memorial Day Nursery.
Mrs. A. C. Link-Essex County PTA.
Dr. Harrold A. Murray-Essex County Medical Society.
Miss Alene D. Simkins-Newark Housing Authority.
Mrs. Dorothy Skeist-League of Women Shoppers.
Jacob L. Trobe-Jewish Children's Home.

Miss Dorothy Dessau-Nat'l Ass'n of Day Nurseries, Inc.

Mrs. Link outlined the plan of the PTA to develop "block mothers" to care for the children of women who wished to volunteer for War work, and said that they were willing to consider broadening the scope of the plan to include that care of children of working mothers. After considerable discussion it was agreed, at the suggestion of Mr. Gordon, to refer the matter to a committee of three (to be appointed by the Chairman), which would meet with representatives of the child-caring agencies to study the plan and then report their findings and conclusions to the Chairman.

Miss Barton summarized Dr. Rolfe's proposed plan for the development of recreational and kindergarten facilities especially to meet the needs of the children of working mothers, and the Committee decided to go on record as approving it. Dr. Rolfe planned to start these groups at 7:30 A.M. to meet the needs of working mothers. It was decided to send to Mayor Murphy and to Directors Byrne and Keenan a telegram endorsing the plan of the Newark Board of Education and urging the Commissioners to make funds available.

Mrs. Klemm submitted the architect's plan for the alteration of Walnut Street School as a nursery center. As the plan seemed adequate, the Chairman asked Mrs. Klemm to assume full responsibility for this project. She agreed to do so, and will appoint her own committee to help her.

Mrs. Klemm reported that she had investigated the basement of Congregation Ahavas Sholem at 145 Broadway, which has been offered to us for a day nursery. She thought the place satisfactory for the accommodation of about twenty children, but she is planning to reinvestigate and report again. Mr. Gordon and Miss Barton gave Mrs. Klemm the names of two churches which she could investigate for the use as possible day nurseries. It was decided, at the suggestion of Mr. Gordon, that the Chairman write to the Ministers Association to find out what resources there were among the churches and synagogues in Newark for the establishment of day nurseries.

Dr. Levy said that the resolution in regard to the acceptance of colored children in day nurseries had been sent to each day nursery in the City, as was agreed upon at the last meeting of the Committee. The reports received from the nurseries on their attendance would seem to indicate that there is no discrimination, but the Chairman felt that the Committee should not abandon this matter. The following figures indicate the attendance at each nursery on the day the Committee's communication was received: Burke Memorial – 50 white – 3 colored; East Side – 111 white – 1 colored; 8th Avenue – 97 white – 2 colored; Friendly Neighborhood – 53 colored; Fuld Neighborhood – 45 white; Holy Angels – 57 white – 2 colored; Holy Rosary – 40 white – 2 colored; Newark Female Charitable – 26 white – 8 colored; Sarah Ward – 73 white 8 colored. The New Jersey Urban League had been requested to appoint a committee of volunteers to effect better cooperation between the day nurseries and colored mothers, and Miss Simkins reported that this committee had been formed. Dr. Levy requested Mr. Gordon to visit all the day nurseries to talk over this question with them in a friendly way, and he agreed to do so.

Dr. Levy read the statement of the Maternal Welfare Committee of the Essex County Medical Society in regard to pregnant women in industry which was submitted by Dr. Kessler. The Committee decided that this statement should be sent to every factory in Newark employing twenty women or more.

Dr. Levy gave the report of Mrs. Nixon of the Milburn-Short Hills Chapter of the American Red Cross on the availability of beds in the suburbs for mothers with newborn babies. As this report is incomplete, Mrs. Nixon will continue to send the Chairman information, as she obtains it.

Miss Barton reported that the sixteen women who took the training Course for Volunteers had completed the Course and were now ready to report for work in the various day nurseries. She said that they would be assigned by Mrs. Trobe, who is in charge of this work at the O[ffice of] C[ivilian] D[efense]. The Committee decided that it should go on record as recognizing the need for additional volunteer workers, and felt that more volunteers should be trained.

Mr. Trobe gave his report on the results of the investigation of the homes submitted by Mr. Burnett of the Public Safety Council of the Newark Defense Council for foster day care of children under two years of age. He said that he felt this method of obtaining foster homes has definite value, and would like to have it tried out in another section of the City. Dr. Levy suggested that Mr. Trobe talk the matter over with Mrs. Link to see whether her "block mother" idea could fit in with his idea of obtaining women for foster day care through the air raid wardens. They could then learn whether this would make available facilities for the care of children of working mother[s].

Mr. Gordon submitted a written report on the work of the working Mothers Information Service. He stated that the committee which is in charge of this service is to meet in ten days to revaluate its work, after which he will report to the Chairman.

Source: File, Newark Defense Council (Unpublished Manuscript), New Jersey Room, Newark Public Library, Newark, New Jersey.

6 Christian Commission for Camp and Defense Communities, "Church Letter on War Communities," Newsletter, 1942

Children and teenagers were profoundly affected by the war. They attended schools that struggled to fill their ranks with qualified staff as male teachers went off to fight and women teachers sought better-paying jobs in defense plants. Many would not see their fathers who were serving in the armed forces and had to wait years before being reunited with them, while their mothers worked long hours in munitions factories. These conditions helped contribute to soaring rates of juvenile delinquency, especially in communities with large numbers of defense plants or military bases. The Christian Commission for Camp and Defense Communities of the Federal Council of Churches sought to coordinate the efforts of member churches to meet the spiritual and other needs of workers and families, especially children. The following two articles appeared in the "Church Letter on War Communities" that circulated to Commission members and to the leadership of membership churches.

JUVENILE DELINQUENCY

Data are presented here from several different sources, dealing in part with the general problem and in part with the situation in specific places.

Wartime Influence on Juvenile Delinquency

Alice Scott Nutt of the Federal Children's Bureau, writing in the November issue of the Bulletin of the Child Welfare League of America, points out that even in normal times juvenile delinquency is a "sizable" problem. Children's courts serving about 40 percent of the population of the country, report yearly to the U.S. Children's Bureau. Data for 1942 are not yet available. For the whole group the increase in delinquency in 1941 over 1940 was only six per cent. But more than three-fifths of the larger courts reported an increase, sometimes a "substantial" one. Some of these reports describe overt acts, such as young girls who practice prostitution; others discuss behavior that is likely to lead to delinquency, such as "the drifting of young girls from rural areas to urban areas and camp areas to seek employment in cheap beer parlors and taverns and the rejection of parental control and supervision by adolescent boys who for the first time in their lives are earning wages—and high wages at that"; still others deal with corrective and preventive agencies, and overcrowded schools.

Even though the economic situation of a family has improved with the industrial boom the child's security may still be threatened, if, for instance the father is serving in the armed forces. The working mother may have an adequate income, yet the children may lack supervision. Delinquent behavior may be "only symptomatic" of the real problems children face. Thus, a young girl may copy an older girl's sexual irregularities without realizing the implications of her actions. The emotional stability of children and adolescents may be seriously affected by the fear and tension of adults and by the quickened tempo of life. Unstable children may have their difficulties increased. Older children may try to "express their patriotism in unwise or socially unacceptable ways," as, for instance the girl who is led into sex delinquencies by her admiration for soldiers or the boy who steals in order to contribute to the salvage drive. Under present conditions adolescents are maturing far more rapidly than during the depression years. Some of them "need help in growing up wisely." Young people react to the great movements going on in the world "even though they may not be entirely conscious of them or articulate about them." Some communities are already organizing themselves to deal with the problem. Others do not yet see its importance. Since the offenses with which children are charged are much the same as formerly "the connection with the war is often missed." Because the conditions fostering juvenile delinquency in a community have grown more intense, without a change in kind, the need for stronger and sometimes different methods of attack is not always recognized.

Wartime delinquency cannot be handled by temporary measures to be dropped right after the war. The services to strengthen the economic and social security of the family must be provided, such as financial aid and case work service for family break downs, health service and medical care, schools, child labor laws, and wholesome recreational facilities. There must be legal provision for inspection and control of health and social conditions

in public spaces, in centers for commercial recreation, and in service industries. It is even more important to have "competent and socially-minded
officials" to enforce the regulatory and protective measures. There must be
adequate facilities for education, social service, vocational guidance and recreation. In some communities there is a danger that in the effort to provide
for adults the needs of children and youth will be forgotten.

More than ever, says Miss Nutt, we "need to preserve essential services
directed toward the prevention and treatment of juvenile delinquency." But
this will be difficult because of the many demands on funds and on skilled
personnel. This calls for careful study of a way to meet the situation without
disrupting essential services.

Delinquency in New York State

The New York State Department of Social Welfare has just issued a report
on juvenile delinquency in upstate New York (not including New York
City). The thirteen "war-industry counties" showed far greater increases in
juvenile delinquency, cases of neglected children, and in those under foster
care than did the rest of the state. (These data have not been analyzed in the
light of population changes.) The percentage of increases in the war-industry
counties for the first six months of 1941 and of 1942 over the average for the
same months from 1938 to 1940 are shown below:

	1941	1942
Delinquency	11.5%	22.4%
Neglect cases	18.5%	39.4%
Cases committed to institutions	20.4%	46.3%
Children under foster care for the first time	17.7%	33.5%

But in the 39 other upstate counties the number of cases of juvenile delinquency, of cases of neglect and delinquency committed to institutions, and
of children receiving foster care for the first time all decreased in the first six
months of 1942 below the average for the six months from 1938 to 1940.
Cases of neglect not requiring institutional care increased 11.9 percent, but
this is less than a third of the increase in the war-industry counties. The
number of children placed in foster homes by their parents or relatives in
war-industry areas increased 39.2 per cent over normal in 1941 and 77.6
per cent in 1942. The number of children placed by agencies also increased

somewhat. Nearly two-thirds of the children placed in foster care in these counties had both parents living, and a quarter of them had had their last home with both parents. The children average a full year younger than those in the rest of the state.

This signifies, the Department of Welfare points out, that families are being broken up by the employment of mothers, or the fathers working in another community, or going into the armed services. Children are being put in foster homes by parents who cannot care for them satisfactorily or by those who are failing to provide the "standards, safeguards and supervision of a normal family home life." In general, the increases in delinquency, neglect and foster care are highest in the sections which have been most seriously affected by wartime conditions or have been affected over the longest period of time. However communities with well-organized social resources have been able to check the "full effect of adverse of wartime influences." A study of the data by counties makes this evident. In a few counties where the number of cases had been dropping from 1938 to 1940 there was an upsurge in 1941 and a decline in 1942 to about the same level as the average of the three years previous. The great increase is found in the counties where delinquency had been increasing before the war boom. Only one war industry county showed a decrease in the percentage of cases of delinquency and neglect in the first six months of 1942 as over against the average from 1938 to 1940. One had an increase of 176.9 per cent and two other increases of more than 80 per cent. ...

Source: Christian Commission for Camp and Defense Communities, "Church Letter on War Communities," No. 2 (December 1942), pp. 23, File 13, Box 5, RG 18, Federal Council of Churches Records, Presbyterian Historical Society, Philadelphia, Pennsylvania.

Study Questions

1 How did the United States pay for the war?
2 What sentiments are expressed in Irving Berlin's song on the income tax? How do his lyrics illustrate the transformation of the income tax as one paid by wealthy Americans to one paid by lower-income groups?
3 How did the rationing system work? Were all Americans willing to abide by the limits it imposed on consumption?
4 How much support existed for working mothers? How available was child care?
5 In what ways were children affected by the war?

Chapter 6   The Arsenal of Democracy

1 Donald M. Nelson, Excerpts from *Arsenal of Democracy: The Story of American War Production*, 1946

World War II involved the unprecedented mobilization of the American economy. This required the federal government to play a strong role in allocating resources, supervising production, and placing limits on prices and wages. Roosevelt seldom liked to concentrate power in the hands of one single administrator and multitudes of New Deal agencies emerged to administer the war-time economy. In this excerpt, Donald Nelson, a businessman who spent his career at the nation's largest retailer of the era, Sears, Roebuck, describes his first meetings with FDR as director of the War Production Board (WPB) in 1942. Nelson recalls not only FDR's setting high goals for defense production, but also the practical difficulties that needed to be overcome to achieve these goals. The WPB had to contend with the continuing power of the War and Navy Departments to procure necessary goods and material directly from business and bypass its authority.

Between Pearl Harbor Sunday and the afternoon of January 13, 1942, when the new War Production Board was outlined by the President to me, I saw him and talked with him just twice. Shortly after Pearl Harbor, Prime

The United States in World War II: A Documentary Reader, First Edition.
Edited by G. Kurt Piehler. Editorial material and organization © 2013 Blackwell Publishing Ltd.
Published 2013 by Blackwell Publishing Ltd.

Minister Churchill and Lord Beaverbrook, the British Minister of Supply, flew to the United States. Their purpose was to co-ordinate military strategy and production plans.

Before the first meeting in the President's study, we had a number of meetings with Lord Beaverbrook in which, drawing on his experiences in England, he tried to convince us that we would have to raise our sights tremendously if we hoped to hold off Japan and at the same time fight Nazi Europe. Lord Beaverbrook talked in what seemed at the time to be fantastic figures for airplane production, tank production, antiaircraft guns, artillery, ammunition, and so on. I remember that he staggered us with his statement that we had to produce 45,000 tanks in 1942. None of our production people thought that this volume was possible, but he stuck to his guns and reminded us that the Germans had crushed Europe by the sheer weight, speed, and fire power of their armored divisions. He spoke earnestly about the necessity for the redesigning of our tanks, for installing bigger guns in them, for heavier armor and more speed, in order to meet the panzers on equal terms.

President Roosevelt had asked all of us to give Lord Beaverbook our most exact estimates of raw materials, facilities, and production potentials. We referred to surveys which had already been made, and we worked feverishly, night and day, consulting with industry, consulting with the Army and the Navy in figuring out how far our supply of materials would go, how far our production facilities could be extended, and how quickly. Before we had time to get our ideas really into shape, the President called me over to his study.

It was about five o'clock in the evening. The President was relaxed, unperturbed, as always the complete master of the situation. Also present were Harry Hopkins; Prime Minister Churchill, sitting on the sofa at the President's right and smoking one of those huge cigars; Lord Beaverbrook; and Mr. Knudsen.

I was the last to arrive, and after I was seated the President said, "I have been thinking about the munitions which this country must produce in order to lick the Germans and the Japs as quickly as possible, and by my usual rule-of-thumb method I have arrived at the following figures."

I remember how startled and alarmed I was when he mentioned 45,000 tanks, 60,000 planes—and ships, guns and ammunition in proportion.

The President continued: "I am going to make a speech before Congress in a few days and tell them what I expect the country to produce. I am going to state these figures publicly."

Someone—I have forgotten who—said: "Mr. President, I doubt that we ought to mention those figures to the public. Won't they give out too much information to the enemy?"

The President answered: "These figures are high because they represent what we simply *have* to produce. I have absolute confidence that the country can do the job, and because I believe these figures will tell our enemies what they are up against, I want to make the figures public."

He did. His message to Congress, a few days later, was explicit, and he set goals which we, who had been closest to the records which were supposed to state the nation's production potentials, thought were completely out of the question. ...

Of course, the immediate problem was to expand the nation's shipbuilding facilities. During the next year and a half, a total of eighty-one shipbuilding yards, with more than 300 ways, were brought into operation, at an estimated cost to the government of more than half a billion dollars. These yards were capable of turning out more than 20,000,000 dead-weight tons of shipping annually.

How simple that sounds now! Three sentences—but they express a revolution in ship construction, they conceal innumerable problems, and an unimaginable amount of extremely hard work; they compress within that one little paragraph one of the secrets of our victory. For we had no sooner got into the war than Axis submarines opened an attack on our commerce which was even more destructive than anything the first World War had seen. Sinkings outran new construction. Production got into a life-or-death race with destruction. To call it a life-or-death race is no exaggeration whatever; for while our general munitions program was swinging into high gear, no conceivable triumph in the production of tanks, guns, ammunition, or other military items would be of the slightest use if the shipping to take it to the fighting fronts were lacking. Admiral Land has remarked that virtually every known world record in shipbuilding was surpassed in American shipyards during 1942 and 1943. Those records *had* to be surpassed. Our national survival depended on it.

With shipbuilding expanding at such a pace, it was not long before the inevitable results began to show up: the shipbuilding program was colliding with other programs. The collision was felt first in the matter of steel plate. In January of 1942 the Maritime Commission was taking 172,000 tons of steel plate; by June that figure had jumped to 321,000 tons, and the end was by no means in sight, for the Commission was estimating that before December 31 it would be needing 450,000 tons a month. This would not have been quite so bad if we had been able to give merchant shipbuilding an absolute top priority, meeting its demands first and then distributing what was left to the other claimants. But any such course was out of the question. We did not have just *one* program that was absolutely vital to victory; we had a dozen or more, and all of them had to go along together. Steel plate was needed by the Navy for its warships, by the Army for its tanks, by Lend-Lease for the requirements of our Allies; it was essential, too, for the building of high-octane gasoline plants, rubber plants, and for the expansion of our overall industrial capacity. All these needs had to be met. What was called for was, obviously, the most careful control of our available supply, to insure that it would be distributed where and when the need was most critical, and in quantities sufficient to meet minimum demands only—for if anyone had a surplus of steel plate on hand the assumption was that someone else was going short.

All of these claimant agencies came to WPB to get their allocations of such essential materials as steel. WPB would allot to each claimant a quantity which came as close as possible to the stated request; it was then up to the claimant agency to divide its quota among its various producers. Thus, in the case of merchant-ship construction, after WPB had decided on the total allocation of steel for this purpose, the Maritime Commission would readjust its orders—in case the allocation as a whole was less in amount than the sum of it requirements—and would notify the mills how much plate would be shipped to each yard. This was an extremely complicated matter to handle even though, as someone once remarked, shipbuilding is principally a fairly simple task of cutting and shaping steel, moving it from place to place, and fastening it together by welding or riveting. In peace time, an ordinary shipyard will carry considerable reserve stocks on hand, as insurance against delays in delivery; and in war time a shipbuilder will naturally try to do the same thing, partly from force of habit and partly as a simple matter of business prudence, even though such a course may be fatal to the success of the program as a whole. To over-simplify the matter considerably: suppose you have ten shipyards in production, and are able to allocate to all ten just enough steel on a month-to-month basis to meet their current needs. If two of the yards obtain a surplus over and above their month-to-month requirements, in order to build up an inventory of three to four months' supply, the other eight are going to get less steel than they should have for current requirements. Consequently, all the yards have to come very close to doing what they would at all costs avoid doing if left to themselves: operate on a hand-to-mouth basis, with inventories reduced to the absolute minimum.

Just to make the problem more complicated, however, there is the unhappy fact, on which the various production agencies stubbed their toes a dozen times during the war, that steel isn't just steel. It comes in myriad sizes and shapes. A shipyard would not merely need so many tons of steel each month; that tonnage had to be divided up into many different kinds and sizes of steel, and if the proper assortment did not come in the proper sequence, the effect on the yard's ability to launch ships was just as bad as if no steel at all had been delivered. For example: we made an extensive survey of the plate situation at various yards in the spring and summer of 1942, and found that one west coast yard (which can be taken as a fair sample of all) needed, each month, no fewer than 763 different kinds of steel plates and 455 steel shapes. Any tangle in the production and shipment of these widely assorted pieces of steel meant an immediate slow-down in the yard's production of ships. If steel for top decks and deck houses arrived first it lay idle, and construction stopped until the steel for the keel and the side platings was delivered. At this particular yard a careful check was made to determine how the shipment of the various categories of plates was being co-ordinated. It developed that the yard had no supply at all for 31 kinds of plates and 109 shapes; on the other hand, it had enough for 50 ships of six varieties of plates and three shapes. Its supplies in the other categories ranged between these two extremes.

There were several reasons for this trouble: Some mills had fallen behind on their orders, while others- were ahead. Some were very prompt in turning out orders which involved large volume and easy processing, but tended to delay production on more difficult items, or on those which were ordered in small quantities. Another factor was the gratifying increase in production speed displayed by many of the yards which were building Liberty ships; they were taking less time than had been anticipated to complete their ships, and consequently were crowding the mills.

Mixed up with these problems was the fact that the yards which were working on standard-type ships—that is, the modern-type vessels whose design and production had been started before the war—were, in general, getting better delivery of steel from the mills than were the yards which concentrated on the Liberty ships. Responsibility for scheduling and ordering steel had been left with these yards. They had had a head start on the emergency yards, and had spread their orders for each ship over several months, placing their orders as far ahead as they felt was necessary. The Maritime Commission was placing the orders for steel for the Liberty ships, and was doing a first-rate job; but the standard yards, taken all in all, were getting better deliveries from the mills; partly, no doubt, because in many cases the mills felt that these yards were their "regular customers," so to speak, and more or less unconsciously tended to favor them. In any case, some steel that was needed elsewhere was piling up at the standard yards, while the emergency shipyards were getting less than they needed for their expected rate of production.

Component parts were another phase of the same problem. The hull of a ship was of no use whatever unless engines, winches, pumps, and various other items were on hand; and in this field the merchant shipbuilding program was in direct competition, once more, with some of the other important programs of our war effort. Each Liberty ship needed, in addition to the hundreds of different kinds of plates and shapes mentioned above, approximately 7,500 different types of individual components. Including the subcontractors, some 6,000 separate concerns were engaged in the production of these items. Contracts had to be placed to cover all of these needs. Each supplier had to be notified to which yard or yards he must ship each item, in terms of ships per month. The ability of each supplier to meet these demands had to be checked, and someone had to see to it that the shipbuilder received on time his own materials and parts. In other words, a very extensive and complex job of planning and scheduling had to be done, and with the shipbuilding program rising so steeply it was inevitable that during the first year there would be a considerable number of bottlenecks.

In general, the problem was simpler with Liberty ships than with high-speed or special-purpose vessels. Most of the things needed for the Liberty ships—from engines and condensers on through piping and rigging to galley equipment—could be produced in adequate volume by existing factories, if a little time were taken to organize production and supply properly. It was not so easy to provide the more complex items required for standard ships. Propulsion equipment, in particular, was a tough item; in some cases the completion of these vessels was delayed for several months while they awaited delivery of turbines, gears, bearings, and the like. The Maritime Commission, however, had tackled the problem of propulsion machinery with a good deal of vigor, and at the time our WPB study was made it was clear that the shortage of turbines and gears was not going to be a seriously limiting factor in the attainment of our goals for 1942 and 1943. The real problem here was that both the Maritime Commission and the Navy were seeking the same types of equipment from the same suppliers. In some cases, Navy orders overrode Maritime Commission orders, with the result that completion of a number of merchant vessels was delayed.

Out of this survey came co-operative action to widen the bottlenecks. Committees representing the Maritime Commission, the Navy, and WPB were set up to co-ordinate efforts for the procurement of material for planning and scheduling. There was some reshuffling of the inventories as among the various yards. Much closer control was maintained over shipments from the mills, and the Maritime Commission broadened and strengthened its planning and scheduling services. Last, but no means least, better centralized direction of that part of the problem which fell in WPB's province was obtained when we secured the appointment, in January, 1943, of William Francis Gibbs as Controller of Shipbuilding. Mr. Gibbs was head of the firm of Gibbs & Cox, and had put through the original production program for the sixty emergency cargo vessels ordered by the British. His efforts admirably supplemented the fine work done by Admiral Land's organization, and not much of 1943 had elapsed before it became fairly clear that the "impossible" merchant shipbuilding program was going to be fulfilled, with a safe margin to spare.

One of the most helpful contributions of WPB to this came in connection with the scheduling procedure we set up for all critical components, such as boilers, fans, pumps, blowers, and valves. The manufacturers of these items were directed by WPB to produce only on a schedule agreed upon. The claimant agencies furnished WPB with accurate lists of their requirements for each item, giving in each case the date on which the necessary quantity must be on hand if the shipbuilding program was to be met. In this way, all of the components which were bought from the agency offices in Washington and those bought by the various procurement agencies in the field, or by prime contractors, were properly listed. It was then possible to arrange an orderly schedule for their production. If it developed, in the process, that the necessary dates could not be met, it was possible to find other sources of supply or to rearrange the schedule to meet the availability of components. The Maritime Commission set up a very efficient Scheduling and Survey Branch to handle its end of this work.

Source: Donald M. Nelson, *Arsenal of Democracy: The Story of American War Production* (New York: Harcourt, Brace, 1946), pp. 185–186, 246–251.

2 Lee Wilson, Excerpt from Interview, 2006

Americans, especially those who were civilians, remember World War II as the "good war" because it brought a full-employment economy and scores of high-wage jobs in defense industries, which stood in sharp contrast to the high unemployment that marked the Great Depression of the 1930s. Demand for workers, combined with pressure exerted by the federal government, encouraged employers to hire women, African Americans, and other minority workers. African Americans left the South seeking work in defense industries in the North and West. In this oral history, Lee Wilson recalls the high wages she earned as a welder in the Kaiser Shipyards in Richmond, California, as well as the sacrifices she had to make regarding her children. Although African Americans who left the South enjoyed greater political rights, they continued to face widespread discrimination in employment and housing, and segregation in many businesses.

Wilson: I went to school there in the shipyard. I think we had Yard 4. I went to welding school and I passed the test. They had 96 hours, you train in 96 hours then they put you out in the yard to do the welding and tacking and whatever that leader man had you to do. And I was over there in the school, I was only in school like three days and they felt that I understood enough to be out in the yard and so they pulled me and put me out in the yard. And that was with a leader man, these are men that have a group, so many welders, so many chippers, so many burners, it's all within this group. And I was the tacker or the welder.

Wilmot: A tacker?

Wilson: Well that is when—the welding is—the tacker—tacking is shorter welder. When you're tacking you weld the place about so long. And from that long on to how ever long that they want you to weld it. And anyway I was a welder and I was out in the yard 30 days and I got a raise and the next 30 days I got a raise. You in school to get 95¢ an hour. That's what we were getting then, 95¢ an hour. The time that we're in school. And when they take you out of school and put you in the yard then you'd be getting $1.05. That was on the dayshift. And $1.05 and then 30 day [*sic*] you get $1.10, another 30 days, $1.15 and on dayshift $1.20, that was as high as they went. And you'd get $1.20. But I was on the dayshift and I had got like $1.15 and I took the welding test and passed the test for to become a journeyman welder. And that was $1.15 on my card that morning and when I brought my card back that evening it was $1.20 because it was $1.10, I skipped $1.15 because I passed the test. And that's right, I skipped $1.15.

Wilmot: So it was $1.20 per—?

Wilson: $1.20 per hour.

Wilmot: Per hour and so you were making—was that a lot more money than you had made in Arkansas?

Wilson: That was a lot of money. That was more than we would make because they were paying like $3 or $4 a week and of course where I worked at when I came here I was making $18.75 a month. And I got paid on the 5th and 20th. And I quit that job when I came out here. And of course out here when I started in the shipyard making—started with $1.05—

Wilmot: $1.20 then you ended up making.

Wilson: You started off, in the shipyard you were—

Wilmot: You were making $64 a week, which is really different than—that's a big difference. Wow.

Wilson: In the shipyard if you were a welder, which I was a welder, when I started on the dayshift, started out in the yard, that was $1.05 an hour and for 30 days then you'd get $1.10 but I didn't do that, I took the ABS test and passed it so I skipped all of that to the highest amount.

Wilmot: Well let me ask you something—hm, of course my mind goes blank. So what did you do with all that money? You suddenly were making more money than you'd ever made in your life. Did you save it? Did you spend—?

Wilson: Well I had two children to take care of.

Wilmot: So you sent it back home?

Wilson: I sent the money back home to my mom to take care of my two children. And see my husband at that time, he was in service but he had just gone in service.

Wilmot: So when he came back 110 days later you continued that job, welding.

Wilson: When he came back from the service, I kept—I continued that job and I worked there until I was laid off in 1946. ...

Wilmot: Who did you work with?

Wilson: Who did I work with?

Wilmot: Were you part of a crew of other women?

Wilson: Yes I was a part of a woman and man crew.

Wilmot: Did you have a female supervisor?

Wilson: No, I had a male.

Wilmot: Okay, and how many women? Was it more women or more men in your crew?

Wilson: It was about the same. Maybe one or two more men than there were women.

Wilmot: Was it mostly black people or was it also integrated with white people?

Wilson: It was integrated.

Wilmot: So it was a mixed group.

Wilson: It was mixed. Sometime you was working with some, is all black. And sometime you're working with some, you the only black. And so I would say it depend on what type work you were doing. And—

Wilmot: Did you experience discrimination in the shipyard? Racial discrimination?

Wilson: Here and there. Well, you know, you don't pay stuff like that no attention.

Wilmot: When you say here and there, what do you mean?

Wilson: Well maybe with this group, you're working with this group, they'll say—you'll hear them talking about the other group, somebody'll get in trouble. If you just keep your mouth closed and be quiet long enough, you hear all what's going on, you don't have to ask nobody. And those who were kind of shy, they were not openly, shall we say, prejudiced, they were not openly prejudiced, they were just like, say it under their breath. They try to pretend, they'd say something but you didn't know what they were talking about or whatever. I never listened to—I'd go to work and do a job. I didn't go to work to socialize. And I go to work and I do what I'm supposed to do. And when time for me to go on my break, I go on my break. When time for me to come back from my break, I come back from my break. I don't wait ten or 15 minutes after my break and here I come back. I'm doing what I'm supposed to do. And I treat you right inasmuch as within me, I'll treat you right. If I can't treat you right, I'd rather not be around you. Stay away from me. I don't get that lonesome that I have to get involved with something that I don't feel comfortable with.

Wilmot: I see what you mean. Was discrimination here out in the West Coast—?

Wilson: Yeah, it's discrimination everywhere you go. If you look for it. If you look for it, you'll find it.

Wilmot: I guess I was going to ask though, was it different or more or less than what you knew back in Arkansas, the experience of racial discrimination?

Wilson: No, the one thing I liked about Arkansas, if people like you they like you. And if they didn't like you, they'll let you know they didn't like you and they don't have nothing to do with you. And I appreciate that.

Wilmot: It was straightforward.

Wilson: Yeah, you don't cover up or pretend that you're something when you're not. Some people are like, "Oh, I just love you, I just love you!" and "I don't know what—don't get nothing near me." I don't like that. Whoever you are, you be whoever you are. You find you live much longer. And you won't have high blood pressure.

Source: Interview with Lee Wilson by Nadine Wilmot, June 22, 2006, pp. 19–20, 28–29, Regional Oral History Office, Bancroft Library, University of California, Berkeley, California. Also available online at http://bancroft.berkeley.edu/ROHO/projects/rosie/.

3 US National War Labor Board, "Statement from the National War Labor Board to the Parties in Dispute Cases," 1944

The 1930s had been an era of labor militancy when the Congress of Industrial Organizations (CIO) had unionized scores of workers in the automobile, steel, glass, rubber, and radio industries using such techniques as sit-down strikes. Prodded by the Roosevelt Administration, most labor unions affiliated with the American Federation of Labor (AFL) and the CIO took a no-strike pledge for the duration of the war. In giving up its ultimate weapon – the strike – labor was dependent on the good faith of employers to bargain reliably and on the federal government through the National War Labor Board to protect its interests. Most of industry also accepted the National War Labor Board because, in a full-employment economy, labor had a strong bargaining position, at least temporarily. Moreover, cost-plus contracts allowed many companies manufacturing war goods to pass on higher labor costs to the federal government. There were exceptions. John L. Lewis led a major coal strike in 1943 that resulted in the Roosevelt Administration threatening to seize the mines and to draft striking coal miners.

Disputes before the War Labor Board, April 1944, pamphlet

Statement from the National War Labor Board to the Parties in Dispute Cases

"It is more than ever necessary in war time that the peaceful processes of collective bargaining be preserved and utilized to the fullest extent. The existence of the National War Labor Board and Regional War Labor Boards, providing machinery for the settlement of disputes, must in no way be considered as a substitute for the bargaining process."

"Labor and management must accept the obligation, so clear and compelling in time of war, to refrain from laying their incidental problems in the lap of the government. This will require, on the part of the unions, that they do not request certification to the Board of disputes which are not of major importance. It will require management in turn to refrain from abusing labor's voluntary surrender of the strike weapon by demonstrating a willingness to bargain collectively in good faith."

William H. Davis, Chairman
National War Labor Board ...

HISTORY

The Origin and Structure of the War Labor Board

The Board was created shortly after Pearl Harbor as the result of a conference called by the President for the representatives of industry and labor who pledged no strikes or lockouts for the duration. They agreed to a tripartite War Labor Board with members chosen in equal numbers from labor, industry, and the general public, as a democratic and practical method for the peaceful settlement of disputes during the war.

As the work of the National Board increased, 12 regional tripartite boards were established to share the load and speed decisions. This has the additional advantage of providing for local settlement of local disputes. ...

The National Board has established tripartite industry commissions in cases where stabilization of a large segment of a particular industry is best achieved by this method. The commissions have the same structure and procedures as the regional and National Boards, and their decisions are final, subject to review by the National Board.

The National Board has also set up industry panels in certain key industries where it is more efficient to handle cases on that basis. Unlike the regional boards and the industry commissions, these panels are not authorized to make the final decisions; they hold hearings and make recommendations to the appropriate board. ...

In addition, the National War Labor Board has given jurisdiction over labor disputes and wage adjustments in the construction industry to a tripartite Wage Adjustment Board.

The Board Gets Its Authority from Presidential Order and from Congress

The tripartite War Labor Board was officially created January 12, 1942 by Executive Order 9017 and given authority to settle finally all labor disputes that might interrupt work which contributes to the effective prosecution of the war.

Congress on October 2, 1942, directed the President to issue an order establishing prices, wages, and salaries. Executive Order 9250 carried out this Congressional directive and placed the responsibility for wage stabilization on the WLB. In 1943, the Board's stabilization powers were more clearly defined by the President's "hold the line" order of April 8, and Justice Byrnes' clarifying directive of May 12.

On June 25, 1943, Congress passed the War Labor Disputes Act, which gave the Board the following powers:

1. To hold public hearings in labor dispute cases which cannot be settled by collective bargaining or conciliation, and which may lead to substantial interference with the war effort,
2. To subpoena parties, witnesses, or documents needed in the settlement of labor disputes or relevant to any inquiry before the Board or any of its agents,
3. To decide the dispute and provide by order the wages and hours and all other terms and conditions ... governing the relations between the parties.

On August 16, 1943, the President issued Executive Order 9370, which provides that the WLB may report cases of non-compliance with its directive orders to the Economic Stabilization Director. The Director in appropriate cases may then issue such directives as he may deem necessary to other Government agencies for the purpose of securing the following action:

1. Against employers—cancellation of Government contracts and priorities, until compliance is secured;
2. Against the unions—withdrawals of privileges, benefits, or rights, as by holding of check-off dues in escrow, pending compliance;
3. Against individuals—modification or cancellation of draft deferments or employment privileges, or both.

The Board Encourage Collective Bargaining

The first obligation of the parties in a dispute to use existing collective bargaining machinery in an effort to reach an agreement between themselves. If this fails, and if no other procedures for adjustment of the dispute are available, they should resort to mediation by the Conciliation Service of the Department of Labor. Only if these measures have been exhausted is the case certified by the Secretary of Labor to the WLB. The WLB will refer back to the parties any cases or issues in which collective bargaining has not been exercised to the fullest extent possible, or in which other available procedures for settlement of the dispute are not utilized. ...

Source: Division of Public Information, National War Labor Board, *Disputes before the War Labor Board* (Washington, DC: Government Printing Office, April 1944), pp. 2–4.

4 Montgomery Ward Department Store, Flyers Distributed to Employees, and International Longshore and Warehouse Union, Flyer to Union Members, 1943, 1944

Labor and capital generally cooperated during the war years as both benefited from a booming economy. Corporate profits soared and membership in labor unions increased, aided by a ruling of the National War Labor Board that required "maintenance of membership" for new employees joining a company with a labor contract in place. A worker joining a company with a valid labor contract had to join the recognized labor union and pay union dues for the duration of the war. The closed shop was often sought by labor in negotiations as a means to increase its bargaining power with employers. Moreover, labor argued the closed shop remained legitimate because a union could only be established if a majority of workers voted to join. Sewell Avery, chairman of Montgomery Ward, a retailer that rivaled Sears, Roebuck in the 1940s, challenged the "maintenance of membership" requirement and, in the view of labor unions seeking to negotiate with him, refused to bargain in good faith, leading to the United Mail Order, Wholesale, and Retail Employees Union going on strike in April 1943. Below are three flyers. The first two were issued by Montgomery Ward to its employees and outline its position. The third flyer, circulated by the International Longshore and Warehouse Workers Union (ILWU), comments on Avery's actions and explains its position on the strike by some Montgomery Ward workers in Chicago.

Flyer Distributed by Montgomery Ward, January 11, 1943

TO ALL MONTGOMERY WARD PEOPLE

1. You are free to join or not join a union, as you wish. The Company fully respects this privilege. Your opportunity with the Company will be the same whether you are a union member or not.
2. You do not have to join a union to work at Wards.
3. Wards is opposed to all forms of the closed shop. Liberty requires that an employee be free to join, to refuse to join, or to resign from a union without losing his job. Liberty requires that an employer be free to employ the person best suited for the work.
4. The President of the United States has commanded Wards to accept for its Chicago plant a form of closed shop called "maintenance of membership." Under this form of closed shop, employees are not free to resign from the union without losing their jobs. Wards is compelled to discharge every union member who fails to maintain his union membership in good standing (non-payment of dues, etc.) This making of membership in a union a condition of holding a job is the closed shop.
5. Wards did not voluntarily agree to this requirement. Wards believes it to be illegal and uneconomic. Wards has accepted it under duress and only because the President of the United States expressly so ordered.
6. Wards is the only retailer in the United States upon whom the President has imposed any form of the closed shop. It is unfair to impose burdens upon Wards and not upon those with whom it is in competition. If the retail industry is to be subjected to the closed shop requirement, it should be legislated by Congress and applied uniformly against all retail establishments.
7. The National War Labor Board has now called a hearing to determine whether the employees at Wards six large stores in Denver, Detroit and

New York City must belong to the union in order to hold their jobs. Wards will continue to oppose this illegal and uneconomic requirement. Wards will reject any demand of the Board that employees be discharged because they fail to maintain their union membership.

8. The President of the United States has no authority to order Wards employees to remain union members in order to hold their jobs. Congress is the only law-making authority. Congress has passed no law requiring the closed shop.

MONTGOMERY WARD & CO.
SEWELL AVERY
President

January 11, 1943

[Flyer Distributed April 1944]

Montgomery Ward & Company

TO ALL MONTGOMERY WARD PEOPLE:

FACTS ABOUT THE STRIKE AT WARDS

1. The contract which Wards signed at Chicago in December, 1942, under duress at the direction of the President, expired December 8, 1943.
2. On November 16, 1943, Wards told the union it would negotiate a new contract covering five of the seven bargaining units established at Chicago. Wards questioned whether the union represented a majority of employees in the mail order house and retail because less than 20 % in those two units were then having union dues checked off from wages.
3. Although five months have elapsed, the union has refused to show that it is the majority choice of the employees by either a card check or an election.
4. Under the law Wards is forbidden to bargain with a union which does not represent a majority.
5. The War Labor Board has illegally ordered Wards to extend the expired contract without requiring the union to prove its majority. Wards has brought suit to have this order set aside.
6. The union has called the strike to force Wards to accept this illegal order.
7. The company stands ready to recognize the union when proof of its representation has been presented.

MONTGOMERY WARD AND COMPANY
SEWELL AVERY
Chairman

Flyer Distributed by the International Longshore and Warehouse Workers, April 1944

ILWU AN[S]WERS MONTGOMERY WARD [April 21, 1944]

TRUE FACTS ABOUT CHICAGO

1. The Company has refused to obey an order of the U.S. Government (by WLB) to recognize the Chicago Union until the question of bargaining agent is settled.
2. The Union in Chicago has applied to the Government (through NLRB) to settle the question of bargaining agent, but this is impossible as long as Wards continues to defy Government orders.
3. By defying the Government the Company is trying to lay the ground-work for getting rid of all Government laws and agencies which protect the rights of labor and will make it possible for Wards to get away with paying its workers about 30 c/ [cents] an hour when the war is over.

NO STRIKES HERE

1. The Company is responsible for the strike in Chicago because it has defied the U.S. Government and provoked the Union into taking strike action.
2. The Chicago Union is a different Union from our Union here.
3. Our Union, ILWU, was organized here on the basis of a no-strike pledge. [T]he ILWU has not gone out on one strike in any part of the country since Pearl Harbor. We will keep the no-strike pledge here in spite of any Company provocation.

WHICH SIDE ARE YOU ON?

1. ON ONE SIDE IS MONTGOMERY WARD AND ON THE OTHER SIDE IS THE UNITED STATES GOVERNMENT.
2. Our Union, the ILWU, stands by the United States Government.
3. If you are on the side of the Government and want to help win the war and the peace that will follow – stay lined up with the Union!

DON'T BE FOOLED
         BUILD THE UNION
                  SUPPORT OUR GOVERNMENT
                           BACK UP ARMED FORCES

Issued by: ILWU Local 219 – 326 West Franklin Street – Lexington 8454

Source: Flyer Distributed by Montgomery Ward, January 11, 1943, Folder 6, Box 25, and Sewell Avery and Appeasement Folder 2, Box 26, Montgomery Ward Collection, American Heritage Center, University of Wyoming, Laramie, Wyoming. I am indebted to John Bussa for locating these documents while conducting research at the American Heritage Center for his undergraduate thesis.

5 Sewell Avery and US Soldiers, Photograph, 1944

Government oversight of the economy required voluntary compliance and cooperation. On April 27, 1944, after refusing to negotiate in good faith with the United Mail Order, Wholesale, and Retail Employees Union and honor the "maintenance of membership" rules imposed by the National War Labor Board, Sewell Avery was blamed by the Roosevelt Administration for giving workers little choice but to strike. To end the labor dispute, Roosevelt ordered the federal government to seize Montgomery Ward and dispatched Attorney General Francis Biddle to oversee the process. Using Army troops, Biddle took over Montgomery Ward's headquarters in Chicago. When Avery refused to leave voluntarily, Army soldiers picked him up by his chair and removed him from his office. This photo was among the most widely circulated of 1944.

Figure 6.1   Guards removing Sewell Avery in a chair from the Montgomery Ward building, April 28, 1944, Chicago, Illinois. © Bettmann/CORBIS.

6 *Washington Post*, "Law and Responsibility," Editorial, 1944

The seizure of Montgomery Ward led to an outcry from the conservative press over unbridled executive authority and the trampling of Americans' individual freedom. The power and influence of organized labor were decried. But even many liberals sympathetic to labor and the Roosevelt Administration took issue with the way the federal government seized Montgomery Ward in April 1944, objecting to the Administration's assertion of the president's constitutional prerogatives as commander in chief in time of war. Presidential authority in war-time continues to be contested and many of the issues raised by this Washington Post *editorial remain relevant.*

Law and Responsibility

In these critical times, especially on the eve of events which will put this war into every household in America, a loyalty to measures which are patently essential to effective prosecution of the war should be taken for granted. We have in mind disciplinary regulations governing work and prices and production. Certainly strikes involving large bodies of workers are inimical to our war effort, whether these strikes occur in plants making munitions of war or in great distributive establishments, such as Montgomery Ward's Chicago properties. Montgomery Ward, however, has been repeatedly cited for engaging in unfair labor practices which have been an impediment to smooth production. Its disputes with its employe[e]s have been frequent. And the evidence strongly indicates that the management is chiefly responsible for the strike that led finally to Government seizure of the company's Chicago properties. The company's hostile attitude, its failure to give full cooperation to Government agencies striving to maintain orderly processes of collective bargaining, thus deserve to be severely condemned.

The seriousness of the interference with our war effort caused by strikes involving the employe[e]s of a mail order house is not, of course, as great as it would be in case of strikes in plants manufacturing war equipment. But it is substantial, as the Attorney General asserts in his opinion sustaining the validity of the executive order. Furthermore, his opinion emphasizes the danger that the Chicago disturbance might spread to other plants and facilities of the company, as well as "breed controversies" in other companies engaged in essential war work. The Attorney General has, in fact, advanced some very strong arguments to support the contention that the Montgomery Ward strike was a most untimely development which the management should have tried to prevent by all means at its disposal. However, the company management has preferred to press the issue of legality. And on that score it can make out a strong case against the methods followed in forcing it to comply with WLB orders.

The legal questions raised in this case should be considered in an atmosphere free from prejudice. For the issues raised are not confined to labor disputes involving Montgomery Ward or other concerns in the same class. The fundamental issue is whether the President has the authority under statutory law or under the Constitution to take over a plant engaged in the distribution of merchandise to civilians. The Attorney General upholds the validity of the seizure on two grounds: (1) that Section 3 of the War Labor Disputes (i.e., the Smith-Connally antistrike) Act gives him necessary authority and (2) that the President's constitutional and statutory powers as Chief Executive and Commander in Chief of the Army and Navy would warrant the seizure even in the absence of Section 3 of the War Labor Disputes Act.

The Attorney General's interpretation of the Smith-Connally Act has already been sharply challenged by certain members of Congress, including Representative Smith. He affirms that the provision permitting seizure of "any plant, mine or facility equipped for the manufacture, production, or mining of any article" used in the war effort was never intended to apply to concerns engaged in retail merchandising. As coauthor of the War Labor Disputes Act Mr. Smith is certainly entitled to express an opinion. Furthermore, the language of the act appears to support his interpretation. Thus the country is again faced by a controversy growing out of the administrative habit of using limited statutes to accomplish purposes not conceived of by their legislative sponsors.

The Attorney General's assumption that the President might exercise the power of seizure without any legislative authorization will give rise to even more violent dissent. For if the President can seize private plants distributing civilian goods whenever, in his judgment, the seizure becomes necessary to prevent injury to the war effort, he might conceivably take over the whole of private industry without so much as asking for congressional approval. One wonders why, if this is the President's notion of his general wartime authority, he bothers to ask Congress for specific authority.

The extension of the powers of the President that would be made possible by acceptance of the sweeping Biddle opinion may well alarm Americans who do not believe that any emergency confers dictatorial powers on the President. In this particular case, seizure is undoubtedly the surest and quickest way of forcing compliance on a recalcitrant concern. But we have labor legislation (the Wagner Act, in fact) that provides means of bringing pressure to bear upon employers who engage in unfair labor practices. It is by no means clear that the present emergency warranted resort to extreme measures before trying out procedures of unquestioned legality.

Source: "Law and Responsibility," Editorial, *Washington Post*, April 28, 1944, p. 8.

7 Janice C. Christensen, Letters to Parents, 1943

In the Soviet Union, women could become military aviators and flew combat missions in fighter planes and bombers. American women could not fly combat missions or officially join the Army Air Force as aviators. But through the Women's Air Force Service Pilots (WASP) program established in 1943, women as civilians could fly military aircraft and perform a variety of support functions on behalf of the Army Air Force. Led by air ace Jacqueline Cochran, WASPs served as test pilots, towed targets, and transported planes to air bases that needed them. Although they were civilians, WASPs had to participate in a rigorous training program that mirrored training accorded to male pilots in the Army Air Force, and they had to wear a distinctive uniform. Efforts to militarize the WASPs and make them part of the Army Air Force failed in late 1944, in part because of resistance from many civilian pilots who feared they would be displaced by women pilots and be subject to conscription. Janice Charlotte Christensen of Waukegan, Illinois, joined the WASPs in March 1942 and completed her training at Avenger Field in Sweetwater, Texas, on September 11, 1943. As a ferry pilot, she served at Romulus Air Field in Michigan until the WASPs were disbanded. In her first letter to her parents, Christensen inaccurately reports that she will be commissioned as an army officer.

8/12/43
43W 5 D-2
318 th AAFFTD
Sweetwater, Texas

Dear Mom,

Well I solo'd the AT 6 about an hour ago and I am giving up for a solo period between 6:00 and 7:30 P.M. Our periods are longer now and so we don't finish till 7:30. We eat at 8:00. This is really a wonderful ship, it cruises at 140 mph, climbs at 110 mph, glides at 100 and lands at 80 to 90 mph. It's an easy step from this ship to any of the fighter ships. We only get 25 hrs in it as we have to have 25 in the AT 17, too.

We will definitely graduate Sept. 11th, so I won't be able to make the reunion but I may stop over if it's convenient.

Myrt is here now, just as slow as ever, but she has a good instructor, so she may make it. I hope she stays till I leave, anyway. I don't want to say goodbye to her.

It's just as hot as ever and there is a good wind today as we are eating and breathing dust. I'll be glad to get out of Texas. I don't know just how long it will take to get home. Transportation is pretty rotten. I'm going to find out about Airlines, too, but it may cost too much. Our pay check sure gets murdered before we see it. The new income tax bites in. How does it affect you, are you getting enough?

Tell Pops, I did appreciate his little cartoon and have had a lot of fun with it.

I've got quite a few rolls of film left. I don't have much time for pictures and there isn't so much to take. I'll probably be able to use them at the base I'm asking for Romulus but don't know that I'll get it.

Miss Cockran [sic] was here last week and she announced that she has the approval for our uniform and they will be issued to us. Slacks, jacket, Trench coat, field jacket, winter flying suit and coveralls for Summer flying. The color is Chilean blue and they will all be tailored. We will have to buy a skirt, black military shoes and black bag. Our headgear will be a beret like Montgomery wears. We will definitely be in the Army in 90 days and will be second lieutenants.

Guess, that's all the news, can you get me some 122 films for my instructor?

Oh yes, we will finish ground school on Tuesday next week, so we'll have half a day to loaf in. We won't be sorry, I'm working on a sun tan for my legs and back. Not as drastically as the first time. It would never do to come home without a little color for my legs.

Can't think of anything else. How about the pictures I ordered. I'll pay you when I get home.

Love,
Janice

11/13/43
Fargo, N.D.

Dear Folks,

Well, this has certainly been a wearing trip so far. Wednesday, when we finally managed to get one good weather report out of them, we cleared out of So. Bend. First of all we ran into some sleet and by the time we had decided it was bad enough to go back we were out of it. Then until we got past Chicago we were alternately in snow and fog. The fog took the ice off the windshield, se we were grateful. It was never a heavy fog or snow, so we kept going. We found clear weather when we reached Joliet but we landed anyway and checked the weather to Madison. They said it was fine with a few light snow flurries so off we went. We had gotten just a little North of Capron when we ran into snow. Of course we proceeded to go through as it wasn't supposed to be heavy. We flew in for just a couple minutes and by that time could barely make each other out. We were about 200 ft above the ground and could just see it. So, Pat signaled for a hasty retreat and we all made a 180 [degree] turn and flew back out of it. We swung along in front of it to see if we could go around and saw that it wasn't possible, so we went back to Joliet. The storm hit Joliet a few minutes after we got there, so we went in to town for the night. The next day we had about 2 inches of snow to clean off the ship and then we couldn't get them started because it was so cold. It took about an hour and a half. We got to Madison without any trouble as it was a nice clear day. We learned there that our 30 ships that had cleared from So. Bend were scattered all over South of Chicago. Every little airport had two or three. We waited in Madison till 1:30 for three of the girls we wanted to catch up with us. However they didn't make it so we cleared for Mpls [Minneapolis] at 5:00 P.M. It was nice and clear and I navigated!! Reached Mpls at 5:00 P.M. so I called Gay's office hoping to catch him before he started home. No one answered so I called the house and Edna was home. Gay wasn't there yet so I went downtown with the other girls and called again, Gay answered and said he'd be right down and pick me up. Edna said he had stewed around for that half hour worrying for fear I wouldn't call back and might not think I was welcome. He certainly is a wonderful relative to have. Zella, Lois and Jerry came over and we stayed up till 2:00 A.M. I was back at the airport at 8:30 A M and all four ships started right away, so we warmed them up and then walked the quarter of a mile back to the terminal. Gay was still waiting as he wanted to see me take off. We checked the weather then and found out we had a 30 mile head wind and it was getting stronger. Anyway we knew we couldn't make Fargo unless it died down so we all went in and had coffee to warm up. By that time we had a 40 mi wind of Mpls., so we walked back down to our ships to be sure they weren't blowing around and had to wade around in the snow looking for chalks. We finally got everything set and walked back, by that time the wind was so strong we could hardly make it. We had more coffee, waited around till 1:30 to be sure the weather wouldn't change and then left. I went up to Gay's office, till he was ready to go home, we picked up Edna and I bought some rum, peppermint schnaps and a pint of whiskey. The fellow let me have the whiskey when he found out what I was doing. Edna had hot buttered rum and Gay and I had schnaps to settle our stomachs because of last night, then we had about five more because it was awful good. Edna had never had schaps before so she had some. After that we went over and visited Jerry and Zella. We followed directions and found their place right away. They are renting but have a nice house and Zella has furnished it beautifully. Coming back we got lost, I guess because we were sober by that time.

Got down to my ship at 9:00 this morning and didn't get it started till 11:00. We were all worn out and frozen. So we warmed up, ate and took off at 1:00, reached Fargo at 3:30 which was too late to get to Winnepeg. I thought I'd never get warm. [T]he hotel here is crummy – no bath or shower.

I[t] looks like we'll have good weather from here on in but can't make any time because the ships are so hard to start now. Even at this rate, though, we should deliver in three more days and be on our way back. I hope my next trip is South, I've seen enough cold weather for a while.

As you already know Edna and Gay have a beautiful place. The creek in their back yard is Minnehaha creek, Jane didn't tell me that. I flew over their house on my way to Fargo but, of course, they were both working.

I've got to make the 9:00 o'clock pick up with this. Guess I've covered every thing anyway.

Love,
Janice

I saw Bob, too.

Source: Collection 54: Janice C. Christensen, US Women and World War II Letter Writing Project, Bryant University, Smithfield, Rhode Island.

8 Dae D. Baird, Letter to Evelyn E. Baird, July 7, 1944

America could only serve as the Arsenal of Democracy if the supplies produced by factories and farms could reach American forces and their Allies abroad. Over 225,000 American civilians served in the US Merchant Marine during World War II and delivered cargoes to American forces and Allies throughout the globe. The risks were great, especially during the early years of the war before the Allied navies curbed the threat posed by German and Japanese naval forces. In 1942, German submarines (U-Boats) routinely sank American merchant ships within sight of the Eastern Seaboard of the United States. Ensign Dae D. Baird, Jr. wrote a series of letters while serving aboard the SS William Bradford as it traveled across the Atlantic and the Mediterranean, through the Suez Canal, and down the Red Sea in order to deliver ammunition and airplane engines destined for the Soviet Union. In the letter below, Baird recounts the final leg of the journey to Iran and the difficulties encountered navigating the Persian Gulf toward the final destination. On the return trip home, the William Bradford *sailed around the Cape of Good Hope and again crossed to Buenos Aires, where it loaded shelled corn. Baird survived the war, but others were less fortunate: Merchant Mariners suffered 6,103 casualties. Because of their civilian status, Merchant Mariners were not accorded veterans' benefits under the GI Bill of Rights passed in 1944.*

July 7, 1944

We have reached our destination and unloading has commenced but before we arrived we had our most trying experience yet.

We entered the Persian Gulf from the Gulf of Oman through the straits of Hormuz which was very narrow and treacherous without incident and for 3 days traversed the Persian Gulf to the entrance of Khor Musa (River Musa). The Gulf while quite wide is not very deep and if [you] … miss the channel there are numerous shoals and hidden sand bars. Well on July 5 having missed the buoy at the entrance to the river when we should've anchored to await developments. It was very hazy so a motor launch was put over the side to try and locate the buoy. In this they were unsuccessful but they did see two other ships that seemed to be anchored some 7 miles away. At nightfall we sent a launch over to them. A pilot boat was near there and as the ships were aground not anchored and the pilot could be of no use to them he came back in the motor launch to us. Upon checking the maps it was found that we were sitting on dry land and yet were anchored in a deep hole. Well the upshot was we had missed the channel and crossed over two sandbars to get to our present position. Well at high tide 11 PM we raised anchor and came out of the hole the same way we went in. (You know I was doing my mental work constantly and) we came out of that place without scraping bottom although there was less than 6 ft clearance most of 20 [meters?]. We anchored again on the channel & everyone breathed a sigh of relief. The next morning we went up the river and docked yesterday evening at Brandar Sha[h]pur in Iran (Persia). This is a place the Germans had up till just before Pearl Harbor when the British took it in a sea battle and now the U.S. Army is in control with about 2000 soldiers. The natives do the unloading under the eye of the Army from 2 piers that will accommodate 6 ships. From here the cargo is sent by rail to Russia. They work the clock around except from 11 AM to 5 PM when everyone is forbidden to work due to the intense heat. They say it is the second hottest place in the earth & I believe it. There is nothing in the town except what the Army has made. A movie

4 nights a week, army canteen with 2 cans of beer a day for the boys. No milk, no ice cream, no swimming and only 11 white women all nurses. The natives are filthy even worse than Egypt and life isn't worth 2 cents to them. The guards & M.G's will shoot them at the slightest infraction of rules and no one cares. Not the Persian Govt. or the Persian people. However the consolation is we would be here as long as we thought and mail from home one delivery this morning and probably twice more before we leave 10 or 12 days from now.

There's lots of red tape many [officials?] to appease but it is gradually being accomplished. We all had to be vaccinated before we could go ashore among other things. Will write again in a few days.

Source: Dae D. Baird, Jr. Papers (09.0169), Institute on World War II and the Human Experience, Department of History, Florida State University, Tallahassee, Florida.

Study Questions

1   Why was it so difficult to build anything during the war? Why did Donald Nelson see government oversight as crucial to ensuring the US military received necessary equipment and supplies?
2   How did the war change the life of Lee Wilson? What did she give up by taking a better-paying job in California?
3   Did Sewell Avery in his public statements deny the right of workers to organize and bargain collectively? Did labor unions and the US government agree with him?
4   Why do you think the image of Sewell Avery being carried out of his office on his own chair by Army soldiers became one of the most popular for 1944? Why was this picture something of a public relations disaster for the Roosevelt Administration? Do you think the Roosevelt Administration exceeded its authority in seizing Montgomery Ward?
5   What crucial role did Women Air Force Service Pilots play in furthering the war effort? Do you think these women should have been granted military status during the war?

Chapter 7   The Quest for Freedom

1   John Haynes Holmes, Excerpt from "The Case of the Jehovah's Witnesses," *The Christian Century*, 1940

*In 1940 the sudden fall of France panicked many Americans. How could the
much-vaunted French Army and nation collapse in a matter of weeks? Many
Americans, including the Roosevelt Administration, attributed part of the
blame to a secret "fifth column" of French citizens who secretly undermined
their country's war effort. Fears of international subversion led to increased
surveillance of such fascist organizations as the German-American Bund.
The Federal Bureau of Investigation (FBI) sought to track and arrest enemy
agents working for the German, Italian, and Japanese governments, but it
also placed under surveillance a number of prominent opponents of
intervention, including Charles Lindbergh. Another group of Americans also
came under suspicion – Jehovah's Witnesses. This small Protestant group
would not only be rebuffed in the US Supreme Court when they attempted
to assert their children's right not to salute the American flag, but also faced
mob violence as well as harassment by local governments when they sought
to proselytize. During World War II, Jehovah's Witnesses continued their
struggle to live according to the tenets of their religion. In a striking victory
for civil liberties and religious freedom, in 1944 the Supreme Court reversed
its original decision and ruled that the children of Jehovah's Witnesses could
not be compelled to salute the American flag. John Haynes Holmes,
a committed pacifist and civil libertarian, wrote this article for the leading
Protestant magazine of the era,* The Christian Century. *A Unitarian minister,*

The United States in World War II: A Documentary Reader, First Edition.
Edited by G. Kurt Piehler. Editorial material and organization © 2013 Blackwell Publishing Ltd.
Published 2013 by Blackwell Publishing Ltd.

he was a firm supporter of the rights of Jehovah's Witnesses to worship God as they saw fit. Throughout the war Holmes spoke out in support of conscientious objectors and argued for greater efforts to rescue European Jewry from the Holocaust.

What is happening to Jehovah's Witnesses in this country today is a thing worth talking about. At the moment they are suffering an experience of assault and violence, humiliation, outrage and injury, which parallels some of the persecutions which are going forward on a larger scale in Europe.

On a recent visit to Washington, where I met and conferred with the chief counsel of Jehovah's Witnesses, I saw a carefully verified list of lawless attacks upon members of this sect during a period of a few weeks ending in the early part of June. This list showed thirty-nine mob outbreaks of greater or less intensity in twenty states running from Wyoming in the west to Maine in the east, from Wisconsin in the north to Texas in the south. Since this date a succession of increasingly savage attacks upon the Witnesses has taken place in various sections of the country, notably Illinois and Maine.

Men and women of various ages and conditions have been raided in their homes and meeting places, set upon by organized mobs led in some cases by officers of the law, held in prison without bail or access to legal counsel, beaten and otherwise physically injured. They have had their property seized and destroyed, their halls stoned and burned, and they themselves have more than once been driven out of town and scattered over the countryside. In one instance, in Texas, a group of nearly one hundred Witnesses, including children and an old woman of 78 years, were lashed like cattle for ten miles down a railroad track in the blazing heat of midday, and left beyond the county line to fend for themselves as best they could. This sounds like the Jews in Germany, but it happens to be Jehovah's Witnesses here in America!

I

One of the most sensational outbreaks against this sect took place in Kennebunk, Maine. With the details of this affair I am familiar, as I have had my summer home in this neighborhood for many years.

Kennebunk is an old, substantial, highly attractive New England town. It has the typical main street lined with shops and offices, a beautiful elm-shaded residential avenue, and an impressive community center comprising the Town Hall, the bank, the library, and a superb, white-towered Unitarian Church. Its population of about 3,500 persons is composed of farmers, tradesmen and fishers, with a considerable factory population employed in a shoe manufacturing plant. Old families abound; traditions and local customs are everywhere; life is prevailingly sober, conservative, self-respecting. The town is Republican, and dry.

Jehovah's Witnesses in Kennebunk comprise a little group of men and women who used a rather shabby one-story wooden building near the railroad station as their headquarters. Certain members of the group occupied this building also as their home. They are Americans of native stock— zealots drawn from the blood and sinew of New England. They have never been popular in the town, but there was no especial feeling against them until the hysteria incident to the German invasion of Holland, Belgium and France swept this country with wild stories of "fifth columns" and "Trojan horses," aggravated in this particular instance by the unfavorable decision of the Supreme Court in the flag-salute cases.

Soon there came murmurs and mutterings against the Witnesses. Small crowds began gathering at nightfall about their headquarters. Threats were spoken and written against them. After some two weeks of agitation, there came an outbreak in which a mob of hundreds of men and boys attacked the Witnesses, looted and set fire to their building, and speedily threatened a lynching. Two members of the mob were shot by the Witnesses; two others were later arrested on a charge of arson, but dismissed after a court hearing. The leaders of the Witnesses were spirited out of town for safekeeping, later arrested, held in heavy bail, and are now awaiting trial in the autumn.

II

Sensational charges against Jehovah's Witnesses were published in the press in connection with this exciting episode. Thus, it was declared that they were "fifth column" nazi agents, and that pictures of Hitler and Stalin were found in their headquarters. It is true that such pictures were searched for by the mob, but it is also true that they were not found. The idea of these humble folk being pro-nazi conspirators has its ludicrous aspects, in view of the peculiarly persistent and conspicuous way in which they had been bringing their activities to the attention of the people of Kennebunk. One does not ordinarily associate conspiracies with public meetings, advertising, open distribution of tracts and literature, and an almost defiant announcement of plans and purposes.

It was charged that the Witnesses had in their possession maps of Kennebunk and vicinity on which had been carefully marked the locations of bridges, public buildings and other works of strategical importance. This evidently with the idea of starting the nazi revolution for the overthrow of the Washington government in a New England village ninety miles north of Boston! It must be confessed that one map was found—just such a map, I imagine, as I have today here in my summer house—but the markings were not of bridges or building at all, but of the homes of citizens to be visited for interviews and tract distribution. Jehovah's Witnesses are evangelists, and they sow the gospel seed systematically from door to door. "When I first came to this town," said a local clergyman to me, "I had a map of this kind, with all the homes of my parishioners clearly marked."

It was charged that the Witnesses had an arsenal of firearms and ammunition in their headquarters, and that without the slightest provocation they shot at an automobile which stopped, purely by chance, in front of their building at a late hour of the night—the episode which unleashed the mob! This automobile, when later examined by the police, was found to be loaded with rocks and stones. There is good evidence that the shooting began when the occupants of the car invaded the property of the Witnesses and began attacking their building.

For a fortnight or more, these threats had been heard like rumblings of an approaching storm. The Witnesses appealed for protection to the local authorities, without response. They turned to the state police, and could get no assurances of aid. Then they addressed the governor, only to be referred back to the state police. Thoroughly alarmed, they secured firearms. This was foolish, and also inconsistent with their non-resistant faith. Still more foolish and inconsistent was their action in firing upon two boys armed only with stones. But these folks were frightened, and they probably remembered an established American principle, duly guaranteed by the United States Constitution, that the right of citizens to bear arms in defense of lives and property shall not be abridged or denied.

III

What happened in Kennebunk has been happening recently with less provocation, fiercer violence and more disastrous results in many other places in the country. Which raises at once the question: why should these Jehovah's Witnesses be attacked in such open and violent fashion? Why all of a sudden, so to speak, should the American people be aroused against a religious sect which is so small in numbers and trivial in importance? ...

... Jehovah's Witnesses have a religion, and they take it seriously. Now, there is nothing more inconvenient, irritating, outrageous than to have in the community a group of people who actually believe their religion, and propose that other people shall believe it as well. Jehovah's Witnesses are New Testament Christians in the sense that they believe what they read in the New Testament. They do not do what most Protestants do—declare vociferously that the New Testament is a divinely inspired volume, every chapter and every word a revelation of the Most High, and then proceed to explain away, by one process or another of rationalization, every text which does not chance to suit their personal comfort, intellectual prejudices and contemporary ideas....

... [Since] the Witnesses believe their religion, and this religion is a religion of crisis—none other than the imminent end of the world—they are a peculiarly aggressive, even obnoxious set of people, at least as judged by ordinary standards of polite, conventional life. Thus, they are not satisfied to enter a town and hold a set of respectable public meetings and services....

... [T]he Witnesses go out on the highways and byways and proclaim their gospel of a world called suddenly to judgment. They ring doorbells and speak personally to the residents of the houses. They carry tracts and circulars and thrust them into the reluctant, even unwilling hands of the passer-by. They even take along talking-machine records, with the machine to operate them, and set them shouting out the messages of damnation and redemption in public squares, on piazzas and in kitchens of private houses, anywhere and everywhere, whether people will listen or whether they will not. All this, to conventional folk, is disquieting, unsetting, alarming. It comes close to disturbing the public peace.... So they try to drive the Witnesses away; they stir up the public authorities against them; in times of excitement and hysteria they organize mobs and beat them up....

Lastly, there is the irritating question of the flag salute. These Witnesses will not salute the American flag, nor will they allow their children to salute it in the public schools. Superficially, this seems to be a defiance of the nation. Especially in times like these is it regarded as an evidence not only of lack of patriotism, but of open sedition or even treason. But to the Witnesses themselves, the flag salute is a question simply of religious fidelity. Their claim is that they can give homage to God alone. They can recognize as worthy of reverence nothing that is made of man's hands, since this is the idolatry that is expressly denounced in the pages of the Holy Writ. God is to them not only supreme, but unique—he is alone, and there is none other. Therefore there cannot only be nothing before him, but nothing even beside him—no object, no symbol, no altar which can divide the loyalty of the soul. Not the kingdoms of this world, nor yet the republics, but the Kingdom of

God only is the country of the true believer, and to God alone, as the Ruler of this Kingdom, must the Christian testify to his allegiance.

It is amazing, when you come to think of it, that this attitude of Jehovah's Witnesses should be questioned or misunderstood, most of all derided and denied. Are not the Witnesses in the best tradition of the Christian spirit in refusing this salutation to the flag? What were the early Christians doing but this very thing when they refused to put their pinch of salt upon the altars of the Roman emperor? That was all the Roman authorities demanded— just this little pinch of salt as evidence of the loyalty of these Christians to the government! But the Christians insisted that the pinch of salt was a matter not of patriotism but of religion. If they made this gesture, they would be denying their sole allegiance, on earth as in heaven, to God and to his Christ. And so they refused—and died! ...

It is no accident that this long and violent succession of outrages against the Witnesses in recent weeks was co-incident with the unfortunate decision of the Supreme Court refusing to interfere with the action of school authorities in demanding the salute.

IV

It is evident that, in this instance of Jehovah's Witnesses, we have an issue as old as Christianity, and as terrible as the persecutions and oppressions of its history....

First, there is the question of religious freedom—the right of a people to worship their own God in their own way, and serve him according to their will. In country after country this right of religious freedom is being abolished. Under all the totalitarian governments, fascist and communist alike, religion is being denied and destroyed as alien to the best interests of the state. Jehovah's Witnesses, crude as may be their faith and naive their expectations, have been among the first in these countries, and now in our country, to meet the awful penalties of tyranny. They are among the few Christian groups in the world today who stand ready to die, as did the early Christians, for the faith that is within them. If religion is to be saved from the new persecutions and perils of our time, it must be in the persons of these Witnesses among others, and perhaps among them first of all.

Second, there is the question of democracy—the duty of this country to protect its humblest citizens in their basic constitutional rights of speech, assembly and worship. If there is danger in America today of the loss of democracy, I see this danger in the invasion not of armies but of ideas from nazi and communist Europe. If we are destroyed as a nation, it will be not by bombs dropped upon us from the skies but by hostilities and hatred. Already, in the mad manias of this hour, the work of fascism is begun. Demands for military conscription, attacks upon civil liberties, mob violence upon innocent and unoffending minorities, reveal already the swift turning of the stream of public sentiment from democracy to tyranny. We shall be conquered by Hitler, if this goes on, long before any nazi troops even look in the direction of these shores. The disease of fascism is catching us, and chief among the symptoms are these outrageous mob assaults upon Jehovah's Witnesses....

Source: John Haynes Holmes, "The Case of Jehovah's Witnesses," *The Christian Century*, July 17, 1940, pp. 896–898.

2 Franklin D. Roosevelt, "Executive Order Reaffirming Policy of Full Participation by all Persons, Regardless of Race, Creed, Color, or National Origin," 1941

In late summer 1941, A. Philip Randolph of the Brotherhood of Sleeping Car Porters threatened to organize a march on Washington, DC, to protest the continued discrimination and segregation of African Americans in the defense industry. In a bid to forestall this march, which would be a public embarrassment to the Roosevelt Administration in the wake of its efforts to highlight the evils of Nazi Germany and muster support for its interventionist policies, FDR issued the following executive order barring discrimination in government-funded defense industries. This executive order established the Fair Employment Practices Committee (FEPC), which operated until 1946. Both this executive order and the FEPC had only a limited impact on protecting the rights of African Americans and other groups. The FEPC's budget allowed investigation of only a small number of cases that were referred to it and it possessed only limited enforcement powers. Nonetheless, this executive order set an important precedent and is the first significant federal action to protect the civil rights of African Americans in the twentieth century.

EXECUTIVE ORDER

REAFFIRMING POLICY OF FULL PARTICIPATION IN THE DEFENSE PROGRAM BY ALL PERSONS, REGARDLESS OF RACE, CREED, COLOR, OR NATIONAL ORIGIN, AND DIRECTED CERTAIN ACTION IN FURTHERANCE OF SAID POLICY.

WHEREAS it is the policy of the United States to encourage full participation in the national defense program by all citizens of the United States, regardless of race, creed, color, or national origin, in the firm belief that the democratic way of life within the Nation can be defended successfully only with the help and support of all groups within its borders; and

WHEREAS there is evidence that available and needed workers have been barred from employment in industries engaged in defense production solely because of consideration of race, creed, color, or national origin, to the detriment of workers' morale and of national unity;

NOW, THEREFORE, by virtue of the authority vested in me by the Constitution and statutes, and as a prerequisite to the successful conduct of our national defense production effort, I do hereby reaffirm the policy of the United States that there shall be no discrimination in the employment of workers in defense industries or government because of race, creed, color, or national origin, and I do hereby declare that it is the duty of employers and of labor organizations, in furtherance of said policy and of this order, to provide for the full and equitable participation of all workers in defense industries, without discrimination because of race, creed, color, or national origin;

And it is hereby ordered as follows:

1. All department and agencies of the Government of the United States concerned with vocational and training programs for defense production shall take special measures appropriate to assure that such programs are administered without discrimination because of race, creed, color, or national origin;

2. All contracting agencies of the Government of the United States shall include in all defense contracts hereafter negotiated by them a provision obligating the contractor not to discriminate against any worker because of race, creed, color, or national origin;

3. There is established in the Office of Production Management a Committee on Fair Employment Practice, which shall consist of a chairman and four other members to be appointed by the President. The chairman and members of the Committee shall serve as such without compensation but shall be entitled to actual and necessary transportation, subsistence and other expenses incidental to performance of their duties. The Committee shall receive and investigate complaints of discrimination in violation of the provisions of this order and shall take appropriate steps to redress grievances which it finds to be valid. The Committee shall also recommend to the several departments and agencies of the Government of the United States and to the President all

measures which may be deemed by it necessary or proper to effectuate the provisions of this order.

Franklin D. Roosevelt

The White House
June 25, 1941.

Source: Executive Order 8802 dated June 25, 1941, General Records of the United States Government (RG 11), US National Archives, Washington, DC. Also available online at http://www.ourdocuments.gov/doc.php?doc=72.

3 Frederick Wells to Harry A. Wann, Memorandum, 1942

War-time unity did not end racial discrimination – African Americans endured segregation within all branches of the military. On leave, African Americans serving in the South often faced degrading treatment when they went off base. Policemen harassed, arrested, and even physically assaulted black servicemen, especially if they intruded into "whites only" areas. This report by an official of the United States Service Organizations (USO) describes the extent of the discrimination black servicemen endured in Jackson, Mississippi, while seeking a few hours of rest from their military duties.

Memo

United Service Organization for National Defense, Inc.

Mid-night

To: Dr. Harry A. Wann   Subject: Soldiers' Survey

From: Frederick Wells   Date: Feb. 13, 1942 12:30 A.M.

Jackson, Mississippi

An arrangement was made through Mr. Bixler's office of the Y. M. C. A., whereby your representatives might contact certain city officials for the purpose of visiting the various streets where both Negro and white Soldiers go to and from their places of recreation. Almost four hours were required to make this early morning survey.

In the White Section, the following streets were reviewed: Capitol Street in the heart of Jackson, Mill and Pearl Streets in the vicinity of the Y. M. C. A. and the large white hotels. Only one Negro Soldier was seen on any of these streets. The general conduct in this section was good. One white Soldier remarked to me that he knew of no friction between Negro and white Soldiers, whatsoever.

In the Negro Section: Upon visiting the Colored section of Rose and Lynch Streets, only three poorly lighted, but crowded cafes were found to be available to the Negro Soldiers. The first visit was made to Coopers Cafe on Lynch near Rose Street. Two doors below Coopers is Ida Drummonds Cafe, both operated by Colored owners. All of these places are crowded from back to front doors with loud noises and laughter, with music, drink and dance flourishing.

Further down the streets there may be found numbers of Soldiers in groups, leaning against buildings, half asleep, or drunk as the case maybe. There are no decent places of amusement for the Negro Soldiers to go, in Jackson, and there are some six to eight hundred of these Soldiers. On occasions of troop movements, there are as many as four to six thousand of these men with no where to go, even for a few hours rest. If they are found on the streets of Jackson, they are immediately abused by white civilian police. These men are sold Boot-leg whisky and this fact in some instances maybe the origin of their trouble.

It has been reported on last Christmas, about mid-night a fight between the Negro Soldiers took place in front of Sheppards Cafe, on Farish Street. A Civilian white policeman came up and attempted to arrest these Soldiers. The Soldiers resisted this arrest, whereupon the civilian policemen proceeded abusing and beating the Negro Soldiers. This commotion terminated into a general brawl. One Soldier was so badly beaten and mal-treated that it was [n]ecessary to remove him to an emergency hospital. This incident is still within the minds of the Negro population of Jackson, who greatly resent such abuses on the part of civilian policemen who are not authorized to arrest men in uniform. There have been subsequent occasions where Negro Soldiers have been pushed off the sidewalks by white civilian policemen. This practice continues whenever Negro Soldiers are found upon the streets not designated for Negro Soldiers. Whereas white soldiers of all descriptions are seen in the streets designated for Negro Soldiers to the great dissatisfaction and co[m]fort of the local Colored Citizens.

The Negro Soldiers are not allowed on the main streets of Jackson on week-ends according to reports given me by local people.

Source: File: Negro Service, Box 209, Papers of American Jewish Welfare Board, Army Navy Division (I-180), American Jewish Historical Society, Center for Jewish History, New York City.

4 Daniel K. Inouye, Excerpt from *Journey to Washington*, 1967

Under Executive Order 9066 issued by President Roosevelt in early 1942,
Japanese Americans living along the West Coast of the continental United
States were forced to leave their homes and live in resettlement camps. The
internment without trial of these Japanese Americans included not only
long-term Japanese immigrants denied American citizenship solely by virtue
of their ancestry, but also their American-born children (Nisei) *who were*
citizens. Demographically, Japanese Americans living in California, Oregon,
and Washington State made up only a small portion of the population and
there was no evidence of any potential subversion or sabotage by this
community aimed at the American war effort. In the case of Hawaii,
Japanese Americans made up a much larger percentage of the population
and potentially could have threatened the war effort. Although there was
some discussion within the military and the Roosevelt Administration about
placing these Japanese Americans in internment camps, the plans were
shelved given the scarcity of shipping and the community's vital role in the
Hawaiian economy. Moreover, fears of potential espionage and sabotage
proved groundless; as Daniel Inouye records in his memoir, many Japanese
Americans were desperate to show their patriotism by enlisting in the armed
services. Although Japanese Americans had fought bravely in World War I
and served in the interwar army, after Pearl Harbor they were discharged
from the armed services and banned from enlisting. In this account, written
after Inouye was elected as US Senator for Hawaii, he describes the struggle
of Japanese Americans to gain the right to serve in the armed forces.

From the very beginning, the younger Japanese in the Islands suffered under a special onus, a deep sense of personal disgrace. They were far removed from the ways of the old country. All their lives they had thought of themselves as Americans. And now, in this time of crisis and peril for America, they were cast from its trust and seemingly lumped with the enemy by official policy. Not only had the War Department turned them down for active service, but those already in the army were transferred to labor battalions. *Nisei* in National Guard units were summarily discharged, and those in the ROTC and Territorial Guard were stripped of their weapons.

But despite every derogation and disparagement, Japanese-Americans fought for a place in the war effort, no matter how small or menial. Older men, including my father, organized their own labor squads and volunteered for garbage details and ditch-digging. University students strung barbed wire and guarded beaches and important intersections, armed only with fury and a massive determination to make a useful contribution. And always, day after discouraging day, they struggled to persuade the government to reverse its anti-*nisei* ruling, writing letters, collecting signatures for petitions and imploring Caucasians of good will to attest to their loyalty....

I passed my college entrance exams and in September 1942, just turned eighteen, I enrolled for a premedical course at the University of Hawaii. For those of us in that wartime class, study as we might, a substantial portion of our thoughts and hopes were directed outside, fixed on that world in conflict, concentrating our fiercest aspirations on the chance that somehow they would allow us into the army. I was still doing my job at the aid station, but with the emergency in Hawaii past and the grim reports of Japanese victories at Bataan and Corregidor, working at the aid station didn't seem like much of a vital contribution any more.

The War Department had given us some small hope that their harsh preconceptions about Japanese-Americans might be changing. A few months earlier, *nisei* Guardsmen and early draftees had been organized into the 100th Infantry Battalion, a combat unit not assigned to any regular outfit. Then, little more than a year after the attack on Pearl Harbor, we got the news that did most to unshackle us from stigma and help us really believe that we would be allowed to fight for our country: the War Department announced that it would accept 4,000 *nisei* volunteers to form a full-fledged combat team for front-line service without restriction, without constraints. The outfit was to be activated on February 1 and would consist of the 442nd Infantry Regiment, the 522nd Field Artillery Battalion and the 232nd Combat Engineer Company.

President Franklin D. Roosevelt, who personally passed on the plan, had this to say about it: "The proposal of the War Department to organize a combat team of loyal American citizens of Japanese descent has my full approval. No loyal citizen of the United States should be denied the democratic right to exercise the responsibilities of his citizenship, regardless of his ancestry. Americanism is a matter of the mind and heart; Americanism is not, and never was, a matter of race or ancestry."

It is hard to express our emotions at this expression of faith by the President. It was as though someone had let us out of some dark place and into the sunlight again. And what chaos in the University auditorium that January morning when Colonel Clarke, head of the ROTC, called us together and announced that the draft boards were now ready to receive our applications for enlistment! It was as though he'd revealed that gold had just been discovered at the foot of Diamond Head. He later told me that he had a little pep talk all prepared for us, how we now had a chance to do our duty as patriotic Americans, but it was about as necessary as telling those navy gunners on December 7 to open fire. As soon as he said that we were now eligible to volunteer, that room exploded into a fury of yells and motion. We went bursting out of there and ran—ran!—the three miles to the draft board, stringing back over the streets and sidewalks, jostling for position, like a bunch of marathoners gone berserk. And the scene was repeated all over Oahu and the other islands. Nearly 1,000 *niseis* volunteered that first day alone, and maybe because I was in better shape than most of them and ran harder, I was among the first 75.

Everything changed that day and, because there are no fairy tale endings in real life, not all the changes were for the best. Dozens of boys I knew from the premed courses crowded into the draft board, some of them with only the rest of that last semester to go before graduation. And the long years of war took their toll on every one of us. Some hadn't the heart to go back to school when peace finally came, and some, with families to support, hadn't the money. Many never came home at all and among those who did there were those so severely wounded that a career in medicine was out of the question. And so it was that of all those students who had entered the University with such high hopes, and with the hopes and prayers of their parents, not a single one ever became a doctor.

The army's original plan called for a *nisei* outfit of 1,500 from the Islands and 2,500 from the mainland. But the crush of volunteers in Hawaii persuaded them to reverse the proportions. We were given three weeks to wind up our affairs—which most of us would have been happy to do in three days—and there were sentimental and sometimes tearful farewell parties from Koko Head to Kahuku. I suppose mine was fairly typical: the parade of aunts and uncles and cousins, the last whispered words—"Be a good boy; be careful; make us proud!"—and the crumpled $5 or $10 bill pressed into my hand.

Source: Senator Daniel K. Inouye with Lawrence Elliott, *Journey to Washington* (Englewood Cliffs, NJ: Prentice-Hall, 1967), pp. 67–68, 74–76.

5 Charles Kikuchi, Diary Entries, 1942

When Charles Kikuchi, a graduate student in social work at the University of California, Berkeley, learned of the Japanese attack on Pearl Harbor, he immediately recorded in his diary that "Anti-Jap feeling is bound to rise to hysterical heights." In May 1942, Kikuchi's misgivings were realized when he, along with other Japanese Americans, was sent by the federal government to a temporary internment center at the Tanforan Race Track near San Bruno, California. Besides the spartan living conditions, the psychological toll on Japanese Americans was enormous, especially for the American-born

Nisei. *As Kikuchi observes, the experience of internment had a profound impact on generational relationships between Japanese-born* Issei *and* Nisei *within Japanese American families and the community. After leaving Tanaforan, Kikuchi was sent to the Gila Relocation Center in Arizona before eventually being allowed to leave the internment camp to resettle in Chicago. He later served in the US Army and after V-J Day settled in New York City, going on to a career as a clinical social worker in the Veterans' Administration. During the war, Professor Dorothy Swaine Thomas of the University of California, Berkeley, hired Kikuchi as a researcher to help document the experiences of Japanese Americans during the war and encouraged him to keep a personal diary.*

May 5, 1942 Tuesday

We got approval to go ahead with the paper and the boys are working hard in order to get the first issue out by Saturday; I'm supposed to write up the section on the employment situation in camp. The whole setup needs centralizing. There are too many conflicting orders about who is supposed to do the hiring, etc. A small number of the Nisei are complaining that the S.F. gang is taking all the choice jobs and just working their friends in—a large part of which is true. It should be on the basis of merit because much of the skills and abilities are not being fully utilized. Mr. Greene, the chief man under Lawson, does not seem to be a dynamic administrator and does not appear to me to be too good a person for such a responsible position....

Today I ran across the first Japan nationalist who reacted violently. He said that Japan "requested" that we be put into a concentration camp so that we have to do it for the sake of Japan. The man seemed pleasant and harmless enough at first, but when he started to talk on this subject, I was amazed to see the bitter look of hatred in his eyes and face. He asked us point-blank whether we were for Japan or America and we said "America" on the basis of our beliefs and education. He got extremely angry and pounded on the table while shouting that we Nisei were fools and that we had better stick by Japan because we could never be Americans; only "Ketos" [white men, literally, hairy people] could be Americans. Since we had Japanese faces we should be for Japan because she would always protect us and not treat us like dogs, etc. We argued for a while but apparently it is no use trying to reason with a person of this type who thinks emotionally. I get fearful of this attitude sometimes because it has been this very thing that makes Americanization so difficult, especially if there is a general tendency to get it from both sides. And I still am not convinced that it is impossible to educate the Issei, although the argument that we are in camp just like them and therefore not Americans is beginning to influence many Nisei. It's a good thing perhaps that I don't understand Japanese because I am not exposed so much to this sort of talk. It makes me feel so uneasy and mad. It gripes me no end to think of being confined in the same place with these Japanists. If they could only realize that in spite of all their past mistreatments, they have not done so bad in America because of the democratic traditions—with its faults. It may be a sense of personal frustration which is projected to a hatred of all "Keto" and deep resentment towards America. I hope we are able to counteract this sort of thing among the young kids. Prof. Obata was in today and he was worried by this same thing—he is an Issei so there are many of them that live by the American way. He wants to direct a camp art class in order to raise the morale—this point needs to be stressed over and over....

The War goes on; men are killed, but this camp is not much aware of that. The Germans have not started the spring offensive although they are challenging the British fleet in the North Sea. Japan is still making gains and is about to cut the China lifeline in Burma, but the Allies are rapidly gaining power. I hope it is not too late....

May 17, 1942 Sunday

The importance of this Assembly Center is that some sort of organizational basis will be developed for self government, and it is not too important for us to perfect anything here, since our stay will be relatively limited in the camp. Some of the younger Nisei think that the Work Corps is a fine idea— if they get prevailing wages—and are anxious to do something as they are getting restless doing nothing here! Work opportunities will continue to be at the minimum here in this camp.

I might as well try to sign up in some way to go as a volunteer among the advance group. Social work is always needed but I wonder what the opportunities will be for me there? Perhaps I should stress the employment field more. Either would be acceptable to me because I could then have the chance to get at the center of things and watch it develop into something—or fall apart. Jack is definitely going to pull out and I don't know what Alice plans to do yet. I suppose that if I did leave first, some provisions can be made for the family to come to the same relocation area. The more I think about it, the more I become convinced that the family will not be a handicap but an asset. It is a stabilizing influence and will help to prevent individual degeneration. Whatever happens, our family can't lose....

Mom and Pop seem to enjoy people coming here to have fun because then they don't have to worry about what is going on. Pop even tried to jitterbug tonight and he was the hit of the evening. I was thinking tonight that the evacuation by itself has already in the past two weeks broken down some of the Japanese culture. Already some of the former causes for cultural conflict have become less intensified—with the Nisei holding the upper hand. We hold the advantage of numbers and the fact that we are citizens.

Many of the parents who would never let their daughters go to dances before do not object so strenuously now. They are slowly accepting the fact that their children cannot stay home night after night doing nothing without some sort of recreational release. Books are still a rarity. Consequently, the Thursday night talent show and the Saturday dances are jammed to capacity. There can no longer be conflict over the types of food served as everybody eats the same things—with forks. We haven't had any Japanese food yet, thank God. The recreational program thus far has been pointed towards the Nisei and there is little for the older folks to do except go visiting.

The Nisei as a whole rejoice that they no longer have to attend Japanese language school. This means that Japanese will be used less and less as the younger children grow up. A very few will be able to read and write it. And if these schools were a source of propaganda for Japan, they have now been eliminated. Thus, it is destined that Japanese will be used less and less among the Japanese here, and by the next generation it no longer will be a necessity to know it. Even among the Issei there will be a greater stress in speaking English so that they can continue to communicate with their children. It almost becomes a necessity. We are not getting any Japanese publications in camp so that even the Issei will be less exposed to the Japanese point of view. The only news that they can get is from the newspaper (American), and the radio, which naturally will stress the American angle. Since short wave radios are not allowed, they can't receive any of the broadcasts from Japan....

The role of the Issei father in the family life has become less dominant because he no longer holds the economic purse strings. This will be true even after the war. Before, this has been the source of their power and it carried a lot of weight. The mother still has a role in the family life, because she still has to sew, do the laundry, and look after the welfare of her children. The only thing she doesn't have to do is cooking! But in general, the control and discipline of the parent have become loosened by the recent events. This may even be harmful if social disorganization develops at too fast a pace without suitable adjustments being made fast enough. But the family will more or less be held together because of the one dominant interest: what does the future hold in store for the Japanese in America? The Nisei consider themselves as Americans and if given a chance to demonstrate their loyalty, the trend will become stronger and stronger. The Issei will have no choice but to follow if they don't want to lose their families altogether.

Source: John Modell (ed.), *The Kikuchi Diary: Chronicle from an American Concentration Camp: The Tanforan Journals of Charles Kikuchi* (Urbana: University of Illinois Press, 1973), pp. 56–57, 81–83.

6 Cesar Chavez, Excerpt from *Cesar Chavez: Autobiography of La Causa*, 1975

After World War II, Cesar Chavez became a driving force behind the organization of Mexican American farm workers on the West Coast. In this excerpt from his memoir, he recalls the discrimination endured by his family and his resistance against it. Wearing particular clothes, specifically "zoot suits," became one way young Mexican Americans displayed their ethnic pride and protested the discrimination visited on them. In June 1943, Mexican Americans wearing zoot suits were attacked in Los Angeles by mobs of servicemen and others, with the local police doing little to protect them. Chavez, a teenager during World War II, went on to serve in the US Navy, only to encounter more discrimination aimed at Mexican American and African American sailors.

When I became a teen-ager I began to rebel about certain things. For example, I rebelled against the home remedies and herbs my mother used. I thought no one knew anything but doctors. And I rebelled against Mexican music. This was the age of the big bands, and I really went for Duke Ellington and Billy Eckstine. We would travel from Delano to Fresno to hear the bands, and in San Jose they had them every week....

And then I rebelled at the conventional way of dressing. I once said I was a pachuco, and I had a very difficult time explaining it. The pachucos wore their hair long, in a duck-tail cut; they wore pegged pants and long coats, long key chains, and a pegged, broad flat hat. Today what people remember are the pachuco riots in the forties in San Jose, Oakland, and Delano. But those riots were not the same as when the barrios and ghettoes exploded in the sixties [1960s]. The rioters were not Mexicans. They were soldiers, marines, and sailors who raided the barrios attacking the pachucos.

I saw clippings of the Los Angeles papers with pictures of pachuco kids with pants torn to the thighs by police. If they had long hair, police clipped them, and if their coats were long, police cut them short. The pachucos would wear shoes with very thick soles, and police would take the soles off....

We needed a lot of guts to wear those pants, and we had to be rebellious to do it, because the police and a few of the older people would harass us. But then it was the style, and I wasn't going to be a square. All the guys I knew liked that style, and I would have felt pretty stupid walking around dressed differently. At Delano dances, for example, all the squares sat across the room from us, and we had a lot more fun than they did.

My mother wasn't violently opposed to our wearing those clothes, though she and my dad didn't like it much, but little old ladies would be afraid of us. And in Delano there was a whole group in the Mexican-American community who opposed pachuco clothes....

The hard thing, though, was the police. We were so gun shy. For sure the cops would stop you anyplace, any time, and we were prepared for that. But when they stopped us at the theater in Merced, it was humiliating. We were thinking of going to the show, but we weren't sure. We were just looking around to see what was playing. A cop, who was just passing by, saw us and got on his radio. Soon two or three police cars arrived, and the officers line us up against the wall. It was a bad scene. They made us take our shoes off, they just almost undressed us there. Then they gave us about ten minutes to get out of town.

We were a minority group of a minority group. So, in a way, we were challenging cops by being with two or three friends and dressing sharp. But in those days I was prepared for any sacrifice to be able to dress the way I wanted to dress. I thought it looked sharp and neat, and it was the style....

We had never experienced discrimination in Yuma when we lived there, but we encountered White Trade Only signs all over California. In Los Angeles we got off the highway and went to East Los Angeles, while in Delano we'd go to Mexican town. We didn't challenge it. Then in the forties we went back to visit Yuma, and there were those signs all over the place, White Trade Only.

My rebellion as a teen-ager wasn't against that, though. It was against Mexican music, my mother's herbs, and some of her religious ideas. But I didn't say I wasn't a Mexican. I didn't feel I wasn't. In fact I was pretty strong about being Mexican. Then after I got married, all of a sudden I began to appreciate mariachis and all those other things I was rebelling against. As I look back, I now understand what was happening. Everywhere we went, to school, to church, to the movies, there was this attack on our culture and our language, an attempt to make us conform to the "American way." What a sin!

I don't know why I joined the navy in 1944; I think mostly to get away from farm labor. I was doing sugar beet thinning, the worst kind of backbreaking job, and I remember telling my father, "Dad, I've had it!"

Neither my mother nor my dad wanted me to go, but I joined up anyway. It was wartime. I suppose my views were pretty much the views of most members of a minority group. They really don't want to serve, but they feel this awesome power above them that's forcing them to do it.

I had little choice, either get drafted or sign up. Since I wanted even less to go into the army, I enlisted in the navy when I was still seventeen.

Those two years were the worst of my life: this regimentation, this super authority that somehow somebody has the right to move you around like a piece of equipment. It's worse than being in prison. And there was lots of discrimination. Before the war, the navy had blacks and Filipinos who were given kitchen jobs, but no Mexicans. The only black man I ever saw who was better than a steward was a painter.

The Mexican-Americans were mostly deck hands. That's what I was. Most of my duty was in small boats, while part of it was land-based. I also was on a crew transport which went to the Mariana Islands, but I never was engaged in combat.

The food in the navy was terrible. I noticed that the Anglos would call the food all kinds of dirty names, and then eat it. On the other hand, if Mexicans didn't like the food, they just didn't eat it. I couldn't understand how Anglos could eat stuff they called by such names.

It was while I was in the navy that the theater incident happened in Delano, a story that's been twisted when it's been told before. I was home with a couple of navy guys from Texas on a seventy-two-hour pass, and we weren't in uniform.

For a long time, movie theaters throughout the San Joaquin Valley were segregated. It was just accepted by the Mexicans then. In Delano, the quarter-section on the right was reserved for Mexicans, blacks, and Filipinos, while Anglos and Japanese sat elsewhere. It had been like that since the theater was built, I guess.

This time something told me that I shouldn't accept such discrimination. It wasn't a question of sitting elsewhere because it was more comfortable. It was just a question that I wanted a free choice of where I wanted to be. I decided to challenge the rule, even though I was very frightened. Instead of sitting on the right, I sat down on the left.

When I was asked to move to the other section, I refused, and the police took me to jail. They didn't book me; they kept me there about an hour. The desk sergeant didn't know with what to charge me. He made a couple of calls. I would guess he called the chief of police and the judge because that's a natural thing to do.

The first call I think was to the chief. I don't know what was said, but the chief probably said, "What about drunk?" because the sergeant said, "Well, he's not drunk," and then he said, "Well, he was wasn't really disturbing the peace." Then I suppose he called a judge or the city attorney. Finally the sergeant gave me a lecture and let me go. He tried to scare me about putting me in jail for life, the typical intimidation they use.

I was angry at what happened, but I didn't know then how to proceed. It was the first time I had challenged rules so brazenly, but in our own way my family had been challenging the growers for some time. That was part of life.

Source: Jacques E. Levy, *Cesar Chavez: Autobiography of La Causa* (Minneapolis: University of Minnesota Press, 1975), pp. 81–85.

Study Questions

1 Why did so many Americans fear Jehovah's Witnesses? Why did John Haynes Holmes think their fears were baseless?
2 What does Franklin D. Roosevelt's executive order mandating fair employment actually accomplish? Does it seek to dismantle segregation in defense industries or the wider society?
3 How were African American servicemen treated when they were on leave in Jackson, Mississippi? What does this say about the limits of patriotic sentiment in America?
4 How did the experience of internment divide the *Nisei* community? How did it impact the family and cultural life?
5 Why did Daniel Inouye express such faith in the American system?
6 How did Cesar Chavez and other Mexican Americans rebel against the discrimination they faced? Why did Chavez resent his naval service?
7 Compare and contrast the experiences of African Americans, Mexican Americans, and the *Nisei* during the war.

Chapter 8   The American Response to the Holocaust

1 Ferdinand M. Isserman, Excerpt from *Sentenced to Death: The Jews in Nazi Germany*, 1933

Soon after Adolf Hitler came to power in Germany in 1933, some Americans sought to sound the alarm regarding the threat posed by his virulent anti-Semitism. As a young child, Ferdinand Isserman immigrated to America with his parents from Antwerp, Belgium, and settled in Newark, New Jersey. Educated at the University of Cincinnati and Hebrew Union College, he served as a rabbi in Toronto, Canada, before coming to St. Louis, Missouri, to lead Temple Israel. Noted for his outreach to Christian clergy and churches to promote ecumenical understanding and tolerance, Isserman visited Germany in 1933 soon after Hitler and the Nazi Party assumed control of the German government. As a result, he witnessed first-hand the brutality of the Nazis in crushing opposition to their rule and the wave of anti-Semitic actions the newly installed regime unleashed against the German Jewish community. In these excerpts from a pamphlet published in 1933, Isserman warned all who would listen of the Nazi threat to German Jewry. Isserman returned to Nazi Germany again in 1935 and 1937.

The United States in World War II: A Documentary Reader, First Edition.
Edited by G. Kurt Piehler. Editorial material and organization © 2013 Blackwell Publishing Ltd.
Published 2013 by Blackwell Publishing Ltd.

For residents of Saint Louis, who are familiar with my views, and who know what I have advocated from the pulpit and platform, some of these preparatory remarks will not be necessary.

Though a member of the United States Army in the world war, I have done all in my power to attempt to heal the wounds between my country and Germany. I have been a friend and not a foe of Germany. I have recognized the injustice of the Treaty of Versailles, and have urged and pleaded for its revision. I did so in Canada, when to speak a kind word for Germany was not too easy.

On November 11, 1930, while delivering the Armistice Day Sermon at the Community Services at Christ Church Cathedral, St. Louis, I pleaded for fair play to Germany, and I urged above all that the war-guilt clause in the Versailles Treaty was unfair and unjust. After that address, an old German-American came up to me and stated "Never in my life will I forget you for these words." I cite this to indicate that I was not anti-German, as I am not anti-any nation. I am anti-Nazi, not only because of the anti-semitism of the Nazis, but also because the philosophy of Naziism is a throw-back to primitive tribalism, ethically and spiritually indefensible, and as outworn as a *Weltanschauung* today as the ox-cart is as a vehicle for transportation. I can conceive of no greater catastrophe for humanity than the spread of the Nazi point of view. It would result in aggressive militant nationalism, war, and then the end of our civilization.

I spent one month in Germany. A good deal of the time I was in Berlin. There I met government officials, Nazis, American and other newspapermen, university professors, religious leaders of all denominations. I also toured through the country and visited other communities. From all these sources, I came to the following conclusions:

1. That there is no hope for the Jews of Germany—that the government aim is their humane extirpation.
2. That atrocities were perpetrated on Jews, Catholics, Socialists, German Nationalists, and other dissenters, and that these atrocities are continuing.
3. That an economic death sentence has been passed upon the Jews of Germany.
4. That only the fear of public opinion, especially that of the United States and Great Britain, has and is preventing a pogrom of all Jews in Germany.
5. That the Jews of Germany live under a sentence of death.

I recognize the sufferings of the German people. These are largely due to the war, and indicate again the need for pacifism. What the war commenced, the depression continued. Being convinced by their present leaders that they are a superior, the superior race; Germans cannot understand why such a race of Viking warriors should have lost the war. To this natural query comes the glib, fictitious Nazi answer— "Our soldiers won the war in the field of battle but were stabbed in the back by Jews, and hence glorious victory was turned into ignominious defeat." On my desk as I write, there is a text-book, issued by the Ministry of Education in Bavaria, detailing German history from 1914–1933, and used in the schools. The book is entitled *Aufruch der Nation*, and on page 15, there is a cartoon showing a Jewish traitor stabbing the victorious German soldier in the back. German vanity is thus satisfied. German soldiers are still the best fighters, and the Jew is the scape-goat, and he must be sacrificed that the Prussian might continue to swagger. Thus people are encouraged not to face the harsh realities of the war and its aftermath, and, living in a world of illusion, believe that if only there had been no Jews in Germany; France, Belgium and Russia would today be German colonies....

Hostages

The silence of many Jews in America about the situation in Germany may be due to the fact that they have relatives there, and that they fear reprisals upon them. American Jewish leaders, too numerous to mention, have such hostages in Germany, and their timidity in the face of the great Jewish calamity may be due to their concern for their own kin. This timidity has played right into the hands of the Nazis. The Nazis fear nothing except force, brute force stronger than their own. Such force exists only outside of Germany. It is the force of nations as big or bigger than Germany. The only factor which may lead the Nazis to mitigate their treatment of Jews is the public opinion of other nations and the pressure of that public opinion made manifest through diplomatic, economic and publicity channels. Especially do the Nazis value British and American public opinion. The Jews of Germany are lost. They can be saved, if at all, through letting the Nazis know that the world will ostracize Germany if it brutally destroys one-half million of its citizens. American Jews who hesitate to expose Naziism in Germany are not helping but harming their relatives. German Jews recognize that only the voice of outraged humanity can save them from pogroms....

The Future

For the Jew there seems to be little chance of the lessening of his burden. The recent statement of Goebbels and Goering indicate where they stand. A Canadian newspaper man had received an appointment for an interview with Goebbels. He was asked to submit seven questions, to which Goebbels would prepare an answer. Two referred to the future of Jews. Goebbels cancelled the interview because of the Jewish questions, which he did not care to answer.

Hitler refused to see a British member of Parliament to whom he had given an appointment when he learned one of the M.P.'s grandparents was Jewish. From both a journalist and a government official, I was informed that Hitler stated that for him the Jewish question was closed and that he no longer cared to discuss it. Recently, a German newspaper which suggested that General Balboa, Italy's hero, was a baptized Jew, was suspended for three months by order of Goering. Its editor was arrested and put in a concentration camp. To call a heroic Italian a Jew, Goering considered an insult to Italy, and hence, the editor responsible for that insult, had jeopardized Germany's foreign policy. This illustrates the intense hatred against Jews in government circles.

The government will not see or deal with Jewish leaders. The men to whom I brought letters of introduction all promised to arrange interviews for me, but never did. A Nazi leader can only lose status by discussing the Jewish problem. If he is disposed to ameliorate conditions of Jewish life, he will lose popularity with the rank and file of the party. If he appears relentless to the Jewish question, he must face the criticism of public opinion and the press of the world. The result is that the Jewish question is the quilled porcupine which no Nazi leader cares to touch. One Nazi leader stated that for 12 years the Nazi Party had spoken about the fruits of victory that they all would enjoy. Now that victory has been achieved, what can the party offer them but the Jews....

A Catholic leader informed me that Jews in Germany must bear a sore burden and that their lot is tragic. A Nazi naively stated that it is hell to be born a Jew. Many German Jews who do not hesitate to face reality, recognize that for the time being German-Jewish history is closed. As one put it, "The old will die here. The youth must migrate. One hundred thousand Jews may be able to settle in other countries. Another one hundred thousand will, by October first, be standing in breadlines. Three hundred thousand will, for a short time, be able to eke out an existence. Above all the children must leave Germany speedily. Thus will the Jew be liquidated in Germany."

A professor, an intellectual apologist for Hitler, stated that the aim of the present government is "the humane extirpation of the Jews." These exact words were phrased by one of the most important Nazis in Germany. Initially, the inhuman extirpation of the Jews was part of the Nazi policy and a pogrom of all Jews was initially contemplated. Only the public opinion of the world prevented that plan from being executed. Humane extirpation is the new goal. The cold pogrom is on. **A paralysis creeps slowly over Jewish life and the shadow of Ghetto memories casts its pall of gloom over the tents of Israel. Without the outraged conscience of humanity, especially of England and of the United States, it is my conviction that today there would not be a single Jew alive in Germany....**

Source: Ferdinand M. Isserman, *Sentenced to Death: The Jews in Nazi Germany* (St. Louis: The Modern View Publishing Co., 1933), pp. 3–4, 25–27.

2 Franklin D. Roosevelt, Public Statement, 1938

On the night of November 9–10, 1938, German officials organized a series of systematic attacks on the Jewish community. Mobs of Nazis, including the Hitler Youth, destroyed 267 synagogues and scores of Jewish-owned businesses. The police stood idly by as Jews were physically assaulted and in some cases raped. The SS and Gestapo rounded up 30,000 Jewish men and sent them to concentration camps. To compound the injustice, German officials fined the Jewish community in order to pay the financial cost of the violence perpetrated against them. American newspapers widely reported the events of Kristallnacht *and on their editorial pages almost uniformly condemned German actions. In his press conference on November 15, President Roosevelt issued the following press release. He also spoke at length of his decision to allow German and Austrian Jews staying in the United States on visitors' visas to remain longer, noting that it would be inhumane to deport these individuals to a regime that committed such crimes. Despite the outcry provoked by* Kristallnacht, *there was little support for scrapping the quotas established by the Immigration Act of 1924, which limited immigration from Europe, and for creating an open door for refugees, as had been the case in the early 1900s when Russian Jews were fleeing the pogroms sanctioned by the czar. The recall of the American ambassador would persist until the German Declaration of War against the United States. Although the United States did not break diplomatic relations with Germany and continued to maintain an embassy, it never seriously sought a negotiated settlement with the Nazis.*

STATEMENT BY THE PRESIDENT

FOR THE PRESS   IMMEDIATE RELEASE   NOVEMBER 15, 1938

The news of the past few days from Germany has deeply shocked public opinion in the United States. Such news from any part of the world would inevitably produce a similar profound reaction among American people in every part of the nation.

I myself could scarcely believe that such things could occur in a twentieth century civilization.

With a view to gaining a first-hand picture of the situation in Germany I asked the Secretary of State to order our Ambassador in Berlin to return at once for report and consultation.

Source: File OF 76C-Jewish 1938, Box 6 (Church Matters), President's Office File, Franklin D. Roosevelt Library, Hyde Park, New York.

3 Robert Taft, Letter to Allan Tarlish, 1939

The United States did offer a safe haven to thousands of refugees fleeing Nazi persecution. The physicist Albert Einstein and the composer Arnold Schoenberg were among German Jews who found safety in America. But the United States, along with most other countries in the world, placed strict limits on the number of refugees that would be allowed to enter. In 1921 and 1924, the US Congress created a quota system that limited immigration from European countries, with an eye to reducing immigration from Southern and Eastern Europe. In response to the Great Depression and increasing unemployment, President Herbert Hoover mandated that before being granted a visa, potential immigrants demonstrate they possessed sufficient financial resources to ensure they would not be a burden on American taxpayers. There were efforts within the Roosevelt Administration, most notably by Secretary of Labor Frances Perkins, to find ways to ease restrictions in order to admit more refugees. In 1938, Democratic Senator Robert Wagner of New York and Republican Congresswoman Edith Rogers of Massachusetts proposed legislation to expand the US quota of immigrants from Germany in order to admit refugee children. But these efforts met with opposition. Within the Roosevelt Administration, the State Department was reluctant to grant visas to refugees seeking to immigrate to the United States and rigorously applied the letter of the law. Even after the German atrocities of Kristallnacht, *the dominant sentiment as expressed by the public and Congress was to maintain strict limits on immigration, and the Rogers-Wagner Act was never passed. In the following letter to the Jewish War Veterans, Republican Senator Robert A. Taft of Ohio, an ardent opponent of intervention, explains why he cannot support this modest modification of current immigration law.*

COPY

UNITED STATES SENATE

Committee on Appropriations

May 10, 1939
Recd: May 16th.

Mr. Allan Tarlish
Jewish War Veterans of United States
Columbus, Ohio

Dear Mr. Tarlish:

I have received your recent communication with regard to the Wagner-Rogers Bill, providing for the admission of 20,000 German children in addition to the regular immigration quota.

I have not found it easy to decide what is the right thing to do with reference to this bill. I have the utmost sympathy with the terrible position of the German refugees, and the appeal for assistance to helpless children is hard to resist.

On the other hand it proposes a substantial modification of the immigration policy which the United States adopted after an unfortunate experience with immigration, and I am loath to vote for any modification of that policy. I do not think anything is more responsible for our present condition than the unrestricted immigration before the world war, which provided cheap labor for the steel mills and the mines.

Particularly at the present time, I think it unwise to encourage immigration. Nearly twenty million people are dependent on the federal government for relief. Among them are millions of children unable to obtain a sufficient amount of food, clothing and housing. It is said that the refugee children will be provided with homes, but if homes are available in America for twenty thousand children, then certainly there are at least 20,000 American children whose condition could be tremendously benefited by access to such homes. Furthermore, there is no assurance that in years to come, when the additional children are looking for jobs, conditions of unemployment will be better than now, and if the refugees obtain jobs, they will displace 20,000 young Americans engaged in the same search.

It is urged that America should contribute its share to relieving the terrific results of oppression in Europe, but America already is admitting 27,000 refugees within the quota and many additional thousands on special and visitors' visas. I believe that we are doing more than our share to relieve the situation. We cannot cure it in any event. No substantial part of the refugee problem can be solved by immigration into any country, because there are practically a million and a half refugees and no country is willing to receive more than a few. The only practical method of dealing with them seems to be some plan for colonization in Asia or Africa.

Finally, the plan of admitting 20,000 children, and separating them from their parents, does not seem desirable to me. It imposes a hardship which may be greater than may result in many cases if these children remain with their families. It inevitably suggests a reunion, and a request for the admission of the children's families at a later time, which it will be hard for any humane person to resist.

I have tried to consider all the arguments that have been urged, and to weigh them carefully and I have come to the conclusion that I shall vote against the bill.

Sincerely yours,
(sgdn) Robert Taft

Source: Jack Sutters (ed.), *American Friends Service Committee, Philadelphia, Volume 2, Part 1, 1932–1939*, in *Archives of the Holocaust*, ed. Henry Friedlander and Sybil Milton (New York: Garland, 1990), pp. 482–483.

4 Breckinridge Long, Diary Excerpts, 1940, 1942–1944

Franklin Roosevelt did not keep a diary or write letters baring his soul. By design, FDR often refused to commit himself to a position until the last possible minute. In meetings with individuals, he listened, asked questions, and often gave the impression he agreed with what they were saying. Moreover, FDR regularly tolerated a high degree of administrative chaos. In 1940, he appointed Breckinridge Long as Assistant Secretary of State in charge of the Visa Division. There is clear evidence that Long reversed earlier efforts to try to bend strict immigration law to admit more Jewish and other refugees fleeing Nazi-held territory. Long's diary raises serious questions about his actions toward refugees and the degree of anti-Semitic feeling within the State Department. Could US consuls abroad have been more proactive in seeking to aid Jews fleeing the grip of the Nazis, or could they have been more permissive in issuing visas? Why the reluctance to speak more vehemently about the plight of the Jews on the world stage? Long's diary makes frequent mention of Stephen Wise, one of the nation's leading Reform rabbis and president of the American Jewish Congress. Wise, a committed Zionist, had regular access to FDR and on several occasions sought to persuade the American government to take action against Germany and to support the creation of a Jewish state in Palestine. Although historians

have been divided on the question of whether Wise could have pressed FDR
more forcefully, it should be mentioned that Roosevelt had a general distrust
of the State Department and often bypassed it on important matters; with
regard to the refugee question, he would do so in 1944. The diary also makes
mention of Cordell Hull, who served as Secretary of State from 1933 to 1944.

September 9, 1940

... A refugee ship from Lisbon at Vera Cruz refused permission to land its passengers there and putting in at Norfolk for coal on its way back to Portugal, and the refugees want to land. Rabbi Wise pleads, as many others do—Sol Bloom and many more—but to do so would be a violation of the spirit of the law if not the letter. We have been generous—but there are limitations....

December 12, 1940

... As regards refugees, which is a continuing and complicated problem, Rabbi Wise and Rabbi Teitelbaum headed a delegation and asked me to accept 3,800 additional names from Lithuania and that part of the present Russian jurisdiction. After a long conversation, I was noncommittal as to what the Department would do but feel it is just a part of the movement to place me and the Department in general in an embarrassing position.

September 12, 1942

... I have accepted a proposal to facilitate the reception here of 1,000 Jewish children from France. Another effort will be made to move 6,000 or 8,000 to this hemisphere. They are derelicts. Their elders are being herded like cattle and ordered deported to Poland or to German work-shops. The appeal for asylum is irresistible to any human instinct and the act of barbarity just as repulsive as the result is appalling. But we can not receive into our own midst *all*—or even a large fraction of the oppressed—and no other country will receive them or even a few thousand, except that the President of Santo Domingo offers to receive and care for 3,500 children. Even Myron Taylor, ... was doubtful of the sincerity of the offer of Trujillo.

September 29, 1942

... Rabbi Wise's son and Dr. Golman [Goldmann] came in with Acheson. They asked to send food to Jews in Warsaw. I said we would agree to $12,000 a month to go to Portugal to buy food there if Treasury would license the transfer of credit. They were pleased. I told Norman Davis and he said his Red Cross would help over there. Then I went to Hull ... We again discussed the political reasons against the humanitarian impulses which had motivated us—and the necessity for us to take into consideration the *political consequences* if we just say "no" for military reasons and oppose the humanitarian decisions of large groups of our citizens—etc. He approved what I had done about the Jewish proposal and would send a letter for the President's consideration ...

October 1, 1942

... The decision [to send food parcels from Portugal was taken] on purely political grounds. The total amount of food involved is infinitesimal. But I did not want that policy along with others to serve as the basis for antagonisms toward us after this war ... so that is our policy.

April 20, 1943

The "Bermuda Conference" on Refugees has been born. It has taken a lot of nursing but is now in existence. One Jewish faction under the leadership of Rabbi Stephen Wise has been so assiduous in pushing their particular cause—in letter and telegrams to the President, the Secretary and Welles—in public meetings to arouse emotions—in full page newspaper advertisements—in resolutions to be presented to the conference—that they are apt to produce a reaction against their interest. Many public men have signed their broadsides and Johnson of Colorado introduced their resolution into the Senate.

One danger in it all is that their activities may lend color to the charges of Hitler that we are fighting this war on account of and at the instigation and direction of our Jewish citizens, for it is only necessary for Nazi propaganda to republish in the press of neutral countries the resolution introduced in the United States Senate and broadsides bearing the names of high Government officials in order to substantiate their charges in the eyes of doubting neutrals. In Turkey the impression grows—and in Spain it is being circulated—and in Palestine's hinderland and in North Africa the Moslem population will be easy believers in such charges. It might easily be a definite detriment to our war effort.

January 24, 1944

The President has appointed a Refugee Board consisting of the Secretaries of State, War, and Treasury—they to appoint a Director to save the refugees in German control. And it is good news for me. This "Director," when chosen, will take over—this insures me staying out. What they can do that I have not done

I cannot imagine. However, they can try. I will advise them, if they want—but the Director should do the work. ... I think it a good move—for local political reasons—for there are 4 million Jews in New York and its environs who feel themselves related to the refugees and because of the persecution of the Jews, and who have been demanding special attention and treatment. This will encourage them to think the persecuted may be saved and possibly satisfy them—politically—but in my opinion the Board will not save any persecuted people I could not save under my recent and long suffering administration.

Source: Breckinridge Long, *The War Diary of Breckinridge Long: Selections from the Years 1939–1944*, ed. Fred L. Israel (Lincoln: University of Nebraska Press, 1966), pp. 128, 161, 282, 283, 307, 336–337.

5 Myron C. Taylor, Memorandum of Conversation, Letter to Cardinal Maglione, 1942

The American response to the Holocaust was complicated by the fact that, until 1943, Germany still had the potential to win the war. Not until the victories of the British at El Alamein, Egypt, in November 1942 and the Soviet Union at Stalingrad in January 1943 did the strategic balance shift in favor of the Allies. American Air Force strategic bombers would not strike targets in Germany until January 1943. Neither the British nor the Americans had the capability to strike the death camps in Poland and the Soviet Union in 1942, the year when the Germans killed the majority of Jews who perished during the Holocaust. Although the United States and Italy were at war in 1942, Pope Pius XII governed the small, independent city-state of Vatican City in the heart of Rome. Consequently, the United States maintained diplomatic relations with Vatican City through the appointment of Myron Taylor as President Roosevelt's personal representative to the pontiff. In 1942, Taylor tried to engage the pontiff on a number of issues that would help the Allied war effort. In a long meeting with Cardinal Maglione, the Secretary of State for the Vatican, summarized in part in the memorandum below, Taylor discussed a range of topics including the pontiff's recent decision to establish diplomatic relations with Japan, Russian intentions, the postwar future, and the plight of refugees and the Jews. Pius XII remained cautious in his condemnation of German actions through much of the war. Some historians attribute this to a bias in favor of Germany and a callous disregard of the fate of the Jews. Others observe that Pius XII did what he could to rescue Jews, including offering haven to the Chief Rabbi of Rome despite the fact that the Vatican was surrounded by Axis territory until the liberation of Rome by Allied forces on June 4, 1944.

Memorandum, Conversation of September 25, 1942 between His Eminence Cardinal Maglione and His Excellency Myron C. Taylor

... Ambassador Taylor stated that there is a general impression, not only in America, but also in Europe and elsewhere – an impression of which His Excellency has personally seen much evidence – that the Holy Father should again speak out against the inhuman treatment of refugees and hostages – and especially of the Jews – in occupied territories. Mr. Taylor also pointed out that this general call for a statement from His Holiness comes not only from Catholics but from Protestants as well, and added that he had heard it in America, in Lisbon, in Madrid, and anywhere that he has gone in recent months. His Eminence, in reply, declared that the Holy See has been working incessantly for the relief of the unfortunate peoples of the occupied countries and very particularly for the refugees and for the Jews. The Secretariat of State and other Vatican agencies, he said, are constantly devoting themselves to these problems. Furthermore, Cardinal Maglione declared, representatives of the Catholic Church in various co[u]ntries have interested themselves in the question and have been quite outspoken in their condemnation of this inhuman treatment of the peoples of their countries. His Holiness has on many occasions condemned this treatment of peoples and of individuals and has declared that the blessing or the malediction of Almighty God would descend upon rulers according to the manner in which they treat the peoples under their rule. This, Cardinal Maglione intimated, was quite a strong statement – as strong, in fact, as it is possible to make without descending to particulars, a course of action which would immediately draw His Holiness into the field of political disputes, require documentary proof, etc. Manifestly, His Eminence added, the Pope should not do this. Mr. Taylor agreed that His Holiness would not be expected to descend to particulars, but only to make His appeal on the higher level. His Excellency pointed out that these declarations of His Holiness had been made some time ago and that it is generally felt that a renewal of the appeal might now be in order and would most certainly be welcomed. To this Cardinal Maglione replied that he had the impression that as late as June 1942 His Holiness had denounced the maltreatment of the peoples of the occupied countries. The difficulty, His Eminence said, lies in the fact that people have short memories in matters of this kind and that many would have the Pope speak out daily in denunciation of these evils. At any rate, His Eminence assured Ambassador Taylor, the Pope will certainly avail Himself of the first opportunity to restate His position in very clear terms.

Letter to Cardinal Maglione, September 26, 1942

My dear Cardinal Maglione:

Vatican City, September 26, 1942

I have the honor to bring to the attention of Your Eminence the following memorandum which has been received by my Government.

"The following was received from the Geneva Office of the Jewish Agency for Palestine in a letter dated August 30th, 1942. That office received the report from two reliable eye-witnesses (Aryans), one of whom came on August 14th from Poland.

"(1) Liquidation of the Warsaw Ghetto is taking place. Without distinction all Jews, irrespective of age or sex, are being removed from the Ghetto in groups and shot. Their corpses are utilized for making fats and their bones for the manufacture of fertilizer. Corpses are even being exhumed for these purposes.

"(2) These mass executions take place, not in Warsaw, but in especially prepared camps for the purpose, one of which is stated to be in Belzek. About 50,000 Jews have been executed in Lemberg itself on the spot during the past month. According to another report, 100,000 have been massacred in Warsaw. There is not one Jew left in the entire district east of Poland, including occupied Russia. It is also reported, in this connection, that the entire non-Jewish population of Sebastopol was murdered. So as not to attract the attention of foreign countries, the butchering of the Jewish population in Poland was not done at one single time.

"(3) Jews deported from Germany, Belgium, Holland, France, and Slovakia are sent to be butchered, while Aryans deported to the East from Holland and France are genuinely used for work.

"(4) Inasmuch as butchering of this kind would attract great attention in the west, they must first of all deport them to the East, where less opportunity is afforded to outsiders of knowing what is going on. During the last few weeks a large part of the Jewish population deported to Lithuania and Lublin has already been executed. That is probably the reason why the deportees were not permitted to have correspondence with any one. A great number of the German refugees were taken to Theresienstadt. This place, however, is only an interim station and the people there await the same fate.

"(5) Arrangements are made for new deportations as soon as space is made by executions. Caravans of such deportees being transported in cattle cars are often seen. There are about forty people in each cattle car. It is especially significant to note that Lithuanian non-Jews are entrusted with fetching the candidates from the death Ghetto in Warsaw.

"(6) It is a tragedy that the Polish population is being incited by the Germans against the Jews and the relationship between the Poles and the Jews has been aggravated to the last degree. In Lemberg this is particularly true."

I should much appreciate it if Your Eminence could inform me whether the Vatican has any information that would tend to confirm the reports contained in this memorandum. If so, I should like to know whether the Holy Father has any suggestions as to any practical manner in which the forces of civilized public opinion could be utilized in order to prevent a continuation of these barbarities.

I avail myself of this occasion to express to Your Eminence the assurances of my highest consideration.

Source: Box 52, Vatican Files, Franklin D. Roosevelt Library, Hyde Park, New York. Also available online at http://www.fdrlibrary.marist.edu/.

6 The *New York Times*, "11 Allies Condemn Nazi War on Jews," 1942

Critics have often faulted the US and other Allied governments for not publicly condemning the Nazi regime for the Holocaust. But the historical record shows that several public warnings were given to the Nazis regarding their crimes against Jews and other nationalities living under German occupation. News about German anti-Semitism and later the mass killing of Jews filled the pages of one of the nation's most influential newspapers, the New York Times, *but often it would be relegated to the back pages. The following article reporting on the joint Allied condemnation of Nazi war crimes appeared on the front page of the* New York Times *on December 18, 1942. Overseas, when British Foreign Secretary Anthony Eden announced the Allied condemnation of German actions, the entire House of Commons stood in silence to express its solidarity with the plight of European Jewry. The BBC broadcast news around the world of the Allied condemnation of Nazi war crimes against the Jews.*

11 ALLIES CONDEMN NAZI WAR ON JEWS

United Nations Issue Joint Declaration of Protest on 'Cold-Blooded Extermination'

Special to THE NEW YORK TIMES.

WASHINGTON, Dec. 17 — A joint declaration by members of the United Nations was issued today condemning Germany's "bestial policy of cold-blooded extermination" of Jews and declaring that "such events can only strengthen the resolve of all freedom-loving people to overthrow the barbarous Hitlerite tyranny."

The nations reaffirmed "their solemn resolution to insure that those responsible for these crimes shall not escape retribution and to press on with the necessary practical measures to this end."

The declaration was issued simultaneously through the State Department here and in London. It was subscribed to by eleven nations, including the United States, Britain and Russia, and also by the French National Committee in London.

The declaration referred particularly to the program as conducted in Poland and to the barbarous forms it is taking.

TEXT OF DECLARATION

The attention of the Belgian, Czechoslovak, Greek, Luxembourg, Netherlands, Norwegian, Polish, Soviet, United Kingdom, United States and Yugoslav Governments and also of the French National Committee has been drawn to numerous reports from Europe that the German authorities, not content with denying to persons of Jewish race in all the territories over which their barbarous rule has been extended, the most elementary human rights, are now carrying into effect Hitler's oft-repeated intention to exterminate the Jewish people in Europe.

From all the occupied countries Jews are being transported in conditions of appalling horror and brutality to Eastern Europe. In Poland, which has been made the principal Nazi slaughterhouse, the ghettos established by the German invader are being systematically emptied of all Jews except a few highly skilled workers required for war industries. None of those taken away are ever heard of again. The able-bodied are slowly worked to death in labor camps. The infirm are left to die of exposure and starvation or are deliberately massacred in mass executions. The number of victims of these bloody cruelties is reckoned in many hundreds of thousands of entirely innocent men, women, and children.

The above-mentioned governments and the French National Committee condemn in the strongest possible terms this bestial policy of cold-blooded extermination. They declare that such events can only strengthen the resolve of all freedom-loving peoples to overthrow the barbarous Hitlerite tyranny. They reaffirm their solemn resolution to insure that those responsible for these crimes shall not escape retribution, and to press on with the necessary practical measures to this end.

Preliminary Steps Taken

The declaration had been forecast through diplomatic conversations that had been conducted in recent days looking to a joint denunciation of the persecution. The nations for some time have been assembling evidence, sifting it, and exchanging it among one another.

Secretary of State Cordell Hull was asked today what practical steps could be taken to reinforce the protest.

Statements have been made by President Roosevelt and heads of other governments during recent months, he replied, in regard to the development of plans, and concrete progress to discover and assemble all possible facts relating to these inhuman acts together with the names of the guilty persons, to the end that they may be apprehended at the earliest possible opportunity, not later than the end of the war, and properly dealt with. These undertakings, he added, are being carried forward now.

The matter has been active for months, not only with reference to Jews but also to other innocent civilians who have been the victims of reprisals and persecution.

President Roosevelt, in a statement on Oct. 25, 1941, denounced the execution of innocent hostages. On Jan. 13, 1942, the representatives of nine governments whose countries are under occupation issued a protest in London and declared that those responsible would be "handed over to justice and tried."

Subsequently the attention of Secretary Hull was formally called to "the barbaric crimes against civilian populations" in occupied countries through a communication from the governments of Belgium, Greece, Luxembourg, Norway, The Netherlands, Poland, Czechoslovakia, Yugoslavia, and the French National Committee.

Roosevelt Statements Recalled

President Roosevelt on Aug. 21, 1942, issued a statement denouncing the persecutions and warning those responsible that "the time will come when they shall have to stand in courts of law in the very countries which they are now oppressing and answer for their acts."

In another statement, on Oct. 7, 1942, President Roosevelt advocated a United Nations Commissions for the Investigation of War Crimes for meting out "just and sure punishment" to the "ringleaders responsible for the organized murder of thousands of innocent persons and the commission of atrocities which have violated every tenet of the Christian faith."

And last week the President gave sympathetic consideration to a proposal of a committee of Jewish organizations in this country, headed by Rabbi

Stephen S. Wise, for a United States commission to consider the persecution of the Jews and to act in conjunction with the United Nations in the matter.

Source: "11 Allies Condemn Nazi War on Jews", *New York Times*, December 18, 1942, pp. 1, 10.

7 Henry Morgenthau, Jr. to Franklin D. Roosevelt, Excerpt from "Personal Report to the President," Memorandum, 1944

Long-time neighbor and friend Henry Morgenthau, Jr. served as FDR's Secretary of the Treasury from 1934 to 1945. Morgenthau was born into a prominent German Jewish family and his father, as an American diplomat, had sought to muster support within the US government to protest Turkish massacres of the Armenian population in the aftermath of World War I. Until Kristallnacht, Morgenthau generally deferred to the State Department on American policy toward Germany and refugees. After 1939, he took a more activist role and explored areas of the world that might serve as new homelands for Jewish refugees. On January 16, 1944, Morgenthau and two of his aides met with FDR to discuss the issues raised in the memorandum reproduced here. At the urging of Morgenthau and his aides, Roosevelt signed an executive order establishing the War Refugees Board. Later in 1944, Morgenthau developed a proposal that called for the dismemberment of Germany into a series of small agricultural states that would be stripped of all heavy industry, in order to ensure it would never make war again. Although FDR initially accepted the Morgenthau Plan, significant opposition from the State and War Departments along with general public disapproval forced him to reverse the policy in favor of a less punitive one.

<hr>

SECRET

PERSONAL REPORT TO THE PRESIDENT

One of the greatest crimes in history, the slaughter of the Jewish people in Europe, is continuing unabated.

This Government has for a long time maintained that its policy is to work out programs to save those Jews and other persecuted minorities of Europe who could be saved.

You are probably not as familiar as I with the utter failure of certain officials in our State Department, who are charged with actually carrying out this policy, to take any effective action to prevent the extermination of the Jews in German-controlled Europe.

The public record, let alone the facts which have not yet been made public, reveals the gross procrastination of these officials. It is well known that since the time when it became clear that Hitler was determined to carry out a policy of exterminating the Jews in Europe, the State Department officials have failed to take any positive steps reasonably calculated to save any of these people. Although they have used devices such as setting up intergovernmental organizations to survey the whole refugee problem, and calling conferences such as the Bermuda Conference to explore the whole refugee problem, making it appear that positive action could be expected, in fact nothing has been accomplished.

The best summary of the whole situation is contained in one sentence of a report submitted on December 20, 1943, by the Committee on Foreign Relations of the Senate, recommending the passage of a Resolution (S.R. 203), favoring the appointment of a commission to formulate plans to save the Jews of Europe from extinction by Nazi Germany. The Resolution had been introduced by Senator Guy M. Gillette in behalf of himself and eleven colleagues, Senators Taft, Thomas, Radcliffe, Murray, Johnson, Guffey, Ferguson, Clark, Van Nuys, Downey and Ellender. The Committee stated:

"We have talked; we have sympathized; we have expressed our horror; the time to act is long past due."

Whether one views this failure as being deliberate on the part of those officials handling the matter, or merely due to their incompetence, is not too important from my point of view. However, there is a growing number of responsible people and organizations today who have ceased to view our failure as the product of simple incompetence on the part of those officials in the State Department charged with handling this problem. They see plain Anti-Semitism motivating the actions of these State Department officials and, rightly or wrongly, it will require little more in the way of proof for this suspicion to explode into a nasty scandal.

In this perspective, I ask you to weigh the implications of the following two cases which have recently come to my attention and which have not as yet become known to the public.

I

WORLD JEWISH CONGRESS PROPOSAL TO EVACUATE
THOUSANDS OF JEWS FROM RUMANIA AND FRANCE

On March 13, 1943, the World Jewish Congress representative in London sent a cable to their offices here. This cable stated that information reaching London indicated it was possible to rescue Jews provided funds were put at the disposal of World Jewish Congress representation in Switzerland.

On April 10, 1943, Sumner Welles cabled our Legation in Bern and requested them to get in touch with the World Jewish Congress representative in Switzerland, who Welles had been informed was in possession of important information regarding the situation of the Jews.

On April 20, 1943, the State Department received a cable from Bern relating to the proposed financial arrangements in connection with the evacuation of the Jews from Rumania and France.

On May 25, 1943, State Department cabled for a clarification of these proposed financial arrangements. This matter was not called to the attention of the Treasury Department at this time although the Treasury has the responsibility for licensing all such financial transactions.

This whole question of financing the evacuation of the Jews from Rumania and France was first called to the attention of the Treasury Department on June 25, 1943.

A conference was held with the State Department relating to this matter on July 15, 1943.

One day after this conference, on July 16, 1943, the Treasury Department advised the State Department that it was prepared to issue a license in this matter.

It was not until December 18, 1943, after having interposed objections for five months, that the State Department, precipitously and under circumstances revealing the fictitious character of their objections, instructed Harrison to issue the necessary license.

During this five months period between the time that the Treasury stated that it was prepared to issue a license and the time when the license was actually issued delays and objections of all sorts were forthcoming from officials in the State Department, our Legation in Bern, and finally the British. The real significance of these delays and objections was brought home to the State Department in letters which I sent to Secretary Hull on November 23, 1943, and December 17, 1943, which completely devastated the excuses which State Department officials had been advancing.

On December 18 I made an appointment to discuss the matter with Secretary Hull on December 20. And then an amazing but understandable thing happened. On the very day I made my appointment the State Department issued a license not withstanding the fact that the objections of our Legation in Bern were still outstanding and that the British had indicated their disapproval for political reasons.

State Department officials were in such a hurry to issue this license that they not only did not ask the Treasury to draft the license (which would have been the normal procedure) but they drafted the license themselves and issued it without even consulting the Treasury as to its terms. Informal discussions with certain State Department officials have confirmed what is obvious from the above-mentioned facts.

This wasn't all that my letter and appointment precipitated. I had told Secretary Hull that I wished to discuss the British objections—in simple terms, the British were apparently prepared to accept the probable death of thousands of Jews in enemy territory because of "the difficulties of disposing of any considerable number of Jews should they be rescued". Accordingly, on that day of "action" for our State Department, December 18, they sent a telegram to the British Foreign Office expressing astonishment at the British point of view and stating that the Department was unable to agree with that point of view.

Breckinridge Long, who is in charge of such matters in the State Department, knew that his position was so indefensible that he was unwilling even to try to defend it at my pending conference with Secretary Hull on December 20. Accordingly, he took such action as he felt was necessary to cover up his previous position in this matter. It is, of course, clear that if we had not made the record against the State Department officials followed by my request to see Secretary Hull, the action which the State Department took on December 18 would either never have been taken at all or would have been delayed so long that any benefits which it might have had would have been lost.

II

SUPPRESSION OF FACTS REGARDING HITLER's EXTERMINATION OF JEWS IN EUROPE

The facts are as follows:

<u>Sumner Welles as Acting Secretary of State requests confirmation of Hitler's plan to exterminate the Jews.</u> Having already received various reports on plight of the Jews, on October 5, 1942 Sumner Welles as Acting Secretary of State sent a cable (2314) for the personal attention of Minister Harrison in Bern stating that leaders of the Jewish Congress had received reports from their representatives in Geneva and London to the effect that many thousands of Jews in Eastern Europe were being slaughtered pursuant to a policy embarked upon by the German Government for the complete extermination of the Jews in Europe. Welles added that he was trying to obtain further information from the Vatican but that other than this he was unable to secure confirmation of these stories. He stated that Rabbi Wise believed that information was available to his representatives in Switzerland but that they were in all lik[e]lihood fearful of dispatching any such reports

through open cables or mail. He than stated that World Jewish Congress officials in Switzerland, Riegner and Lichtheim, were being requested by Wise to call upon Minister Harrison; and Welles requested Minister Harrison to advise him by telegram of all the evidence and facts which he might secure as a result of conferences with Riegner and Lichtheim.

State Department receives confirmation that the extermination was being rapidly carried out. Pursuant to Welles' cable of October 5 Minister Harrison forwarded documents from Riegner confirming the fact of extermination of the Jews (in November 1942), and in a cable of January 21, 1943 (482) relayed a message from Riegner and Lichtheim which Harrison stated was for the information of the Under Secretary of State (and was to be transmitted to Rabbi Stephen Wise if the Under Secretary should so determine). This message described a horrible situation concerning the plight of Jews in Europe. It reported mass executions of Jews in Poland; the Jews were required before execution to strip themselves of all their clothing which was then sent to Germany; in Germany deportations were continuing; many Jews were being deprived of rationed foodstuffs; no Jews would be left in Prague or Berlin by the end of March, etc.; and in Rumania 130,000 Jews were deported to Transnistria; about 60,000 had already died and the remaining 70,000 were starving; living conditions were indescribable; Jews were deprived of all their money, foodstuffs and possessions; they were housed in deserted cellars, and occasionally twenty to thirty people slept on the floor of one unheated room; disease was prevalent, particularly fever; urgent assistance was needed.

Sumner Welles furnishes this information to the Jewish organizations. Sumner Welles furnished the documents received in November to the Jewish organizations in the United States and authorized them to make the facts public. On February 9, 1943 Welles forwarded the messages contained in cable 482 of January 21 to Rabbi Stephen Wise.

The receipt of this message intensified the pressure on the State Department to take some action.

Certain State Department officials attempt to stop this Government from obtaining further information from the very source from which the above evidence was received. On February 10, the day after Welles forwarded the message contained in cable 482 of January 21 to Rabbi Wise, and in direct response to this cable, a most highly significant cable was dispatched to Minister Harrison. This cable, 354 of February 10, read as follows:

"Your 482, January 21
"In the future we would suggest that you do not accept reports submitted to you to be transmitted to private persons in the United States unless such action

is advisable because of extraordinary circumstances. Such private messages circumvent neutral countries' censorship and it is felt that by sending them we risk the possibility that steps would necessarily be taken by the neutral countries to curtail or forbid our means of communication for confidential official matter. HULL (SW)"

The cable was signed for Hull by "SW" (Sumner Welles). But it is significant that there is not a word in it that would even suggest to the person signing that it was designed to countermand the Department's specific requests for information on Hitler's plans to exterminate the Jews. The cable has the appearance of being a normal routine message which a busy official would sign without question. On its face it is most innocent and innocuous, yet when read together with the previous cables is it anything less than an attempted suppression of information requested by this Government concerning the murder of Jews by Hitler?

It is also significant that the message which provoked the ban on further communications of this character was not addressed to private persons at all but was addressed to Under Secretary Welles at his own request and the information contained therein was only to be transmitted to the World Jewish Congress if Welles deemed it advisable.

Thereafter on April 10, 1943, Sumner Welles again requested our Legation for information (cable 877). Apparently he did not realize that in cable 354 (to which he did not refer) Harrison had been instructed to cease forwarding reports of this character. Harrison replied on April 20 (cable 2460) and indicated that he was in a most confused state of mind as a result of the conflicting instructions he had received. Among other things he stated:

"May I suggest that messages of this character should not (repeat not) be subjected to the restriction imposed by your 354, February 10, and that I be permitted to transmit messages from R more particularly in view of the helpful information which they may frequently contain?"

The fact that cable 354 is not the innocent and routine cable that it appears to be on its face is further highlighted by the efforts of State Department officials to prevent this Department from obtaining the cable and learning its true significance.

The facts relating to this attempted concealment are as follows:

(i)   Several men in our Department had requested State Department officials for a copy of the cable of February 10 (354). We had been advised that it was a Department communication; a strictly political communication, which had nothing to do with economic matters; that it had only had a very limited distribution within the Department, the only ones having anything to do with it being the European Division, the Political Adviser and Sumner Welles; and that a copy could not be furnished to the Treasury.

(ii) At the conference in Secretary Hull's office on December 20 in the presence of Breckinridge Long I asked Secretary Hull for a copy of cable 354, which I was told would be furnished to me.

(iii) By note to me of December 20, Breckinridge Long enclosed a paraphrase of cable 354. This paraphrase of cable 354 specifically <u>omitted any reference to cable 482 of January 21—thus destroying the only tangible clue to the true meaning of the message.</u>

(iv) I would never have learned the true meaning of cable 354 had it not been for chance. I had asked one of the men in my Department to obtain all the facts on this matter. He had previously called one of the men in another Division of the State Department and requested permission to see the relevant cables. In view of the Treasury interest in this matter, this State Department representative obtained cable 354 and the cable of January 21 to which it referred and showed these cables to my representative.

The facts I have detailed in this report, Mr. President, came to the Treasury's attention as a part of our routine investigation of the licensing of the financial phases of the proposal of the World Jewish Congress for the evacuation of Jews from France and Rumania. The facts may thus be said to have come to light through accident. How many others of the same character are buried in State Department files is a matter I would have no way of knowing. Judging from the almost complete failure of the State Department to achieve any results, the strong suspicion must be that they are not few.

This much is certain, however. The matter of rescuing the Jews from extermination is a trust too great to remain in the hands of men who are indifferent, callous, and perhaps even hostile. The task is filled with difficulties. Only a fervent will to accomplish, backed by persistent and untiring effort can succeed where time is so precious.

Henry Morgenthau
Jan. 16, 1944

Source: Henry Morgenthau, "Personal Report to the President," in *The Abandonment of the Jews: America and the Holocaust 1941–1945*, ed. David S. Wyman, Vol. 8 (New York: Garland Publishing, 1990), pp. 194–202.

8 Harold Porter, Letter to Parents, 1945

The Nazis had placed most of the major extermination camps in Eastern Europe. But there were also a number of concentration camps within Germany that imprisoned political opponents, enemy captives, and Jews. One of the oldest camps was Dachau, located near Munich, established soon after Adolf Hitler assumed power in 1933. In the closing years of the war, inmates were given starvation rations and were literally worked to death. Moreover, even as the Nazi regime was collapsing, the SS continued to carry out the Final Solution and kill as many Jews as possible. In the following letter, US Army Sergeant Harold Porter, serving with the 116th Evacuation Hospital, wrote to his parents describing the conditions he encountered at Dachau shortly after liberation and the efforts of American forces to aid the survivors.

7 May 1945

Dear Mother and Father,

You have, by this time, received a letter mentioning that I am quartered in the concentration camp at Dachau. It is still undecided whether we will be permitted to describe the conditions here, but I'm writing this now to tell you a little, and will mail it later when we are told we can.

It is difficult to know how to begin. By this time I have recovered from my first emotional shock and am able to write without seeming like a hysterical gibbering idiot. Yet, I know you will hesitate to believe me no matter how objective and factual I try to be. I even find myself trying to deny what I am looking at with my own eyes. Certainly, what I have seen in the past few days will affect my personality for the rest of my life.

We knew a day or two before we moved that we were going to operate in Dachau, and that it was the location of the most notorious concentration camps, but while we expected things to be grizzly, I'm sure none of us knew what was coming. It is easy to read about atrocities, but they must be seen before they can be believed. To think that I once scoffed at Valtin's book "Out of the Night" as being preposterous! I've seen worse sights than any he described.

The trip south from Oettingen was pleasant enough. We passed through Donauworth and Ashbach and as we entered Dachau, the country, with the cottages, rivers, country estates and Alps in the distance, was almost like a tourist resort. But as we came to the center of the city, we met a train with a wrecked engine — about fifty cars long. Every car was loaded with bodies.

There must have been thousands of them — all obviously starved to death. This was a shock of the first order, and the odor can best be unimagined. But neither the sight nor the odor were anything when compared with what we were still to see.

Marc Coyle reached the camp two days before I did and was a guard so as soon as I got there I looked him up and he took me to the crematory. Dead SS troopers were scattered around the grounds, but when we reached the furnace house we came upon a huge stack of corpses piled up like kindling, all made so that their clothes wouldn't be wasted by the burning. There were furnaces for burning six bodies at once, and on each side of them was a room twenty feet square crammed to the ceiling with more bodies — one big stinking rotten mess. Their faces purple, their eyes popping and with a ludicrous grin on each one. They were nothing but bones & skin. Coyle had assisted at ten autopsies the day before (wearing a gas mask) on ten bodies selected at random. Eight of them had advance T.B., all had typhus and extreme malnutrition symptoms. There were both women and child in the stack in addition to the men.

While we were inspecting the place, freed prisoners drove up with wagon loads of corpses removed from the compound proper. Watching the unloading was horrible. The bodies squooshed and gargled as they hit the pile and the odor could almost be seen.

Behind the furnaces was the execution chamber, a windowless cell twenty feet square with gas nozzles every few feet square across the ceiling. Outside, in addition to a huge mound of charnel bone fragments, were the carefully sorted and stacked clothes of the victims — which obviously numbered in the thousands. Although I stood there looking at it, I couldnt believe it. The realness of the whole mess is just gradually dawning on me, and I doubt if it ever will on you.

There is a rumor circulating which says that the war is over. It probably is — as much as it ever will be. We've all been expecting the end for several days, but were not too excited about it because we know that it does not mean too much as far as our immediate situation is concerned. There was no celebrations — it's difficult to celebrate anything with the morbid state we're in.

The Pacific theater will not come immediately for this unit; we have around 36,000 potential and eventual patients here. The end of the work for everyone else is going to be just the beginning for us.

Today was a scorching hot day after several rainy cold ones. The result of the heat on the corpses is impossible to describe, and the situation will probably get worse because their disposal will certainly take time.

My arm is sore from a typhus shot so I'm ending here for the present. More will follow later. I have lots to write about now.

Love,
Harold

Source: Sonya Porter Collection, Dwight D. Eisenhower Library, Abilene, Kansas. Available online at http://www.eisenhower.archives.gov/.

9 David Max Eichhorn, Sermon, 1945

As American troops advanced through North Africa, Sicily, France, and Germany they liberated scores of Jews and other victims of Nazi terror. Rabbis serving as chaplains in the US Army played an important role in aiding liberated Jews to find food and shelter and arranging for them to contact family in America. They also alerted the Jewish Welfare Board and other Jewish organizations in America of the desperate needs of European Jewry who survived the Holocaust. Many Jewish chaplains, often aided by Protestant and Roman Catholic chaplains and Jewish GIs, sought to rekindle spiritual life among Jews who had survived the horrors of Nazi rule. On May 6, 1945, Rabbi David Max Eichhorn addressed the Jewish survivors of Dachau and sought to offer words of comfort during a service that would be filmed by the US Army Signal Corps. Eichhorn prior to the war had served a congregation in Tallahassee, Florida, and also served as the first Hillel Director of Florida State College for Women (Florida State University) and the University of Florida.

My Jewish brethren at Dachau,

In the portion which we read yesterday in our holy Torah, we found these words … "Proclaim freedom through the world to all the inhabitants thereof; a day of celebration shall this be for you, a day when every man shall return to his family and to his rightful place in society."

In the United States of America, in the city of Philadelphia, upon the exact spot where 169 years ago a group of brave Americans met and decided to fight for American independence, there stands a marker upon which is written these very same words: "Proclaim freedom throughout the world to all the inhabitants thereof." From the beginning of their existence as a liberty-loving and independent people, the citizens of America understood that not until all the peoples of the world were free would they be truly free, that not until tyranny and oppression had been erased from the hearts of all men and all nations would there be a lasting peace and happiness for themselves. Thus it has been that, throughout our entire history, whenever and wherever men have been enslaved, Americans have fought to set them free, whenever and whatever dictators have endeavored to destroy democracy and justice and truth, Americans have not rested content until these despots have been overthrown.

Today I come to you in a dual capacity—as a soldier in the American Army and as a representative of the Jewish community of America. As an American soldier, I say to you that we are proud, very proud, to be here, to know that we have had a share in the destruction of the most cruel tyranny of all time. As an American soldier, I say to you that we are proud, very proud, to be with you as comrades-in-arms, to greet you and salute you as the bravest of the brave. We know your tragedy. We know your sorrows. We know that upon you was centered the venomous hatred of power-crazed madmen, that your annihilation was decreed and planned systematically and ruthlessly. We know, too, that you refused to be destroyed, that you fought back with every weapon at your command, that you fought with your bodies, your minds and your spirit. Your faith and our faith in God and in humanity have been sustained. Our enemies lie prostrate before us. The way of life which together we have defended still lives and it will live so that all men everywhere may have freedom and happiness and peace.

I speak to you also as a Jew, as a rabbi in Israel, as a teacher of that religious philosophy which is dearer to all of us than life itself. What message of comfort and strength can I bring to you from your fellow-Jews? What can I say that will compare in depth or intensity to that which you have suffered and overcome? Full well do I know and humbly do I confess the emptiness of mere words in this hour of mingled sadness and joy. Words will not bring the dead back to life nor right the wrongs of the past ten years. This is not time for words, you will say, and rightfully so. This is a time for deeds, deeds of justice, deeds of love ... Justice will be done. We have seen with our own eyes and we have heard with our own ears and we shall not forget. As long as there are Jews in the world, "Dachau" will be a term of horror and shame. Those who labored here for their evil master must be hunted down and destroyed as systematically and as ruthlessly as they sought your destruction. ... And there will be deeds of love. It is the recognized duty of all truly religious people to bestir themselves immediately to assist you to regain health, comfort and some measure of happiness as speedily as humanly possible. This must be done. This can be done. This will be done. You are not and you will not be forgotten men, my brothers. In every country where the lamps of religion and decency and kindness still burn, Jews and non-Jews alike will expend much time and energy and money as it is needful to make good that pledge which is written in our holy Torah and inscribed on that marker in Philadelphia, city of Brotherly Love.

We know that abstractions embodied in proclamations and celebrations must be followed by more concrete, more helpful fulfillments. We do not intend to brush aside the second part of the Divine promise ... Every man who has been oppressed must and will be restored to his family and to his rightful place in society. This is a promise and a pledge which I bring to you from your American comrades in arms and your Jewish brethren across the seas. ...

Source: David Max Eichhorn, *The GI's Rabbi: World War II Letters of David Max Eichhorn*, ed. Greg Palmer and Mark S. Zaid (Lawrence: University Press of Kansas, 2004), pp. 188–190.

10 Simon Chilewich, Letter to Family, 1945

Simon Chilewich and his immediate family managed to escape Poland on the eve of World War II. Chilewich's father, a successful Russian-born merchant based in Warsaw, gained entry visas from the US State Department and the entire family arrived in New York City in September 1939. Chilewich was educated in Poland and at the London School of Economics, and worked as a manager in a leather factory outside of Asheville, North Carolina, before joining the US Army in 1944. Fluent in English, Polish, Russian, and German, Chilewich served as a sergeant in a special army intelligence unit that interrogated German prisoners of war. As the war drew to an end in Europe, Chilewich disguised himself as a Russian officer – Major Andrenko – in order to gain the necessary authority to hasten the surrender of German forces in Leipzig. While impersonating a Soviet officer, he also took it upon himself to ensure the Germans provided badly needed medical care to Holocaust survivors. In this letter to his family, Chilewich describes his joy at being able to provide several survivors of Hitler's death camps with a traditional Friday night kiddush meal, and how this experience has aged him. The letter opens by commenting on the hope he and his father shared for a better postwar world and the efforts at the international conference held in San Francisco, California, to establish the United Nations.

Germany 14 May 1945

My Dear Folks,

Thanks God today received several of your letters. I was so excited that although there were several of them I read them all twice and have put some aside for another going over.

First, thanks very much for your birthday greetings. I knew very well that you remembered the 25 April and was quite flattered with Daddy's defense to the San Francisco Conference. Just because we are on the subject of this conference it is my opinion from the few observations which I was able to make in Europe and in Germany in particular, that the purpose and results of this conference are of primary importance for world peace.—It is my extreme hope that the guidance of the delegates will be able to devise a true machinery to preserve peace in Europe but present developments certainly point to it that the problem is a very complicated one and so far at least— there seems to be a considerable lack of this understanding.—Personally I was rather sorry to see that the agenda is clouded up with relatively insig- nificant problems which may, I hope not, effect to some extent the solving of major issues.

Well lets stop talking about San Francisco—which you probably talk all day long about it—and lets come back to my birthday (After all also an important matter—I am sure for Kobele it definitely was once 26 years ago).

I wrote you already that I had a few "goodies" from you and from England, and since on the 25 we were traveling, — on the 26 we got to celebrate.

Now comes something interesting. I spent my birthday in Germany in the company of a few soldier friends and Jewish girls. Yes just that. Jewish girls, ex Auschwitz Concentration camp inmates, by some ten miracles saved their lives from total brutality and gangsterism. They were all young 18–22 years originally from Czechoslovakia and Hungary. It was a small group of girls who were able to successfully manage an escape from the labor detail the Nazis were evacuating a few days before the arrival of U.S. troops and so they lived to tell the tail [sic]. I … [can]not to tell you what it meant to me to see these girls — sit and talk with them. In our small way we have done what we could for the girls — but although they were hungry and almost naked they were only interested in one thing … a friendly Jewish hand. It was a definite thrill for me to notice that although young and having lived through so much the girls had such a hunger for everything that was Jewish.

I can't describe to you what it meant and how it felt being with them — it was about the best treat I could imagine for my birthday. Suddenly I felt abt. 20 years older — as a Father to all of them and it certainly felt very bad within me to know how little we can for these saved souls. First we visited the manager of the factory which has employed them — and have seen to it that they got fed as human beings and not only the watery soup which they have been getting for years and which was still being dished out to them despite the presence of American authorities. In this connection I found out with the help of Major Andrenko (about whom I will tell you a lot some other time) that the Germans do not understand requests—but they do listen to strict and clear cut orders. We therefore did not request but ordered a menu for the girls and I can tell you that within hours they had everything including chocolate and cigarettes and also apologize that they had only a choice between butter or jam. Not a pound of this food was given by the Allies — it was all provided by the Germans and evidently it was there. A few trips here and there provided clothes for the girls including under-wear, silk stockings, leather shoes etc. The climax was reached when we brought some wine and held Kiddish for them on Friday night. Well I better not start to than to describe it all to you because one has to be a poet to describe the looks, emotions, happiness and thrill. As a guest of honor on this Friday evening we had DR. ISAAK ALTER, a young Polish doctor from Poland whom I met in a hospital and who quietly approached me with the question "*Seit et's a yid?*" [Are you Jewish?] Conversation revealed that he had faked papers and was hiding as an aryan in Lodz from where he was ordered to go to ... ., Germany to take care of a department for foreigners. We inspected his ward consisting for all sorts of half alive patients, Poles, Russians, French, some Jews mostly Prisoners of war and Concentration camp inmates. What this doctor went through in his private life and in con-nection with curing of his patients is beyond description. Any film which I have so far seen paying tribute to men in white is underestimating his work and efforts. When he stood there in the middle of the ward surrounded by beds on which half alive people were looking at him with eyes of hope and confidence—and how he distributed smiles — instead of food — and good words instead of medicine—compared only with an angel who brings com-fort but realizes the hopelessness of the situation. And have also — in spite of the presence of American troops the war criminal management of the hospital continued their previous practice of depriving the patients of food and medicine in fact of the necessary treatments and operations. A visit of Major Andrenko, I assure quickly altered the situation and believe me it was a great satisfaction to see the next day smiling faces of the patients because the first time in years they were properly fed.

Believe me the patients got 3 full meals a day including 70 gr. butter, 300 gr. meat, white bread, coffee and even wine and glucose. For your informa-tion these normal rations consisted of 7 gr. butter, 250 gr. bread and 1 liter soup per day. The ward now has a normal number of good nurses and 3 doctors except Alter — and so we hope — that maybe some of the poor people will again see life. However, this all is such a fraction — such a drop in the ocean and there would be so much more good which we could do comparatively without any trouble or effort, definitely without any cost, if only we had the [understanding?] on German psychology and forgot their crocodile tears and experiences of sorrow and regret to the extent that we turn around and start having pity for the Germans.

From the papers and reports I see that there are various economic approaches on how to occupy Germany and undoubtedly the delegates of San Francisco have much better qualifications to judge the matter better than myself — but it seems to me that a part of Mein Kampf Hitler has won for Germany. Germany is in a way the richest country on the continent — they have much more of everything than France & Belgium and undoubtedly more than Holland and Poland. You will therefore understand that it burns one up even to read about a possibility of our distributing food reserves in Germany. I hope that it will never come to the point or else they will have really won a great victory. Knowing how beautifully they have misrepresented the true picture to the occupying authorities and believe me they are experts in misrepresentation. Personally, I do not doubt that all their statistics of food are fictitious — since my small experience has shown me that every household has still some food reserves back since 1941 and 1942...

Source: Unpublished letter from photocopy of original letter, personal collection of editor.

Study Questions

1   Were the fears Rabbi Ferdinand M. Isserman expressed in 1933 regarding the fate of German Jewry justified? How did US public officials react to the persecution of European Jewry prior to 1939?
2   Compare and contrast the actions of Breckinridge Long and Myron Taylor with regard to the Holocaust.
3   How much did government and the informed public know about the extent of Nazi crimes against European Jewry prior to 1945?
4   Why did Secretary of the Treasury Morgenthau think the State Department was complicit in Germany's murder of the Jews?
5   How did American GIs respond to the liberation of the concentration and death camps?

Chapter 9   From Strategic Bombing to the Atomic Bomb

1   Albert Einstein, Letter to Franklin D. Roosevelt, 1939

The physicist Albert Einstein's theories of relativity revolutionized understandings of the universe and earned him a Nobel Prize as well as worldwide acclaim. Because he was Jewish, Einstein fled Nazi Germany and accepted an offer to work at the Institute for Advanced Study in Princeton, New Jersey. In 1939, the Hungarian-born physicist Leo Szilard persuaded Einstein to sign this letter to President Roosevelt. Given Einstein's pacifist leanings, he would later regret signing it and the role it played in convincing the American government to begin development of the atomic bomb. At first, the Roosevelt Administration moved slowly to implement the recommendations proposed in the letter, but after the attack on Pearl Harbor the United States initiated the Manhattan Project to build an atomic bomb. American efforts incorporated a team of British scientists who had been working on a similar project in 1941, as well as scores of Jewish refugees who had fled Germany and occupied Europe. Without the influx of this talent, the development of the bomb would have taken much longer and would not likely have been completed by 1945.

The United States in World War II: A Documentary Reader, First Edition.
Edited by G. Kurt Piehler. Editorial material and organization © 2013 Blackwell Publishing Ltd.
Published 2013 by Blackwell Publishing Ltd.

Old Groves Road
Nassau Point
Peconic, Long Island

August 2nd, 1939

F.D. Roosevelt
President of the United States
White House
Washington, D.C.

Sir:

Some recent work by E. Fermi and L. Szilard, which has been communicated to me in manuscript, leads me to expect that the element uranium may be turned into a new and important source of energy in the immediate future. Certain aspects of the situation which has arisen seem to call for watchfulness and, if necessary, quick action on the part of the Administration. I believe therefore that it is my duty to bring to your attention the following facts and recommendations:

In the course of the last four months it has been made probable — through the work of Joliot in France as well as Fermi and Szilard in America — that it may become possible to set up a nuclear chain reaction in a large mass of uranium, by which vast amounts of power and large quantities of new radium-like elements would be generated. Now it appears almost certain that this could be achieved in the immediate future.

This new phenomenon would also lead to the construction of bombs, and it is conceivable — though much less certain — that extremely powerful bombs of a new type may thus be constructed. A single bomb of this type, carried by boat and exploded in a port, might very well destroy the whole port together with some of the surrounding territory. However, such bombs might very well prove to be too heavy for transportation by air.

The United States has only very poor ores of uranium in moderate quantities. There is some good ore in Canada and the former Czechoslovakia, while the most important source of Uranium is Belgian Congo.

In view of this situation you may think it desirable to have some permanent contact maintained between the Administration and the group of physicists working on chain reactions in America. One possible way of achieving this might be for you to entrust with this task a person who has your confidence and who could perhaps serve in an unofficial capacity. His task might comprise the following:

a)   to approach Government Departments, keep them informed of the further development, and put forward recommendations for Government

action, giving particular attention to the problem of securing a supply of
uranium ore for the United States;

b)   to speed up the experimental work, which is at present being carried on
within the limits of the budgets of University laboratories, by providing
funds, if such funds be required, through his contacts with private persons who are willing to make contributions for this cause, and perhaps
also by obtaining the co-operation of industrial laboratories which have
the necessary equipment.

I understand that Germany has actually stopped the sale of uranium from
the Czechoslovakian mines which she has taken over. That she should have
taken such early action might perhaps be understood on the ground that the
son of the German Under-Secretary of State, von Weizsucker is attached to
the Kaiser-Wilhelm-Institut in Berlin where some of the American work on
uranium is now being repeated.

Yours very truly,
Albert Einstein

Source: Franklin D. Roosevelt Library, Hyde Park, New York.

2 US Army Air Force, Air War Plan Division, Excerpts from "Munitions Requirements of the AAF for the Defeat of our Potential Enemies," 1941

*In the opening decades of the twentieth century, military thinkers and leaders
were divided on how airplanes should be used in warfare. Many army and
naval leaders discounted aviation, seeing it merely as an adjunct to existing
forces and doctrine. For instance, battleship admirals stressed the role of
aircraft as a way to scout for the enemy fleet. During the interwar years,
airpower advocates claimed that aviation had the potential to revolutionize
warfare and bring in an element of decisiveness. The Italian army officer and
theorist Giulio Douhet argued that civilians should be deliberately targeted
in order to force an enemy nation to quickly press for peace. In contrast, the
US Army Air Force developed a doctrine of strategic bombing that eschewed
the targeting of civilians and stressed the destruction of the enemy's vital
centers, such as key factories, in order to achieve victory. This doctrine led
the Army Air Force to procure the heavily armed B-17 aircraft and the
Norden bomb sight that increased the accuracy of aerial bombing. A few
months before the attack on Pearl Harbor, a team of Army Air Force officers
assigned to the newly developed Air War Plans Division (AWPD) developed
what was widely known as AWPD/1 as part of a large Victory Plan that*

President Roosevelt asked the War and Navy Departments to prepare.
It should be noted that the British had already switched their air operations
strategy. In the opening years of the war, the Royal Air Force had avoided
striking civilian targets, but after London was bombed by German aircraft
during the Battle of Britain in 1940, it retaliated by engaging in area
bombing of enemy cities. Through much of the war the Army Air
Force focused on many targets highlighted in this plan, with varying
degrees of success.

Munitions Requirements of the AAF for the Defeat of our Potential Enemies (AWPD/1)

...

2. *Air Mission*:
    a. To wage a sustained air offensive against German military power, supplemented by air offensives against other regions under enemy control which contribute toward that power (ABC-1).
    b. To support a final offensive, if it becomes necessary to invade the continent.
    c. In addition, to conduct effective air operations in connection with Hemisphere Defense and a strategic defensive in the Far East.
3. *Situation*:
    a. The center of the Axis system is in Germany. Hence, that is where pressure must be applied ultimately. Italy has been relegated to a position of secondary importance.
    b. The German offensive against Russia and other German war operations have placed a considerable strain upon the economic structure of the Reich, and the Russian Campaign has engaged a major portion of the German Army and most of the German Air Force in Eastern Europe.
    c. The declaration of war by Germany against Russia improved the conditions for enforcing the sea blockade and the means of applying pressure through economic warfare. Even in the event of Russian collapse, the German economic structure will continue to operate under heavy strain, and there will be a period of at least a year before [the] Russian economy could be resuscitated and incorporated into the German system.
    d. The extent of the economic strain on Germany is indicated by the following: at present there are 6 ½ million men under arms in the Germany Army, 1 million in the German Navy, and 1 ½ million in the

German Air Force. Behind this armed front there are 8 ½ million men engaged in armaments works alone, about half of whom are working in steel industries. Nearly 17 million men are directly engaged in this war, to the exclusion of all normal civil pursuits and production. Hence, there is a very heavy drain on the social and economic structure of the state. Destruction of that structure will virtually break down the capacity of the German nation to wage war. The basic conception on which this plan is based lies in the application of air power for the breakdown of the industrial and economic structure of Germany. This conception involves the selection of a system of objectives vital to continued German war effort, and to the means of livelihood of the German people, and tenaciously *concentrating all bombing* toward the destruction of those objectives. The most effective manner of conducting such a decisive offensive is by the destruction of precise objectives, at least initially. As German morale begins to crack, area bombing of civil concentrations may be effective.

e. It is improbable that a land invasion can be carried out against Germany proper within the next three years. If the air offensive is successful, a land offensive may not be necessary. Our air bases in England and elsewhere must be made secure, primarily by ground forces, and the lines of communication by sea must also be made secure.

4.

a. *Possible Lines of Action.* Based on an analysis of military and economic factors, the following lines of action for an air offensive can be set up for consideration.

(1) *Lines of action whose accomplishment will accomplish the air mission in Europe.*

(a) Disruption of a major portion of the Electric Power System of Germany.

(b) Disruption of the German transportation system.

(c) Destruction of the German oil and petroleum system.

(d) Undermining of German morale by air attack of civil concentrations.

(2) *Lines of action representing intermediate objectives, whose accomplishment may be essential to the accomplishment of the principal objectives listed above.*

(a) Neutralization of the German Air Force.

(1) By attack of its bases.

(2) By attack of aircraft factories.
(engine and airframe)

(3) By attack of aluminum and magnesium factories.

5. *Discussion of Possible Lines of Action. ...*
   f.   *Morale.* Timeliness of attack is most important in the conduct of air operations directly against civil morale. If the morale of the people is already low because of sustained suffering and deprivation and because the people are losing faith in the ability of the armed forces to win a favorable decision, then heavy and sustained bombing of cities may crush that morale entirely. However, if these conditions do not exist, then area bombing of cities may actually stiffen the resistance of the population, especially if the attacks are weak and sporadic. Hence, no specific number of targets is set up for this task. Rather it is believed that the entire bombing effort might be applied toward this purpose when it becomes apparent that the proper psychological conditions exist. ...

Source: Haywood S. Hansell, Jr., *The Air Plan That Defeated Hitler* (Atlanta: Self-Published, 1972), pp. 298–300, 304–305.

3 Pius XII, Memorandum on Bombing of Civilians, and Myron Taylor, Informal Notes for Discussion with Msgr. Montini, 1942

Most Americans raised few objections to the air war against either Germany or Japan. The US Air Force in Europe relied on strategic bombing of military targets as well as factories, transportation facilities, and oil refineries. It coordinated attacks with the Royal Air Force that centered on night-time area bombing, which deliberately sought to attack civilian housing. Later in the war, the American Air Force switched from strategic bombing to area bombing of Japanese cities that would produce enormous casualties. It is estimated that 100,000 civilians died during the Tokyo fire raids of March 1945. Religious leaders – although not uniformly – were among the few persistent critics of aerial bombing that threatened civilians. During the war, both publicly and privately, Pope Pius XII urged combatants to follow the just war tradition and avoid deliberate attacks on civilians, especially in the case of aerial bombing. Pius XII also unsuccessfully appealed to American and British officials to spare Rome from bombing and protested when bombs landed on papal territory outside of the Vatican. The following excerpt from the Roosevelt Papers deals with appeals by Pius in September 1942 to Roosevelt through his personal representative, Myron Taylor. Taylor not only passed on the memorandum from Pius to FDR, but also summarized his conversation with the Vatican official, Monsignor Montini, who later became Pope Paul VI.

MEMORANDUM OF HIS HOLINESS POPE PIUS XII
RE BOMBING CIVILIAN POPULATIONS
SEPTEMBER 26 1942

The Holy See has always been, and still is greatly preoccupied, out of a heart filled with constant solicitude, with the fate of civil populations defenseless against the aggressions of war.

Since the outbreak of the present conflict no year has passed, that We have not appealed in Our public utterances to all the belligerents, — men who also have human hearts moulded by a mother's love — to show some feeling of pity and charity for the sufferings of civilians, for helpless women and children, for the sick and the aged, on whom a rain of terror, fire, destruction and havoc pours down out of a guiltless sky. (Nov. 1940, Easter 1941). Our appeal was little heeded, as the world knows, and tens of thousands know to their own personal grief.

Now We have been asked to take occasion of this visit of Your Excellency to repeat Our appeal in a personal way, and ask you to carry it to your esteemed President of the United States, of whom Your Excellency is so worthy and so valued a Representative. To refuse to comply with such a request would seem to bespeak little confidence in the noble sentiments of Christian brotherhood and generous sympathy for innocent victims of wrong, of which Your Excellency and the President have given conspicuous proof.

We lay Our appeal, therefore, before you in behalf of countless human beings, children of our one, same Father in heaven; and if aerial bombardments must continue to form part of this harrowing war, let them with all possible care be directed only against objects of military value and spare the homes of non-combattants [sic] and the treasured shrines of art and religion.

INFORMAL NOTES OF MR. TAYLOR FOR DISCUSSION WITH MSGR. MONTINI ON SUNDAY, SEPTEMBER 27, 1942, ON THE SUBJECT OF BOMBING

I am not clear whether the Holy See has condemned the bombing of London, Warsaw, Rotterdam, Belgrade, Coventry, Manila, Pearl Harbor, and places in the South Pacific. A list, together with photographs of Catholic Church property in England damaged by German bombs up to February 1, 1941, is attached.

It might be misunderstood, now that the United Nations are strong enough to bomb military objectives in Germany, to raise the question, because there will be many conflicting reactions. Of course, civilian populations will suffer because of the very character of bombing itself, as it can not be controlled as can some other features of war making; but it is not intended that the United Nations would engage in indiscriminate bombing as was done in the British towns and is evidenced by the long list of hospitals, churches, private residences, and commercial centers which a visit to those communities will indicate. That is especially true in London, where the whole region around St. Paul's is leveled to the ground and where no military objectives existed; nor did munition production plants exist in that area. There is the danger of the Vatican's being called partisan. It has already been called so. Deplorable inhumanities in Germany against civilian populations are even more reprehensible than the attacks on all her neighbors whom she invaded. The Germans set a pattern for ruthlessness; the United Nations have not initiated it nor copied it. The Germans deliberately bombed many of the peaceful cathedral towns of England. The United Nations have no such objective. Their objectives are carefully planned. The civilian population in military areas, munition and vital transportation centers, have been warned and should leave those centers. The workmen in the military and munition plants in those areas are as truly military as those at the front line of battle. Now that the rising power of the United Nations' air forces has exceeded that of Germany, it might be interpreted that pressure was being exerted by the Axis on the Holy See in an effort to limit an important military arm which the United Nations did not introduce in this war but to sap its strength and render it ineffective in the face of German military claims that through air alone would the war be won. We quote:

"All German authorities who have dealt with the subject have made it clear that they believe air superiority to be decisive. General Goering, speaking on January 11th, 1941, said: 'When you consider the power of the Luftwaffe, no one can doubt the issue of the war.' Major Wolf Bley, the German air expert, said on June 27th last: 'The Axis leaders have turned the decisive importance of the Luftwaffe into a weapon which ensures victory.' Field-Marshal Kesselring, of the Luftwaffe, when asked in April, 1941, which weapon of war would prove decisive, replied: 'The air arm must decide the issue. We shall regard the Luftwaffe's aim as achieved when military occupation can follow more or less without fighting.' Hitler evidently considered overwhelming air power to be decisive when he referred to the projected conquest of Britain in 1940 with the words: 'There are no longer any islands.'"

I shall undertake (1) to discourage, in London and Washington, indiscriminate bombing and to urge that targets be confined to munitions plants and communication centers; (2) to have the public warned to move away from danger zones.

Source: File: "Bombing of Rome," Vatican Diplomatic Relations, Box 51 President Secretary's File, Franklin D. Roosevelt Library, Hyde, Park, New York.

4 Interim Committee, Excerpt from Notes of Meeting, 1945

*The Manhattan Project did produce an atomic bomb, but not until after
Germany surrendered. At the urging of Secretary of War Henry Stimson,
President Harry S. Truman created an ad hoc committee shortly after he assumed
the presidency in April 1945 to consider the future of the atomic bomb in the
postwar era as well as the question of how the bomb should be used in the present
war. For members of the Interim Committee, which included senior government
officials like Stimson and Secretary of State James Byrnes, as well as scientists
such as Karl Compton and James Conant, who had advised the Roosevelt and
Truman Administrations on science policy, there was little doubt the bomb
should be used. It should be added that a number of scientists who worked on
the Manhattan Project did have reservations about using the bomb on the civilian
populations of Japan, but their protests had little impact on the final decision.*

NOTES OF THE INTERIM COMMITTEE MEETING
FRIDAY, 1 JUNE 1945
11:00 A.M - 12:30 P.M., 1:45 P.M.- 3:30 P.M.

PRESENT:

Members of the Committee
Secretary Henry L. Stimson, Chairman
Hon. Ralph A. Bard
Dr. Vannevar Bush
Hon. James F. Byrnes
Hon. William L. Clayton
Dr. Karl T. Compton
Dr. James B. Conant
Mr. George L. Harrison
Invited Industrialists
Mr. George H. Bucher, President
of Westinghouse – manufacture
of equipment for the electromagnetic process.
Mr. Walter S. Carpenter, President of Du Pont Company –
construction of the Hanford Project.
Mr. James Rafferty, Vice President of Union Carbide –
construction and operation of gas diffusion plant in Clinton.
Mr. James White, President of Tennessee Eastman – production
of basic chemicals and construction of the RDX plant at
Holston, Tennessee.

By Invitation
General George C. Marshall
Major Gen. Leslie H. Groves
Mr. Harvey H. Bundy
Mr. Arthur Page

... USE OF THE BOMB:

Mr. Byrnes recommended, and the Committee agreed, that the Secretary of War should be advised that, while recognizing that the final selection of the target was essentially a military decision, the present view of the Committee was that the bomb should be used against Japan as soon as possible; that it be used on a war plant surrounded by workers' homes; and that it be used without prior warning. It was the understanding of the Committee that the (plutonium?) small bomb would be used in the test and that the large bomb (gun mechanism) would be used in the first strike over Japan....

... PUBLICITY:

Mr. Harrison pointed out that the discussions and tentative conclusions of yesterday's meetings had already rendered obsolete the draft Presidential statement prepared by Arthur Page. In the past few days the Secretary [of War] had held discussions with Generals Marshall and Arnold concerning targets and would probably discuss this question further with Admiral King and General Marshall. This Committee was not considered competent to make a final decision on the matter of targets, this being a military decision. Accordingly, Mr. Harrison suggested that he be empowered by the Committee to confer with those members of the Committee who would be available as the situation with regard to targets developed and to have prepared new draft statements for the consideration of the full Committee at its next meeting.

Source: Notes on Meeting of the Interim Committee, June 1, 1945, Miscellaneous Historical Documents Collection, Harry S. Truman, Independence, Missouri. Available online at www.trumanlibrary.org/whistlestop/study_collections/bomb/large/index.php.

5 Senior Military Advisors, Excerpts from Minutes of Meeting, 1945

In this meeting to consider the future strategy in the war against Japan, Truman's chief advisors did not see one single factor as ending the war in June 1945. Instead, his advisors, especially General George Marshall, saw a land invasion of Japan as essential; equally important, Marshall stressed the need to ensure the Soviet Union entered the war. In assessing the decision of whether the atomic bomb should have been used against Japanese civilians, historians have debated the cost in American lives of a land invasion of Japan. Some historians argue that the destruction of two Japanese cities and the killing of thousands of civilians saved hundreds of thousands of American lives. Although one can never be certain what the casualties of an invasion of the home island would have been, the estimate of possible casualties in this first phase of the projected invasion of Japan is quite modest compared to the numbers that have been cited by some advocates for the use of the bomb.

Minutes of Meeting held at the White House on Monday, 18 June 1945 at 1530

PRESENT

The President
Fleet Admiral William D. Leahy
Fleet Admiral E. J. King
General of the Army G. C. Marshall

Lieut. General I. C. Eaker [Army Air Force]
    (Representing General of the Army H. H. Arnold)
The Secretary of War, Mr. Stimson
The Secretary of the Navy, Mr. Forrestal
The Assistant Secretary of War, Mr. McCloy

SECRETARY

Brig. General A. J. McFarland
...

THE PRESIDENT stated that he had called the meeting for the purpose of informing himself with respect to the details of the campaign against Japan set out in Admiral Leahy's memorandum to the Joint Chiefs of Staff of 14 June. He asked General Marshall if he would express his opinion.

GENERAL MARSHALL pointed out that the present situation with respect to operations against Japan was practically identical with the situation which had existed in connection with the operations proposed against Normandy. He then read, as an expression of his views, the following digest of a memorandum prepared by the Joint Chiefs of Staff for presentation to the President (J.C.S. 1388):

Our air and sea power has already greatly reduced movement of Jap shipping south of Korea and should in the next few months cut it to a trickle if not choke it off entirely. Hence, there is no need for seizing further positions in order to block Japanese communications south of Korea.

General MacArthur and Admiral Nimitz are in agreement with the Chiefs of Staff in selecting 1 November as the target date to go into Kyushu because by that time.

a.   If we press preparations we can be ready.
b.   Our estimates are that our air action will have smashed practically every industrial target worth hitting in Japan as well as destroying huge areas in the Jap cities.
c.   The Japanese Navy, if any still exists, will be completely powerless.
d.   Our sea action and air power will have cut Jap reinforcement capabilities from the mainland to negligible proportions.

Important considerations bearing on the 1 November date rather than a later one are the weather and cutting to a minimum Jap time for preparation of defenses. If we delay much after the beginning of November the weather situation in the succeeding months may be such that the invasion of Japan, and hence the end of the war, will be delayed for up to 6 months.

An outstanding military point about attacking Korea is the difficult terrain and beach conditions which appear to make the only acceptable assault areas Fusan in the southeast corner and Keijo, well up the western side. To get to Fusan, which is a strongly fortified area, we must move large and vulnerable assault forces past heavily fortified Japanese areas. The operation appears more difficult and costly than assault on Kyushu. Keijo appears an equally difficult and costly operation. After we have undertaken either one of them we still will not be as far forward as going into Kyushu.

The Kyushu operation is essential to a strategy of strangulation and appears to be the least costly worth-while operation following Okinawa. The basic point is that a lodgement in Kyushu is essential, both to tightening our strangle hold of blockade and bombardment on Japan, and to forcing capitulation by invasion of the Tokyo Plain.

We are bringing to bear against the Japanese every weapon and all the force we can employ and there is no reduction in our maximum possible application of bombardment and blockade, while at the same time we are pressing invasion preparations. It seems that if the Japanese are ever willing to capitulate short of complete military defeat in the field they will do it when faced by the completely hopeless prospect occasioned by (1) destruction already wrought by air bombardment and sea blockade, coupled with (2) a landing on Japan indicating the firmness of our resolution, and also perhaps coupled with (3) the entry or threat of entry of Russia into the war.

With reference to clean-up of the Asiatic mainland, our objective should be to get the Russians to deal with the Japs in Manchuria (and Korea if necessary) and to vitalize the Chinese to a point where, with assistance of American air power and some supplies, they can mop out their own country.

Casualties. Our experience in the Pacific war is so diverse as to casualties that it is considered wrong to give any estimates in numbers. Using various combinations of Pacific experience, the War Department staff reaches the conclusion that the cost of securing a worthwhile position in Korea would almost certainly be greater than the cost of the Kyushu operation. Points on the optimistic side of the Kyushu operation are that: General MacArthur has not yet accepted responsibility for going ashore where there would be disproportionate casualties. The nature of the objective area gives room for maneuver, both on the land and by sea. As to any discussion of specific operations, the following data are pertinent:

Campaign	U.S. Casualties Killed, wounded, missing	Jap Casualties Killed and Prisoners (Not including wounded)	Ratio U.S. to Jap
Leyte	17,000	78,000	1:4.6
Luzon	31,000	156,000	1:5.0
Iwo Jima	20,000	25,000	1:1.25
Okinawa	34,000 (Ground)	81,000	1:2
	7,700 (Navy)	(not a complete count)	
Normandy (1st 30 days)	42,000		

The record of General MacArthur's operations from 1 March 1944 through 1 May 1945 shows U.S. 13,742 killed compared to 310,165 Japanese killed, or a ratio of 22 to 1.

There is reason to believe that the first 30 days in Kyushu should not exceed the price we have paid for Luzon. It is a grim fact that there is not an easy, bloodless way to victory in war and it is the thankless task of the leaders to maintain their firm outward front which holds the resolution of their subordinates. Any irresolution in the leaders may result in costly weakening and indecision in the subordinates. It was this basic difficulty with the Prime Minister [Winston Churchill] which clouded and hampered all our preparations for the cross-channel operation now demonstrated as having been essential to victory in Europe.

An important point about Russian participation in the war is that the impact of Russian entry on the already hopeless Japanese may well be the decisive action levering them into capitulation at that time or shortly thereafter if we land in Japan.

In considering the matter of command and control in the Pacific war which the British wish to raise at the next conference, we must bear in mind the point that anything smacking of combined command in the Pacific might increase the difficulties with Russia and perhaps with China. Furthermore the obvious inefficiencies of combined command may directly result in increased cost in resources and American lives....

Source: "Minutes of Meeting Held at the White House on Monday, 18 June 1945 at 1530," Top Secret Source: Record Group 218, Records of the Joint Chiefs of Staff, Central Decimal Files, 1942–1945, Box 198 334 JCS (2-2-45) Mtg 186th–194th. Also available online on the website of the National Security Archive, George Washington University, at http://www.gwu.edu/~nsarchiv/NSAEBB/NSAEBB162.

6 Heads of Governments, United States, China, and the United Kingdom, Potsdam Declaration, 1945

At the last meeting of the Big Three of World War II – Harry S. Truman, Winston Churchill, and Joseph Stalin – at Potsdam, Germany, in July 1945, significant divisions emerged between the Western Allies and the Soviet Union. But the need to defeat Japan still remained paramount in the eyes of Truman, and at Potsdam the Soviet Union confirmed that it would soon enter the war against Japan. During the conference, the United States and the United Kingdom, with the agreement of China, issued the Potsdam declaration demanding the surrender of Japan. This policy was not new, but adhered to Franklin D. Roosevelt's policy of unconditional surrender first announced at the Casablanca Conference with Prime Minister Churchill in 1943.

PROCLAMATION BY THE HEADS OF GOVERNMENTS, UNITED STATES, CHINA, AND THE UNITED KINGDOM

(1) We, the President of the United States, the President of the National Government of the Republic of China and the Prime Minister of Great Britain, representing the hundreds of millions of our countrymen, have conferred and agree that Japan shall be given an opportunity to end this war.

(2)   The prodigious land, sea and air forces of the United States, the British
       Empire and of China, many times reinforced by their armies and air
       fleets from the west are poised to strike the final blows upon Japan.
       This military power is sustained and inspired by the determination of
       all the Allied nations to prosecute the war against Japan until she
       ceases to resist.

(3)   The result of the futile and senseless German resistance to the might of
       the aroused free peoples of the world stands forth in awful clarity as
       an example to the people of Japan. The might that now converges on
       Japan is immeasurably greater than that which, when applied to the
       resisting Nazis, necessarily laid waste to the lands, the industry and the
       method of life of the whole German people. The full application of our
       military power, backed by our resolve, *will* mean the inevitable and
       complete destruction of the Japanese armed forces and just as inevita-
       bly the utter devastation of the Japanese homeland.

(4)   The time has come for Japan to decide whether she will continue to be
       controlled by those self-willed milita[r]istic advisers whose unintelli-
       gent calculations have brought the Empire of Japan to the threshold of
       annihilation, or whether she will follow the path of reason.

(5)   Following are our terms. We will not deviate from them. There are no
       alternatives. We shall brook no delay.

(6)   There must be eliminated for all time the authority and influence of
       those who have deceived and misled the people of Japan into embark-
       ing on world conquest, for we insist that a new order of peace, security
       and justice will be impossible until irresponsible militarism is driven
       from the world.

(7)   Until such a new order is established *and* until there is convincing
       proof that Japan's war-making power is destroyed, points in Japanese
       territory to be designated by the Allies shall be occupied to secure the
       achievement of the basic objectives we are here setting forth.

(8)   The terms of the Cairo Declaration shall be carried out and Japanese
       sovereignty shall be limited to the islands of Honshu, Hokkaido,
       Kyushu, Shikoku and such minor islands as we determine.

(9)   The Japanese military forces, after being completely disarmed, shall be
       permitted to return to their homes with the opportunity to lead peace-
       ful and productive lives.

(10)   We do not intend that the Japanese shall be enslaved as a race or
       destroyed as [a] nation, but stern justice shall be meted out to all war
       criminals, including those who have visited cruelties upon our prison-
       ers. The Japanese Government shall remove all obstacles to the revival
       and strength[en]ing of democratic tendencies among the Japanese

people. Freedom of speech, of religion, and of thought, as well as respect for the fundamental human rights shall be established.

(11) Japan shall be permitted to maintain such industries as will sustain her economy and permit the exaction of just reparations in kind, but not those industries which would enable her to re-arm for war. To this end, access to, as distinguished from control of raw materials shall be permitted. Eventual Japanese participation in world trade relations shall be permitted.

(12) The occupying forces of the Allies shall be withdrawn from Japan as soon as these objectives have been accomplished and there has been established in accordance with the freely expressed will of the Japanese people a peacefully inclined and responsible government.

(13) We call upon the Government of Japan to proclaim now the unconditional surrender of all the Japanese armed forces, and to provide proper and adequate assurances of their good faith in such action. The alternative for Japan is prompt and utter destruction.

POTSDAM July 26, 1945 ...

Source: US Department of State, *Foreign Relations of the United States: The Conference of Berlin*, 2 vols. (Washington, DC: Government Printing Office, 1960), Vol. 2, pp. 1474–1476.

7 Henry Stimson, Diary Excerpts, 1945

The dropping of atomic bombs on Hiroshima and Nagasaki, as well as the entry of the Soviet Union into the Pacific War on August 8, 1945, empowered the peace faction in the Japanese government, which recognized the war was lost. Moreover, Soviet troops met with spectacular success in Manchuria and Japanese military positions were quickly overrun. In fact, there were some concerns in the American government that the Soviet Union might join the land invasion of Japan and have a legitimate claim to an occupation zone on the home islands. At the same time, neither the atomic bomb nor the Soviet entry into the war was decisive enough to compel an immediate Japanese surrender without guarantees for the future of the emperor. As this excerpt from the diary of Secretary of War Henry Stimson conveys, there existed significant disagreement within the American government over modifying the Potsdam Declaration and allowing the emperor to remain on the throne. In the end, while Japan itself surrendered unconditionally, it was given assurances that the imperial institution would be retained by the Allied Powers. Moreover, Emperor Hirohito, while stripped of his political power, was allowed to remain on the throne and was never charged or tried for any war crimes, despite the fact that he retained ultimate control of the Japanese government during the war. Even though a number of senior Japanese leaders were tried by the Tokyo War Crimes Tribunal set up by the Allies after Japan's surrender, Emperor Hirohito was never even called to testify before it.

Friday, August 10, 1945

Today was momentous. We had all packed up and the car was waiting to take us to the airport where we were headed for our vacation when word came from Colonel McCarthy at the Department that the Japanese had made an offer to surrender. Furthermore they had announced it in the clear. That busted our holiday for the present and I raced down to the office, getting there before half past eight. There I read the messages. Japan accepted the Potsdam list of terms put out by the President "with the understanding that the said declaration does not comprise any demand which prejudices the prerogatives of his majesty as a sovereign ruler". It is curious that this was the very single point that I feared would make trouble. When the Potsdam conditions were drawn and left my office where they originated, they contained a provision which permitted the continuance of the dynasty with certain conditions. The President and Byrnes struck that out. They were not obdurate on it but thought they could arrange it in the necessary secret negotiations which would take place after any armistice. There has been a good deal of uninformed agitation against the Emperor in this country mostly by people who know no more about Japan than has been given them by Gilbert and Sullivan's "Mikado", and I found today that curiously enough it had gotten deeply embedded in the minds of influential people in the State Department. Harry Hopkins is a strong anti-Emperor man in spite of his usual good sense and so are Archibald MacLeish and Dean Acheson – three very extraordinary men to take such a position.

As soon as I got to the Department I called up Connolly at the White House and notified him that I was not going away and would be standing by if he wanted me. Not more than ten minutes afterwards they called back to say that the President would like me to come right over, so I hurried around there and joined in the conference consisting of the President, Byrnes, Forrestal, Admiral Leahy, and the President's aides. Byrnes was troubled and anxious to find out whether we could accept this in light of the public statements by Roosevelt and Truman. Of course during three years of a bitter war there have been bitter statements made about the Emperor. Now they come to plague us. Admiral Leahy took a good plain horse-sense position that the question of the Emperor was a minor matter compared with delaying a victory in the war which was now in our hands.

The President then asked me what my opinion was and I told him that I thought that even if the question hadn't been raised by the Japanese we would have to continue the Emperor ourselves under our command and supervision in order to get into surrender the many scattered armies of the Japanese who would own no other authority and that something like this use of the Emperor must be made in order to save us from a score of bloody Iwo Jima and Okinawas all over China and the New Netherlands. He was the only source of authority in Japan under the Japanese theory of the State. I also suggested that something like an armistice over the settlement of the question was inevitable and that it would be a humane thing and the thing that might effect the settlement if we stopped the bombing during that time – stopped it immediately. My last suggestion was rejected on the ground that it couldn't be done at once because we had not yet received in official form the Japanese surrender, having nothing but the interception to give it to us, and that so far as we were concerned the war was still going on. This of course was a correct but narrow reason, for the Japanese had broadcast their offer of surrender through every country in the world. After considerable discussion we adjourned to wait the arrival of the final notice.

When we adjourned Byrnes and I went into another room to discuss the form of the paper and I told him the desire of Marshall to have one of the conditions of our negotiations with Japan the surrender of the American prisoners in their hands to some accessible place where we could send planes to get them. By this time the news was out and the howling mob was in front of the White House, access to which by the public was blockaded on Pennsylvania avenue.

I drove back to the Department and entered into conference with Marshall and McCloy who had just returned from his overseas trip while I was at the White House. Bundy, Lovett, and Harrison and I were together and I later called in Colonel Van Slyck who had written the intelligent article I had shown the President the other day on the form of a surrender; and also General Weckerling of G-2 who has not been quite so intelligent on this matter as he might be, together with Mr. Robert A. Kinney and Mr. William R. Braisted who are acting as Japanese experts for the G-2 people. We started in in accordance with a request that Byrnes had made of me at our talk on the drafting of the whole terms of surrender including the answer to the present Japanese offer. On the latter I found for once that McCloy was rather divergent from me. He was intrigued with the idea that this was the opportunity to force upon Japan through the Emperor a program of free speech, etc. and all the elements of American free government. I regarded this as unreal and said that the thing to do was to get this surrender through as quickly as we can before Russia, who has begun invading Manchuria, should get down in reach of the Japanese homeland. I felt it was of great importance to get the homeland into our hands before the Russians could put in any substantial claim to occupy and help rule it. After all this discussion I called Byrnes on the telephone and discussed the matter with him. He told me he had drafted the answer to the Japanese notice and that he would like me to see it. So I sent over Kyle to the Department and got it. While a compromise, it was much nearer my position than McCloy's and after a while McCloy agreed that it was good enough from his standpoint. I thought it was a pretty wise and careful statement and stood a better chance of being accepted than a more outspoken one. It asserted that the action of the Emperor must be dominated by the Allied Commander, using the singular in order to exclude any condominium such as we have in Poland. He had asked me in the morning who was the commander that had been agreed upon among our forces and I told him I thought it was MacArthur although there had been quite an issue between the Army and Navy to have a dual command, MacArthur and Nimitz.

By this time it was lunchtime and I ate a hasty lunch and had to hurry over to the Cabinet meeting at two o'clock.

During the morning Forrestal had called me up for the purpose of telling me he was heart and soul with me in regard to the proposition of shutting off attack and saving life during the time we discussed this. He told me that they were planning another big attack by Halsey and he was afraid this would go on. As a matter of fact, at the present time it is under order to go on.

After a fifteen or twenty minutes delay, which is unusual in this Administration, the President and Byrnes came in from a conference which had been going on in the other room and the President announced to the Cabinet that we had received official notice from Japan through the intermediary, Sweden, and that Byrnes had drawn a reply to it of which they thought they could get an acceptance from Great Britain, China, and perhaps Russia, with all of whom they were communicating. The paper was in the exact form that Byrnes had read me over the telephone and which I told him I approved.

After the Cabinet Byrnes had another talk with me and asked me if we in the War Department could draft the follow-up papers to effectuate the terms of surrender. I told him that if he wanted me to I would start McCloy on it at once and get it ready as soon as possible. He was very grateful.

When I got back to the Department I found McCloy had been working on it all the time we were at Cabinet and with the aid of the draft which had been started by the Staff some time before, he had the papers pretty nearly ready. He read them to me and Marshall and then undertook to perfect them and get them ready for tomorrow morning when I will go over them again and get them off to the State Department.

This has been a pretty heavy day. Leveritt came up and massaged me, and Mabel and I sat on the porch together and tried to cool off after our efforts.

Saturday, August 11, 1945

My rather strenuous efforts yesterday had their consequences in a sleepless night but I am otherwise feeling fairly well. I want to get away. I have been over the terms of surrender papers which were outlined yesterday and drafted last night and they are on their way to Byrnes. The four other powers to have approved the Byrnes form of reply to the Japanese offer. The British rather question the compulsion to sign put on the Emperor. The Chinese were very jubilant and the Russians accepted, but stated that they would like to discuss the Supreme Commander. So thus far it looks as if things were going pretty well. I do not see how the Japanese can hold out against this united front. I am planning to go away now as soon as I can.

Source: Diary entries, Friday and Saturday, August 10 and 11, 1945, Henry Stimson Diary, Manuscripts and Archives, Yale University Library, New Haven, Connecticut. (Also available on microfilm.)

8 Kurt Vonnegut, "Wailing Shall Be in All the Streets," 2008

A native of Indianapolis, Indiana, Kurt Vonnegut was one of America's most highly regarded novelists of the postwar era. As a young infantryman, Vonnegut served only a few days in combat before being captured at the Battle of the Bulge and sent to the German city of Dresden as a prisoner of war. Vonnegut narrowly escaped death during the devastating air raids launched by American and British bombers against the city on February 14–15, 1945. His experience formed the basis for one of his most popular and highly regarded novels, Slaughterhouse Five. *In the following essay, published after his death in 2007, Vonnegut reflects on the question of whether it is morally acceptable to kill civilians deliberately in war-time, especially unarmed women and children.*

It was a routine speech we got during our first day at basic training, delivered by a wiry little lieutenant. "Men, up to now you've been good, clean,

American boys with an American's love for sportsmanship and fair play. We're here to change that. Our job is to make you the meanest, dirtiest bunch of scrappers in the history of the World. From now on you can forget the Marquess of Queensberry Rules and every other set of rules. Anything and everything goes. Never hit a man above the belt when you can kick him below it. Make the bastard scream. Kill him any way you can. Kill, kill, kill, do you understand?

His talk was greeted with nervous laughter and general agreement that he was right. "Didn't Hitler and Tojo say the Americans were a bunch of softies? Ha! They'll find out." And of course, Germany and Japan did find out: a toughened-up democracy poured forth a scalding fury that could not be stopped. It was a war of reason against barbarism, supposedly, with the issues at stake on such a high plane that most of our feverish fighters had no idea why they were fighting—other than that the enemy was a bunch of bastards. A new kind of war, with all destruction, all killing approved. Germans would ask, "Why are you Americans fighting us?" "I don't know, but we're sure beating the hell out of you," was a stock answer.

A lot of people relished the idea of total war: it had a modern ring to it, in keeping with our spectacular technology. To them it was like a football game: "Give 'em the axe, the axe, the axe ..." Three small-town merchants' wives, middle-aged and plump, gave me a ride when I was hitch-hiking home from Camp Atterbury. "Did you kill a lot of them Germans?" asked the driver, making cheerful small-talk. I told her I didn't know. This was taken for modesty. As I was getting out of the car, one of the ladies patted me on the shoulder in motherly fashion: "I'll bet you'd like to get over and kill some of them dirty Japs now, wouldn't you?" We exchanged knowing winks. I didn't tell those simple souls that I had been captured after a week at the front; and more to the point, what I knew and thought about killing dirty Germans, about total war. The reason for my being sick at heart then and now has to do with an incident that received cursory treatment in the American newspapers. In February, 1945, Dresden, Germany was destroyed, and with it over one hundred thousand human beings. I was there. Not many know how tough America got.

I was among a group of one hundred and fifty infantry privates, captured in the Bulge breakthrough and put to work in Dresden. Dresden, we were told, was the only major German city to have escaped the bombing so far. That was in January, 1945. She owed her good fortune to her unwarlike countenance: hospitals, breweries, food-processing plants, surgical supply houses, ceramics, musical instrument factories, and the like. Since the war, hospitals had become her prime concern. Every day hundreds of wounded came into the tranquil sanctuary from the east and west. At night we would hear the dull rumble of distant air raids. "Chemnitz is getting it tonight," we used to say, and speculated what it might be like to be under the yawning bomb-bays and the bright young men with their dials and cross-hairs. "Thank heaven we're in an 'open city,'" we thought, and so thought the thousands of refugees—women, children, and old men—who came in a forlorn stream from the smouldering wreckage of Berlin, Leipzig, Breslau, Munich.... They flooded the city to twice its normal population.

There was not war in Dresden. True, planes came over nearly every day and the sirens wailed, but the planes were always en route elsewhere. The alarms furnished a relief period in a tedious work day, a social event, a chance to gossip in the shelters. The shelters, in fact, were not much more than a gesture, casual recognition of the national emergency: wine cellars and basements with benches in them and sand bags blocking the windows, for the most part. There were a few more adequate bunkers in the center of the city, close to the government offices, but nothing like the staunch subterranean fortress that rendered Berlin impervious to her daily pounding. Dresden had no reason to prepare for attack—and thereby hangs a beastly tale.

Dresden was surely among the World's most lovely cities. Her streets were broad, lined with shade-trees. She was sprinkled with countless little parks and statuary. She had marvelous old churches, libraries, museums, theaters, art galleries, beer gardens, a zoo, and a renowned university. It was at one time a tourist's paradise. They would be far better informed on the city's delights than am I. But the impression I have is that in Dresden—in the physical city—were the symbols of the good life; pleasant, honest, and intelligent. In the Swastika's shadow those symbols of the dignity and hope of mankind stood waiting, monuments to truth. The accumulated treasure of hundreds of years, Dresden spoke eloquently of those things excellent in European civilization wherein our debt lies deep. I was a prisoner, hungry, dirty, and full of hate for our captors, but I loved that city and saw the blessed wonder of her past and the rich promise of her future.

In February, 1945, American bombers reduced this treasure to crushed stone and embers; disemboweled her with high-explosives and cremated her with incendiaries. The atom bomb may represent a fabulous advance, but it is interesting to note that primitive TNT and thermite managed to exterminate in one bloody night more people than died in the whole London blitz. Fortress Dresden fired a dozen shots at our airmen. Once back at their bases and sipping hot coffee, they probably remarked, "Flak unusually light tonight. Well, guess it's time to turn in." Captured British pilots from tactical fight units (covering front-line troops) used to chide those who had flown heavy bombers on city raids with, "How on Earth did you stand the stink of boiling urine and burning perambulators?"

A perfectly routine piece of news: "Last night our planes attacked Dresden. All planes returned safely." The only good German is a dead one: over one hundred thousand evil men, women, and children (the able-bodied were at the fronts) forever purged of their sins against humanity. By chance I met a bombardier who had taken part in the attack. "We hated to do it," he told me.

The night they came over we spent in an underground meat locker in a slaughterhouse. We were lucky, for it was the best shelter in town. Giants stalked the Earth above us. First came the soft murmur of their dancing on the outskirts, then the grumbling of their plodding toward us, and finally the ear-splitting crashes of their heels upon us—and thence to the outskirts again. Back and forth they swept: saturation bombing.

"I screamed and I wept and I clawed the walls of our shelter," an old lady told me. "I prayed to God to 'please, please, please, dear God, stop them.' But he didn't hear me. No power could stop them. On they came, wave after wave. There was no way we could surrender; no way to tell them we couldn't stand it anymore. There was nothing anyone could do but sit and wait for morning." Her daughter and grandson were killed.

Our little prison was burned to the ground. We were to be evacuated to an outlying camp occupied by the South African prisoners. Our guards were a melancholy lot, aged Volkssturmers and disabled veterans. Most of them were Dresden residents and had friends and families somewhere in the holocaust. A corporal, who had lost an eye after two years on the Russian front, ascertained before we marched that his wife, his two children, and both of his parents had been killed. He had one cigarette. He shared it with me.

Our march to new quarters took us on the city's edge. It was impossible to believe that anyone survived in its heart. Ordinarily the day would have been cold, but occasional gusts from the colossal inferno made us sweat. And ordinarily the day would have been clear and bright, but an opaque and towering cloud turned noon to twilight. A grim procession clogged the outbound highways; people with blackened faces streaked with tears, some bearing wounded, some bearing dead. They gathered in the fields. None spoke. A few with Red Cross arm-bands did what they could for the casualties.

Settled with the South Africans, we enjoyed a week without work. At the end of it communications were reestablished with higher headquarters and we were ordered to hike seven miles to the area hardest hit. Nothing in the district had escaped the fury. A city of jagged building shells, of splintered statuary and shattered trees; every vehicle stopped, gnarled and burned, left to rust or rot in the path of the frenzied night. The only sounds other than our own were those of falling plaster and their echoes. I cannot describe the desolation properly, but I can give an idea of how it made us feel, in the words of a delirious British soldier in a makeshift P.W. hospital:

"It's frightenin', I tell you. I would walk down one of them bloody streets and feel a thousand eyes on the back of me 'ead. I would 'ear 'em whisperin' behind me. I would turn around to look at 'em and there wouldn't be a bloomin' soul in sight. You can feel 'em and you can 'ear 'em but there's never anybody there." We knew what he said was so.

For "salvage" work we were divided into small crews, each under a guard. Our ghoulish mission was to search for bodies. It was rich hunting that day and the many thereafter. We started on a small scale—here a leg, there an arm, and an occasional baby—but struck a mother lode before noon. We cut our way through a basement wall to discover a reeking hash of over one hundred human beings. Flame must have swept through before the building's collapse sealed the exits, because the flesh of those within resembled the texture of prunes. Our job, it was explained, was to wade into the shambles and bring forth the remains. Encouraged by cuffing and guttural abuse, wade in we did. We did exactly that, for the floor was covered with an unsavory broth from burst water mains and viscera. A number of victims, not killed outright had attempted to escape through a narrow emergency exit. At any rate, there were several bodies packed tightly into the passageway. Their leader had made it halfway up the steps before he was buried up to his neck in falling brick and plaster. He was about fifteen, I think.

It is with some regret that I here besmirch the nobility of our airmen, but boys, you killed an appalling lot of women and children. The shelter I described and innumerable others like it were filled with them. We had to exhume their bodies and carry them to mass funeral pyres in the parks—so I know. The funeral pyre technique was abandoned when it became apparent how great was the toll. There was not enough to do it nicely, so a man with a flamethrower was sent down instead, and he cremated them where they lay. Burned alive, suffocated, crushed—men, women, and children indiscriminately killed. For all the sublimity of the cause for which we fought, we surely created a Belsen of our own. The method was impersonal, but the result was equally cruel and heartless. That, I am afraid, is a sickening truth.

When we had become used to the darkness, the odor, and the carnage, we began musing as to what each of the corpses had been in life. It was a sordid game: "Rich man, poor man, beggar man, thief ..." Some had fat purses and jewelry, others had precious foodstuff. A boy had his dog still leashed to him. Renegade Ukrainians in German uniform were in charge of our operations in the shelters proper. They were roaring drunk from adjacent wine cellars and seemed to enjoy their job hugely. It was a profitable one, for they stripped each body of valuables before we carried it to the street. Death became so commonplace that we could joke about our dismal burdens and cast them about like so much garbage. Not so with the first of them, especially the young: we had lifted them onto stretchers with care, laying them out with some semblance of funeral dignity in their last resting place before the pyre. But our awed and sorrowful propriety gave way, as I said, to rank callousness. At the end of a grisly day we would smoke and survey the impressive heap of dead accumulated. One of us flipped his cigarette butt into the pile: "Hell's bells," he said, "I'm ready for Death anytime he wants to come after me."

A few days after the raid the sirens screamed again. The listless and heart-sick survivors were showered this time with leaflets. I lost my copy of the epic, but remember that it ran something like this: "To the people of Dresden: We were forced to bomb your city because of the heavy military traffic your railroad facilities have been carrying. We realize that we haven't always hit our objectives. Destruction of anything other than military objectives was unintentional, unavoidable fortunes of war." That explained the slaughter to everyone's satisfaction, I am sure, but it aroused no little contempt for the American bomb-sight. It is a fact that forty-eight hours after the last B-17 had droned west for a well-earned rest, labor battalions had swarmed over the damaged rail yards and restored them to nearly normal service. None of the rail bridges over the Elbe was knocked out of commission. Bomb-sight manufacturers should blush to know that their marvelous devices laid bombs down as much as three miles wide of what the military claimed to be aiming for. The leaflet should have said, "We hit every blessed church, hospital, school, museum, theater, your university, the zoo, and every apartment building in town, but we honestly weren't trying hard to do it. C'est la guerre. So sorry. Besides, saturation bombing is all the rage these days, you know."

There was tactical significance: stop the railroads. An excellent maneuver, no doubt, but the technique was horrible. The planes started kicking high-explosives and incendiaries through their bomb-bays at the city limits, and for all the pattern their hits presented, they must have been briefed by a Ouija board. Tabulate the loss against the gain. Over one hundred thousand non-combatants and a magnificent city destroyed by bombs dropped wide of the stated objectives: the railroads were knocked out for roughly two days. The Germans counted it the greatest loss of life suffered in a single raid. The death of Dresden was a bitter tragedy, needlessly and willfully executed. The killing of children—"Jerry" children or "Jap" children, or whatever enemies the future may hold for us—can never be justified.

The facile reply to great groans such as mine is the most hateful of all clichés, "fortunes of war," and another, "They asked for it. All they understand is force." Who asked for it? The only thing who understands is force? Believe me, it is not easy to rationalize the stamping out of vineyards where the grapes of wrath are stored when gathering up babies in bushel baskets or helping a man dig where he thinks his wife may be buried. Certainly enemy military and industrial installations should have been blown flat, and woe unto those foolish enough to seek shelter near them. But the "Get Tough America" policy, the spirit of *revenge*, the approbation of all destruction and killing, has earned us a name for obscene brutality, and cost the World the possibility of Germany's becoming a peaceful and intellectually fruitful nation in anything but the most remote future.

Our leaders had a carte blanche as to what they might or might not destroy. Their mission was to win the war as quickly as possible, and, while they were admirably trained to do just that, their decisions as to the fate of certain priceless World heirlooms—in one case Dresden—were not always judicious. When, late in the war, with the Wehrmacht breaking up on all fronts, our planes were sent to destroy this last major city, I doubt if the question was asked, "How will this tragedy benefit us, and how will that benefit compare with the ill-effects in the long run? Dresden, a beautiful city, built in the art spirit, symbol of an admirable heritage, so anti-Nazi that Hitler visited it but twice during his whole reign, food and hospital center so bitterly needed now—plowed under and salt strewn in the furrows.

There can be no doubt that the Allies fought on the side of right and the Germans and the Japanese on the side of wrong. World War II was fought for near-Holy motives. But I stand convinced that the brand of justice in which we dealt, wholesale bombings of civilian populations, was blasphemous. That the enemy did it first has nothing to do with the moral problem. What I saw of our air war, as the European conflict neared an end, had the earmarks of being an irrational war for war's sake. Soft citizens of the American democracy learned to kick a man below the belt and make the bastard scream.

The occupying Russians, when they discovered that we were Americans, embraced us and congratulated us on the complete desolation our planes had wrought. We accepted their congratulations with good grace and proper modesty, but I felt then as I feel now, that I would have given my life to save Dresden for the World's generations to come. That is how everyone should feel about every city on Earth.

Source: Kurt Vonnegut, "Wailing Shall Be in All the Streets," in *Armageddon in Retrospect and Other New and Unpublished Writings on War and Peace* (New York: G. P. Putnam's Sons, 2008), pp. 32–45.

Study Questions

1   Why did Albert Einstein urge the United States to develop an atomic bomb? In the end, would the atomic bomb be used against Germany?
2   Before the United States entered the war, how did the Army Air Force foresee using air power? Did it plan to make civilians a primary target?
3   What limits does Pius XII want the United States to place on the air campaign against Germany? Were any of them acceptable to the US government?
4   Did American leaders think only the atomic bomb would lead to the Japanese surrender? What other factors were deemed important? What role was the Soviet Union to play?
5   What predictions did military leaders make regarding the invasion of Japan?
6   Why does Kurt Vonnegut condemn the bombing of Dresden? Does he condemn all use of air power?

Chapter 10   Visions of a Postwar World

1 Henry Luce, Excerpt from "The American Century," *Life*, 1941

The New York-based publisher of such influential magazines as Time, Life, *and* Fortune, *Henry Luce exerted tremendous influence over public opinion. Although he was opposed to much of the New Deal, Luce, along with his second wife Clare Boothe Luce, was a committed internationalist who prior to Pearl Harbor favored providing aid to Great Britain in the struggle against Germany. In this article, written for the weekly picture magazine* Life *on the eve of America's entry into World War II, Luce not only called on Americans to embrace internationalism, but also argued that the nation and the world were at a pivotal turning point. In short, average citizens of the republic needed to recognize that the United States had a unique role to play abroad and that this entailed obligations as well as opportunities.*

... In 1919 we had a golden opportunity, an opportunity unprecedented in all history, to assume the leadership of the world—a golden opportunity handed to us on the proverbial silver platter. We did not understand that opportunity. [Woodrow] Wilson mishandled it. We rejected it. The opportunity persisted. We bungled it in the 1920's and in the confusion of the 1930's we killed it.

The United States in World War II: A Documentary Reader, First Edition.
Edited by G. Kurt Piehler. Editorial material and organization © 2013 Blackwell Publishing Ltd.
Published 2013 by Blackwell Publishing Ltd.

To lead the world would never have been an easy task. To revive the hope of that lost opportunity makes the task now infinitely harder than it would have been before. Nevertheless, with the help of all of us, [Franklin D.] Roosevelt must succeed where Wilson failed.

THE 20ᵀᴴ CENTURY IS THE AMERICAN CENTURY

Some facts about our time

Consider the 20ᵗʰ century. It is not only in the sense that we happen to live in it but ours also because it is America's first century as a dominant power in the world. So far, this century of ours has been a profound and tragic disappointment. No other century has been so big with promise for human progress and happiness. And in no one century have so many men and women and children suffered such pain and anguish and bitter death. ...

AMERICA'S VISION OF OUR WORLD

How it shall be created

... It is for America and for America alone to determine whether a system of free economic enterprise—an economic order compatible with freedom and progress—shall or shall not prevail in this century. We know perfectly well that there is not the slightest chance of anything faintly resembling a free economic system prevailing in this country if it prevails nowhere else. What then does America have to decide? Some few decisions are quite simple. For example: we have to decide whether or not we shall have for ourselves and our friends freedom of the seas—the right to go with our ships and our ocean-going airplanes where we wish, when we wish and as we wish. The vision of America as the principal guarantor of the freedom of the seas, the vision of America as the dynamic leader of world trade, has within it the possibilities of such enormous human progress as to stagger the imagination. Let us not be staggered by it. Let us rise to its tremendous possibilities. Our thinking of world trade today is on ridiculously small terms. For example, we think of Asia as being worth only a few hundred million a year to us. Actually, in the decades to come Asia will be worth to us exactly zero—or else it will be worth to us four, five, ten billion dollars a year. And the latter are the terms we must think in, or else confess a pitiful impotence.

Closely akin to the purely economic area and yet quite different from it, there is the picture of an America which will send out through the world its technical and artistic skills. Engineers, scientists, doctors, movie men, makers of entertainment, developers of airlines, builders of roads, teachers and educators. Throughout the world, these skills, this training, this leadership is needed and will be eagerly welcomed, if only we have the imagination to see it and the sincerity and good will to create the world of the 20th Century.

But now there is a third thing which our vision must immediately be concerned with. We must undertake now to be the Good Samaritan of the entire world. It is the manifest duty of this country to undertake to feed all the people of the world who as a result of this worldwide collapse of civilization are hungry and destitute—all of them, that is, whom we can from time to time reach consistently with a very tough attitude toward all hostile governments. For every dollar we spend on armaments, we should spend at least a dime in a gigantic effort to feed the world—and all the world should know that we have dedicated ourselves to this task. Every farmer in America should be encouraged to produce all the crops he can, and all that we cannot eat—and perhaps some of us could eat less—should forthwith be dispatched to the four quarters of the globe as a free gift, administered by a humanitarian army of Americans, to every man, woman and child on this earth who is really hungry.

*

But all this is not enough. All this will fail and none of it will happen unless our vision of America as a world power includes a passionate devotion to great American ideals. We have some things in this country which are infinitely precious and especially American—a love of freedom, a feeling for the equality of opportunity, a tradition of self-reliance and independence and also of cooperation. In addition to ideals and notions which are especially American, we are the inheritors of all the great principles of Western civilization—above all Justice, the love of Truth, the ideal of Charity. ...

America as the dynamic center of ever-widening spheres of enterprise, America as the training center of the skillful servants of mankind, America as the Good Samaritan, really believing again that it is more blessed to give than to receive, and America as the powerhouse of the ideals of Freedom and Justice—out of these elements surely can be fashioned a vision of the 20th century to which we can and will devote ourselves in joy and gladness and vigor and enthusiasm. ...

Source: Henry R. Luce, "The American Century," *Life*, February 17, 1941, pp. 64–65.

2 Wendell Willkie, Excerpt from *One World*, 1943

Wendell L. Willkie of Indiana, a successful attorney and corporate executive, ran as the Republican candidate for president in 1940. Defeated by FDR, Willkie was a committed internationalist who supported Roosevelt's

interventionist policies to provide aid to Great Britain in 1941. After Pearl
Harbor, he urged Roosevelt to send him on a world tour to gather
information and to display American war-time unity. In 1942, FDR granted
Willkie an Air Force plane and crew that took him around the globe. In One
World, *Willkie wrote about his observations on such diverse places as Africa,*
the Middle East, Turkey, the Soviet Union, and China. Although he did not
visit India, he took note of the independence movement there and the
support it enjoyed among many colonial peoples of the world. In contrast to
the isolationist wing of the Republican Party, led by Ohio Senator Robert
Taft, Willkie envisioned the United States playing an active role in the
postwar world, as well as dealing with racial discrimination at home.

The temptation is great, in all of us, to limit the objectives of a war. Cynically, we may hope that the big words we have used will become smaller at the peace table, that we can avoid the costly and difficult readjustments which will be required to establish and defend real freedom for all peoples.

Many men and women I have talked with from Africa to Alaska asked me the question which has become almost a symbol all through Asia: what about India? Now I did not go to India. I do not propose to discuss that tangled question. But it has one aspect, in the East, which I should report. From Cairo on, it confronted me at every turn. The wisest man in China said to me: "When the aspiration of India for freedom was put aside to some future date, it was not Great Britain that suffered in public esteem in the Far East. It was the United States."

This wise man was not quarreling with British imperialism in India when he said this—a benevolent imperialism, if you like. He does not happen to believe in it, but he was not even talking about it. He was telling me that by our silence on India we have already drawn heavily on our reservoir of good will in the East. People of the East who would like to count on us are doubt-ful. They cannot ascertain from our attitude toward the problem of India what we are likely to feel at the end of the war about all the other hundreds of millions of Eastern peoples. They cannot tell from our vague and vacillating talk whether or not we really do stand for freedom, or what we mean by freedom.

In China, students who were refugees a thousand miles from their homes asked me if we were going to try to take back Shanghai after the war. In Beirut, Lebanese asked me if their relatives in Brooklyn—one third of all the Lebanese in the world live in the United States—would help to persuade the British and French occupying forces to leave Syria and the Lebanon after the war and let them run their own country.

In Africa, in the Middle East, throughout the Arab world, as well as in China and the whole Far East, freedom means the orderly but scheduled abolition of the colonial system. Whether we like it not or not, this is true. ...

It has been a long while since the United States had any imperialistic designs toward the outside world. But we have practiced within our own boundaries something that amounts to race imperialism. The attitude of the white citizens of this country toward the Negroes has undeniably had some of the unlovely characteristics of an alien imperialism—a smug racial superiority, a willingness to exploit an unprotected people. We have justified it by telling ourselves that its end is benevolent. And sometimes it has been. But so sometimes have been the ends of imperialism. And the moral atmosphere in which it has existed is identical with that in which men—well-meaning men—talk of "the white man's burden."

But that atmosphere is changing. Today it is becoming increasingly apparent to thoughtful Americans that we cannot fight the forces and ideas of imperialism abroad and maintain any form of imperialism at home. The war has done this to our thinking.

Source: Wendell L. Willkie, *One World* (New York: Simon and Schuster, 1943), pp. 183–184, 190.

3 Langston Hughes, "My America," *Journal of Educational Sociology,* 1943

African American leaders were keenly aware of the contradictions inherent in a war waged against fascism abroad while many white Americans accepted discrimination and disenfranchisement at home. Langston Hughes, a leading poet of the Harlem Renaissance, contributed this article to a special issue of the Journal of Educational Sociology *dedicated to promoting ethnic, religious, and racial cooperation among Americans. In it, Hughes outlines many of the barriers his fellow black Americans faced despite their ancestry dating back for generations. At the same time, he strikes a note of hope and singles out political leaders, black and white, who were working to create a more just America. Among the leaders he applauds is the black actor, singer, and intellectual Paul Robeson, the writer Pearl Buck, best known for her novels about China, Wendell Willkie, and Henry Wallace, former Secretary of Agriculture and Vice President of the United States from 1941 to 1945. Hughes refers to Roosevelt as a proponent of democracy; he is most likely referring to FDR, but he may also have meant Eleanor Roosevelt, who remained far more willing to embrace the cause of African American equality. Eleanor not only pushed FDR to consult with black leaders, but personally lent her support to creating the Tuskegee Airmen, the first group of African American Army Air Force aviators, and arranged for a black civilian pilot to take her up in his airplane to show her confidence in the ability of African Americans as pilots.*

This is my land America. Naturally, I love it—it is home—and I am vitally concerned about its mores, its democracy, and its well-being. I try now to look at it with clear, unprejudiced eyes. My ancestry goes back at least four generations on American soil—and, through Indian blood, many centuries more. My background and training is purely American—the schools of Kansas, Ohio, and the East. I am old stock as opposed to recent immigrant blood.

Yet many Americans who cannot speak English—so recent is their arrival on our shores—may travel about the country at will securing food, hotel, and rail accommodations wherever they wish to purchase them. I may not. These Americans, once naturalized, may vote in Mississippi or Texas, if they live there. I may not. They may work at whatever job their skills command. But I may not. They may purchase tickets for concerts, theaters, lectures wherever they are sold throughout the United States. I may not. They may repeat the Oath of Allegiance with its ringing phrase of "liberty and justice for all," with a deep faith in its truth—as compared to the limitations and oppressions they have experienced in the Old World. I repeat the oath, too, but I know that the phrase about "liberty and justice" does not fully apply to me. I am an American—but I am a colored American.

I know that all these things I mention are not *all* true for *all* localities *all* over America. Jim Crowism varies in degree from North to South, from mixed schools and free franchise of Michigan to the tumbledown colored schools and open terror at the polls of Georgia and Mississippi. All over America, however, against the Negro there has been an economic color line of such severity that since the Civil War we have been kept most effectively, as a racial group, in the lowest economic brackets. Statistics are not needed to prove this. Simply look around you on the Main Street of any American town or city. There are no colored clerks in any of these stores—although colored people spend their money there. There are practically never any colored street-car conductors or bus drivers—although these public carriers run over streets for which we pay taxes. There are no colored girls at the switchboards of the telephone company—but millions of Negroes have phones and pay their bills. Even in Harlem, nine times out of ten, the man who comes to collect your rent is white. Not even that job is given a colored man by the great corporations owning New York real estate. From Boston to San Diego, the Negro suffers from job discrimination.

Yet America is a land where, in spite of its defects, I can write this article. Here the voice of democracy is still heard—Roosevelt, Wallace, Willkie, Agar, Pearl Buck, Paul Robeson. America is a land where the poll tax still holds in the South but opposition to the poll tax grows daily. America is a land where lynchers are not yet caught—but Bundists are put in jail, and majority opinion condemns the Klan. America is a land where the best of all democracies has been achieved for some people—but in Georgia, Roland Hayes, world-famous singer, is beaten for being colored and nobody is jailed—nor can Mr. Hayes vote in the State where he was born. Yet America is a country where Roland Hayes *can* come from a log cabin to wealth and fame—in spite of the segment that still wishes to maltreat him, physically and spiritually, famous though he is.

This segment, however, is not all of America. If it were, millions of Negroes would have no heart for this war in which were are now engaged. If it were, we could see no difference between our ideals and Hitler's, in so far as our own dark lives are concerned. But we know, on the other hand, that America is a land in transition. And we know it is within our power to help in its further change toward a finer and better democracy than any citizen has known before. The American Negro believes in democracy. We want to make it real, complete, workable, not only for ourselves—the thirteen million dark ones—but for all Americans all over the land.

Source: Langston Hughes, "My America," *Journal of Educational Sociology*, 16 (February 1943): 334–336.

4 Winston Churchill, Franklin D. Roosevelt, Joseph Stalin, "Yalta Conference Public Statement," 1945

In February 1945, a grievously ill Roosevelt journeyed to the war-devastated region of the Crimea to meet with British Prime Minister Winston Churchill and Soviet leader Joseph Stalin to discuss a strategy for bringing the war in Europe and Asia to a successful conclusion. Although Soviet and Western Allies (Britain, Canada, and the United States) had taken the war to German soil, both sides remained suspicious that the other would agree to a negotiated settlement with the Nazis. During the conference Roosevelt remained committed to continuing the Grand Alliance after victory in Germany and gained Stalin's assurance that the Soviet Union would enter the war against Japan after the struggle in Europe had ended. Eager to fulfill a long-standing pledge to create a new international organization – the

United Nations – to replace the League of Nations, the agreement at Yalta
settled a crucial sticking point between the Soviets and the United States
over the role the great powers would play in the Security Council. It also set
in motion an international conference that met in San Francisco in April
1945 to write a charter for the United Nations Organization. A significant
portion of the Yalta conference centered on the future of Germany. The
leaders decided to partition Germany into zones of occupation, but also
established machinery to govern the nation. Among the most contentious
issues that would lead to the collapse of the Grand Alliance soon after the
war ended was the question of control over areas liberated by the Soviet
Union. Although FDR appears to have accepted that the Soviet Union
would have a dominant role in Eastern Europe, it is clear that he wanted
inclusive governments formed there, in part to mollify strong political
opposition from Polish Americans and other Eastern European groups in
the United States. The failure of the Soviet Union to hold what the United
States deemed free and fair elections in Poland, and the engineering of a
coup against the government of Czechoslovakia, would be among the causes
of the Cold War.

... The following statement is made by the Prime Minister of Great Britain, the President of the United States of America, and the Chairman of the Council of People's Commissars of the Union of Soviet Socialist Republics on the results of the Crimean Conference:

The Defeat of Germany

We have considered and determined the military plans of the three allied powers for the final defeat of the common enemy. The military staffs of the three allied nations have met in daily meetings throughout the Conference. These meetings have been most satisfactory from every point of view and have resulted in closer co-ordination of the military effort of the three Allies than ever before. The fullest information has been interchanged. The timing, scope and co-ordination of new and even more powerful blows to be launched by our armies and air forces into the heart of Germany from the East, West, North and South have been fully agreed and planned in detail.

Our combined military plans will be made known only as we execute them, but we believe that the very close working partnership among the three staffs attained at this Conference will result in shortening the war. Meetings of the three staffs will be continued in the future whenever the need arises.

Nazi Germany is doomed. The German people will only make the cost of their defeat heavier to themselves by attempting to continue a hopeless resistance.

The Occupation and Control of Germany

We have agreed on common policies and plans for enforcing the unconditional surrender terms which we shall impose together on Nazi Germany after German armed resistance has been finally crushed. These terms will not be made known until the final defeat of Germany has been accomplished. Under the agreed plan, the forces of the Three Powers will each occupy a separate zone of Germany. Coordinated administration and control has been provided for under the plan through a Central Control Commission consisting of the Supreme Commanders of the Three Powers with headquarters in Berlin. It has been agreed that France should be invited by the Three Powers, if she should so desire, to take over a zone of occupation, and to participate as a fourth member of the Control Commission. The limits of the French zone will be agreed by the four governments concerned through their representatives on the European Advisory Commission.

It is our inflexible purpose to destroy German militarism and Nazism and to ensure that Germany will never again be able to disturb the peace of the world. We are determined to disarm and disband all German armed forces; break up for all time the German General Staff that has repeatedly contrived the resurgence of German militarism; remove or destroy all German military equipment; eliminate or control all German industry that could be used for military production; bring all war criminals to just and swift punishment and exact reparation in kind for the destruction wrought by the Germans; wipe out the Nazi Party, Nazi laws, organizations and institutions, remove all Nazi and militarist influences from public office and from the cultural and economic life of the German people; and take in harmony such other measures in Germany as may be necessary to the future peace and safety of the world. It is not our purpose to destroy the people of Germany, but only when Nazism and Militarism have been extirpated will there be a hope for a decent life for Germans, and a place for them in the comity of nations.

Reparation by Germany

We have considered the question of the damage caused by Germany to the Allied Nations in this war and recognized it as just that Germany be obliged to make compensation for this damage in kind to the greatest extent possible. A Commission for the Compensation of Damage will be established.

The Commission will be instructed to consider the question of the extent and methods for compensating damage caused by Germany to the Allied Countries. The Commission will work in Moscow.

United Nations Conference

We are resolved upon the earliest possible establishment with our allies of a general international organization to maintain peace and security. We believe that this is essential, both to prevent aggression and to remove the political, economic and social causes of war through the close and continuing collaboration of all peace-loving peoples.

The foundations were laid at Dumbarton Oaks. On the important question of voting procedure, however, agreement was not there reached. The present conference has been able to resolve this difficulty.

We have agreed that a conference of United Nations should be called to meet at San Francisco in the United States on April 25, 1945, to prepare the charter of such an organization, along the lines proposed in the informal conversations at Dumbarton Oaks.

The Government of China and the Provisional Government of France will be immediately consulted and invited to sponsor invitations to the Conference jointly with the Governments of the United States, Great Britain and the Union of Soviet Socialist Republics. As soon as the consultation with China and France has been completed, the text of the proposals on voting procedure will be made public.

Declaration on Liberated Europe

The Premier of the Union of Soviet Socialist Republics, the Prime Minister of the United Kingdom, and the President of the United States of America have consulted with each other in the common interests of the peoples of their countries and those of liberated Europe. They jointly declare their mutual agreement to concert during the temporary period of instability in liberated Europe the policies of their three governments in assisting the peoples liberated from the domination of Nazi Germany and the peoples of the former Axis satellite states of Europe to solve by democratic means their pressing political and economic problems.

The establishment of order in Europe and the rebuilding of national economic life must be achieved by processes which will enable the liberated peoples to destroy the last vestiges of Nazism and Fascism and to create democratic institutions of their own choice. This is a principle of the Atlantic Charter— the right of all peoples to choose the form of government under which they will live—the restoration of sovereign rights and self-government to those peoples who have been forcibly deprived of them by the aggressor nations.

To foster the conditions in which the liberated peoples may exercise these rights, the three governments will jointly assist the people in any European liberated state or former Axis satellite state in Europe where in their judgment conditions require (a) to establish conditions of internal peace; (b) to carry out emergency measures for the relief of distressed people; (c) to form interim governmental authorities broadly representative of all democratic elements in the population and pledged to the earliest possible establishment through free elections of governments responsive to the will of the people; and (d) to facilitate where necessary the holding of such elections.

The three governments will consult the other United Nations and provisional authorities or other governments in Europe when matters of direct interest to them are under consideration.

When, in the opinion of the three governments, conditions in any European liberated state or any former Axis satellite state in Europe make such action necessary, they will immediately consult together on the measures necessary to discharge the joint responsibilities set forth in this declaration.

By this declaration we reaffirm our faith in the principles of the Atlantic Charter, our pledge in the Declaration by the United Nations, and our determination to build in co-operation with other peace-loving nations world order under law, dedicated to peace, security, freedom and general well-being of all mankind.

In issuing this declaration, the Three Powers express the hope that the Provisional Government of the French Republic may be associated with them in the procedure suggested.

Poland

A new situation has been created in Poland as a result of her complete liberation by the Red Army. This calls for the establishment of a Polish Provisional Government which can be more broadly based than was possible before the recent liberation of western Poland. The Provisional Government which is now functioning in Poland should therefore be reorganized on a broader democratic basis with the inclusion of democratic leaders from Poland itself and from Poles abroad. This new government should then be called the Polish Provisional Government of National Unity.

M. Molotov, Mr. Harriman and Sir A. Clark Kerr are authorized as a Commission to consult in the first instance in Moscow with members of the present Provisional Government and with other Polish democratic leaders from within Poland and from abroad, with a view to the reorganization of the present Government along the above lines. This Polish Provisional Government of National Unity shall be pledged to the holding of free and unfettered elections as soon as possible on the basis of universal suffrage and secret ballot. In these elections all democratic and anti-Nazi parties shall have the right to take part and to put forward candidates.

When a Polish Provisional Government of National Unity has been properly formed in conformity with the above, the Government of the U.S.S.R., which now maintains diplomatic relations with the present Provisional Government of Poland, and the Government of the United Kingdom and the government of the United States will establish diplomatic relations with the new Polish Provisional Government of National Unity, and will exchange ambassadors by whose reports the respective Governments will be kept informed about the situation in Poland.

The three Heads of Government consider that the eastern frontier of Poland should follow the Curzon line with digressions from it in some regions of five to eight kilometers in favor of Poland. They recognize that Poland must receive substantial accessions of territory in the north and west. They feel that the opinion of the new Polish Provisional Government of National Unity should be sought in due course on the extent of these accessions and that the final delimitation of the western frontier of Poland should thereafter await the Peace Conference.

Yugoslavia

We have agreed to recommend to Marshal Tito and Dr. Subasic that the Agreement between them should be put into effect immediately, and that a new government should be formed on the basis of that Agreement.

We also recommend that as soon as the new Government has been formed, it should declare that:

(i) The Anti-fascist Assembly of National Liberation (Avnoj) should be extended to include members of the last Yugoslav Parliament (Skupschina) who have not compromised themselves by collaboration with the enemy, thus forming a body to be known as a temporary Parliament; and,
(ii) legislative acts passed by the anti-Fascist Assembly of National Liberation (AVNOJ) will be subject to subsequent ratification by a Constituent Assembly.

There was also a general review of other Balkan questions.

Meetings of Foreign Secretaries

Throughout the Conference, besides the daily meetings of the Heads of Governments and the Foreign Secretaries, separate meetings of the three Foreign Secretaries and their advisers have also been held daily.

These meetings have proved of the utmost value and the Conference agreed that permanent machinery should be set up for regular consultation between the three Foreign Secretaries. They will, therefore, meet as often as may be necessary, probably about every three or four months. These meetings will be held in rotation in the three capitals, the first meeting being held in London, after the United Nations Conference on World Organization.

Unity for Peace as for War

Our meeting here in the Crimea has reaffirmed our common determination to maintain and strengthen in the peace to come that unity of purpose and of action which has made victory possible and certain for the United Nations in this war. We believe that this is a sacred obligation which our Governments owe to our peoples and to all the peoples of the world.

Only with continuing and growing co-operation and understanding among our three countries and among all the peace-loving nations can the highest aspiration of humanity be realized—a secure and lasting peace which will, in the words of the Atlantic Charter, "afford assurance that all the men in all the lands may live out their lives in freedom from fear and want."

Victory in this war and establishment of the proposed international organization will provide the greatest opportunity in all history to create in the years to come the essential conditions of such a peace.

(*Signed*)
WINSTON S. CHURCHILL
FRANKLIN D. ROOSEVELT
J. STALIN
February 11, 1945

Source: Charles I. Bevans, *Treaties and Other International Agreements of the United States of America, 1776–1949*, Vol. 3: *Multilateral, 1931–1945* (Washington, DC: Government Printing Office, 1969), pp. 1005–1012.

5 United Nations, Excerpt from Charter, 1945

One of the enduring legacies of World War II would be the formation of the United Nations, an international organization dedicated to promoting peace and security in the world. Although Woodrow Wilson had played a pivotal role in creating the League of Nations in 1919 as part of the Treaty of Versailles, the American people remained divided over whether they should abandon traditional isolationism and commit themselves to an international organization, which many feared would limit American sovereignty in questions of war and peace. Unable to overcome these reservations, Wilson's proposal fell short of the necessary two-thirds majority in the US Senate to ratify the League of Nations covenants, and the United States never joined the organization. World War II convinced many erstwhile isolationists to embrace internationalism, and when the treaty creating the United Nations Organization was put before the US Senate, it garnered near-unanimous consent, with only two dissenting votes. In forging the United Nations, FDR sought a balance between Wilsonian internationalism and the demands of power politics. He wanted to create an international organization that would be powerful enough to stop future aggression and preserve a peaceful world order. As a result, the Charter granted the Security Council far-reaching powers to maintain peace and security. In contrast to the General Assembly, in which every nation had an equal vote, the United Nations Security Council would be dominated by the great powers and the permanent five members could veto any action of this body. The power of veto did limit the United Nations' effectiveness during the Cold War as both the Soviet Union and the United States vetoed actions that were against their interests. Under the US Constitution, treaties once ratified become the law of the land and Security Council resolutions have served as the legal basis for American intervention during the Korean War (1950), Persian Gulf War (1990), and Afghanistan War (2001).

Charter of the United Nations, June 26, 1945

WE THE PEOPLES OF THE UNITED NATIONS DETERMINED to save succeeding generations from the scourge of war, which twice in our lifetime has brought untold sorrow to mankind, and to reaffirm faith in fundamental human rights, in the dignity and worth of the human person, in the equal rights of men and women and of nations large and small, and to establish conditions under which justice and respect for the obligations arising from treaties and other sources of international law can be maintained, and to promote social progress and better standards of life in larger freedom, AND

FOR THESE ENDS to practice tolerance and live together in peace with one another as good neighbours, and to unite our strength to maintain international peace and security, and to ensure, by the acceptance of principles and the institution of methods, that armed force shall not be used, save in the common interest, and to employ international machinery for the promotion of the economic and social advancement of all peoples, HAVE RESOLVED TO COMBINE OUR EFFORTS TO ACCOMPLISH THESE AIMS. Accordingly, our respective Governments, through representatives assembled in the city of San Francisco, who have exhibited their full powers found to be in good and due form, have agreed to the present Charter of the United Nations and do hereby establish an international organization to be known as the United Nations.

CHAPTER I

PURPOSES AND PRINCIPLES

Article 1

The Purposes of the United Nations are:

1. To maintain international peace and security, and to that end: to take effective collective measures for the prevention and removal of threats to the peace, and for the suppression of acts of aggression or other breaches of the peace, and to bring about by peaceful means, and in conformity with the principles of justice and international law, adjustment or settlement of international disputes or situations which might lead to a breach of the peace;
2. To develop friendly relations among nations based on respect for the principle of equal rights and self-determination of peoples, and to take other appropriate measures to strengthen universal peace;
3. To achieve international co-operation in solving international problems of an economic, social, cultural, or humanitarian character, and in promoting and encouraging respect for human rights and for fundamental freedoms for all without distinction as to race, sex, language, or religion; and
4. To be a centre for harmonizing the actions of nations in the attainment of these common ends.

Article 2

The Organization and its Members, in pursuit of the Purposes stated in Article 1, shall act in accordance with the following Principles.

1. The Organization is based on the principle of the sovereign equality of all its Members.
2. All Members, in order to ensure to all of them the rights and benefits resulting from membership, shall fulfill in good faith the obligations assumed by them in accordance with the present Charter.
3. All Members shall settle their international disputes by peaceful means in such a manner that international peace and security, and justice, are not endangered.
4. All Members shall refrain in their international relations from the threat or use of force against the territorial integrity or political independence of any state, or in any other manner inconsistent with the Purposes of the United Nations.
5. All Members shall give the United Nations every assistance in any action it takes in accordance with the present Charter, and shall refrain from giving assistance to any state against which the United Nations is taking preventive or enforcement action.
6. The Organization shall ensure that states which are not Members of the United Nations act in accordance with these Principles so far as may be necessary for the maintenance of international peace and security.
7. Nothing contained in the present Charter shall authorize the United Nations to intervene in matters which are essentially within the domestic jurisdiction of any state or shall require the Members to submit such matters to settlement under the present Charter; but this principle shall not prejudice the application of enforcement measures under Chapter VII.

CHAPTER II

MEMBERSHIP

Article 3

The original Members of the United Nations shall be the states which, having participated in the United Nations Conference on International Organization at San Francisco, or having previously signed the Declaration by United Nations of 1 January 1942, sign the present Charter and ratify it in accordance with Article 110.

Article 4

1. Membership in the United Nations is open to all other peace-loving states which accept the obligations contained in the present Charter and, in the judgment of the Organization, are able and willing to carry out these obligations.

2. The admission of any such state to membership in the Nations will be effected by a decision of the General Assembly upon the recommendation of the Security Council. ...

CHAPTER V

THE SECURITY COUNCIL

Composition

Article 23

1. The Security Council shall consist of fifteen Members of the United Nations. The Republic of China, France, the Union of Soviet Socialist Republics, the United Kingdom of Great Britain and Northern Ireland, and the United States of America shall be permanent members of the Security Council. The General Assembly shall elect ten other Members of the United Nations to be non-permanent members of the Security Council, due regard being specially paid, in the first instance to the contribution of Members of the United Nations to the maintenance of international peace and security and to the other purposes of the Organization, and also to equitable geographical distribution.

2. The non-permanent members of the Security Council shall be elected for a term of two years. In the first election of the non-permanent members after the increase of the membership of the Security Council from eleven to fifteen, two of the four additional members shall be chosen for a term of one year. A retiring member shall not be eligible for immediate re-election.

3. Each member of the Security Council shall have one representative. ...

CHAPTER VII

ACTION WITH RESPECT TO THREATS TO THE PEACE, BREACHES OF THE PEACE, AND ACTS OF AGGRESSION

Article 39

The Security Council shall determine the existence of any threat to the peace, breach of the peace, or act of aggression and shall make recommendations, or decide what measures shall be taken in accordance with Articles 4 and 42, to maintain or restore international peace and security.

Article 40

In order to prevent an aggravation of the situation, the Security Council may, before making the recommendations or deciding upon the measures provided for in Article 39, call upon the parties concerned to comply with such provisional measures as it deems necessary or desirable. Such provisional measures shall be without prejudice to the rights, claims, or position of the parties concerned. The Security Council shall duly take account of failure to comply with such provisional measures.

Article 41

The Security Council may decide what measures not involving the use of armed force are to be employed to give effect to its decisions, and it may call upon the Members of the United Nations to apply such measures. These may include complete or partial interruption of economic relations and of rail, sea, air, postal, telegraphic, radio, and other means of communication, and the severance of diplomatic relations.

Article 42

Should the Security Council consider that measures provided for in Article 41 would be inadequate or have proved to be inadequate, it may take such action by air, sea, or land forces as may be necessary to maintain or restore international peace and security. Such action may include demonstrations, blockade, and other operations by air, sea, or land forces of Members of the United Nations.

Article 43

1. All Members of the United Nations, in order to contribute to the maintenance of international peace and security, undertake to make available to the Security Council, on its and in accordance with a special agreement or agreements, armed forces, assistance, and facilities, including rights of passage, necessary for the purpose of maintaining international peace and security.
2. Such agreement or agreements shall govern the numbers and types of forces, their degree of readiness and general location, and the nature of the facilities and assistance to be provided.
3. The agreement or agreements shall be negotiated as soon as possible on the initiative of the Security Council. They shall be concluded between the Security Council and Members or between the Security Council and groups of Members and shall be subject to ratification by the signatory states in accordance with their respective constitutional processes.

Article 44

When Security Council has decided to use force it shall, before calling upon a Member not represented on it to provide armed forces in fulfilment of the obligations assumed under Article 43, invite that Member, if the Member so desires, to participate in the decisions of the Security Council concerning the employment of contingents of that Member's armed forces.

Article 45

In order to enable the Nations to take urgent military measures, Members shall hold immediately available national air-force contingents for combined international enforcement action. The strength and degree of readiness of these contingents and plans for their combined action shall be determined, within the limits laid down in the special agreement or agreements referred to in Article 43, by the Security Council with the assistance of the Military Committee.

Source: General Records of the United States Government, 1778-1992, RG 11, US National Archives, Washington, DC. Also available online at http://www.our documents.gov/doc.php?flash=true&doc=79.

6 Robert Jackson, Excerpts from Opening Address at Nuremberg War Crimes Trial, 1945

As promised during the war, the United States and other Allied countries held German and Japanese leaders accountable for the war crimes they committed. The United States, Great Britain, the Soviet Union, and France established the International Military Tribunal at Nuremberg, Germany, to try the top Nazi leaders. The Nuremberg Trials, which were held from November 1945 to October 1946, set an important precedent in establishing an international court to try individuals for violating established laws of war. But Nuremberg also set new precedents by prosecuting Nazi leaders for engaging in a conspiracy to wage aggressive war and for crimes against humanity. It also introduced to international jurisprudence what is now the widely accepted principle that an individual must disobey an illegal command and cannot escape criminal culpability with the excuse that "I was only following orders." US Supreme Court Justice Robert Jackson, who served as the lead prosecutor for the United States, gathered and presented evidence to a court made up of judges from the United States, Great Britain, the Soviet Union, and France. In the excerpted document presented below, Justice Jackson outlined the charges against Hermann Goering, Rudolph Hess, Albert Speer, General Alfred Jodl, and other major Nazi leaders.

Robert H. Jackson, Opening Address for the United States, November 21, 1945

May it please Your Honors:

The privilege of opening the first trial in history for crimes against the peace of the world imposes a grave responsibility. The wrongs which we seek to condemn and punish have been so calculated, so malignant and so devastating, that civilization cannot tolerate their being ignored because it cannot survive their being repeated. That four great nations, flushed with victory and stung with injury stay the hand of vengeance and voluntarily submit their captive enemies to the judgment of the law is one of the most significant tributes that Power has ever paid to Reason.

This tribunal, while it is novel and experimental, is not the product of abstract speculations nor is it created to vindicate legalistic theories. This inquest represents the practical effort of four of the most mighty of nations, with the support of seventeen more, to utilize International Law to meet the greatest menace of our times—aggressive war. The common sense of mankind demands that law shall not stop with the punishment of petty crimes by little people. It must also reach men who possess themselves of great power and make deliberate and concerted use of it to set in motion evils which leave no home in the world untouched. It is a cause of this magnitude that the United Nations will lay before Your Honors.

In the prisoners' dock sit twenty-odd broken men. Reproached by the humiliation of those they have led almost as bitterly as by the desolation of those they have attacked, their personal capacity for evil is forever past. It is hard now to perceive in these men as captives the power by which as Nazi leaders they once dominated much of the world and terrified most of it. Merely as individuals their fate is of little consequence to the world.

What makes this inquest significant is that these prisoners represent sinister influence that will lurk in the world long after their bodies have returned to dust. They are living symbols of racial hatreds, of terrorism and violence, and of the arrogance and cruelty of power. They are symbols of fierce nationalisms and of militarism, of intrigue and war-making which have embroiled Europe generation after generation, crushing its manhood, destroying its homes, and impoverishing its life. They have so identified themselves with the philosophies they conceived and with the forces they directed that any tenderness to them is a victory and an encouragement to all the evils which are attached to their names. Civilization can afford no compromise with the social forces which would gain renewed strength if we deal ambiguously or indecisively with the men in whom those forces now precariously survive.

What these men stand for we will patiently and temperately disclose. We will give you undeniable proofs of incredible events. The catalog of crimes will omit nothing that could be conceived by a pathological pride, cruelty, and lust for power. These men created in Germany, under the *Fuehrerprinzip*, a National Socialist despotism equalled only by the dynasties of the ancient East. They took from the German people all those dignities and freedoms that we hold natural and inalienable rights in every human being. The people were compensated by inflaming and gratifying hatreds toward those who were marked as "scape-goats". Against their opponents, including Jews, Catholics, and free labor the Nazis directed such a campaign of arrogance, brutality, and annihilation as the world has not witnessed since the pre-Christian ages. They excited the German ambition to be a "master race," which of course implies serfdom for others. They led their people on a mad gamble for domination. They diverted social energies and resources to the creation of what they thought to be an invincible war machine. They overran their neighbors. To sustain the "master race" in its war-making, they enslaved millions of human beings and brought them into Germany, where these hapless creatures now wander as "displaced persons". At length bestiality and bad faith reached such excess that they aroused the sleeping strength of imperiled civilization. Its united efforts have ground the German war machine to fragments. But the struggle has left Europe a liberated yet prostrate land where a demoralized society struggles to survive. These are the fruits of the sinister forces that sit with these defendants in the prisoners' dock. ...

This war did not just happen—it was planned and prepared for over a long period of time and with no small skill and cunning. The world has perhaps never seen such a concentration and stimulation of the energies of any people as that which enabled Germany twenty years after it was defeated, disarmed, and dismembered to come so near carrying out its plan to dominate Europe. Whatever else we may say of those who were the authors of this war, they did achieve a stupendous work in organization, and our first task is to examine the means by which these defendants and their fellow conspirators prepared and incited Germany to go to war.

In general, our case will disclose these defendants all uniting at some time with the Nazi Party in a plan which they well knew could be accomplished only by an outbreak of war in Europe. Their seizure of the German state, their subjugation of the German people, their terrorism and extermination of dissident elements, their planning and waging of war, their calculated and planned ruthlessness in the conduct of warfare, their deliberate and planned criminality toward conquered peoples, all these are ends for which they acted in concert; and all these are phases of the conspiracy, a conspiracy which reached one goal only to set out for another and more ambitious one. We shall also trace for you the intricate web of organizations which these men formed and utilized to accomplish these ends. We will show how the entire structure of offices and officials was dedicated to the criminal purposes and committed to use of the criminal methods planned by these defendants and their co-conspirators, many of whom war and suicide have put beyond reach.

It is my purpose to open the case, particularly under Count One of the Indictment, and to deal with the Common Plan or Conspiracy to achieve ends possible only by resort to crimes against peace, war crimes, and crimes against humanity. My emphasis will not be on individual barbarities and perversions which may have occurred independently of any central plan. One of the dangers ever present is that this trial may be protracted by details of particular wrongs and that we will become lost in a "wilderness of single instances." Nor will I now dwell on the activity of individual defendants except as it may contribute to exposition of the common plan.

The case as presented by the United States will be concerned with the brains and authority back of all the crimes. These defendants were men of a station and rank which does not soil its own hands with blood. They were men who knew how to use lesser folk as tools. We want to reach the planners and designers, the inciters and leaders without whose evil architecture the world would not have been for so long scourged with the violence, and lawlessness, and wracked with the agonies and convulsions, of this terrible war.

... Crimes Against the Jews

The most savage and numerous crimes planned and committed by the Nazis were those against the Jews. These in Germany, in 1933, numbered about 500,000. In the aggregate, they had made for themselves positions which excited envy, and had accumulated properties which excited the avarice of the Nazis. They were few enough to be helpless and numerous enough to be held up as a menace.

Let there be no misunderstanding about the charge of persecuting Jews. What we charge against these defendants is not those arrogances and pretensions which frequently accompany the intermingling of different peoples and which are likely despite the honest efforts of government, to produce regrettable crimes and convulsions. It is my purpose to show a plan and design, to which all Nazis were fanatically committed, to annihilate all Jewish people. These crimes were organized and promoted by the Party leadership, executed and protected by the Nazi officials, as we shall convince you by written orders of the Secret State Police itself.

The persecution of the Jews was a continuous and deliberate policy. It was a policy directed against other nations as well as against the Jews themselves. Anti-Semitism was promoted to divide and embitter the democratic peoples and to soften their resistance to the Nazi aggression. ...

Anti-Semitism also has been aptly credited with being a "spear head of terror." The ghetto was the laboratory for testing repressive measures. Jewish property was the first to be expropriated, but the custom grew and included similar measures against anti-Nazi Germans, Poles, Czechs, Frenchmen, and Belgians. Extermination of the Jews enabled the Nazis to bring a practiced hand to similar measures against Poles, Serbs, and Greeks. The plight of the Jew was a constant threat to opposition or discontent among other elements of Europe's population—pacifists, conservatives, communists, Catholics, Protestants, socialists. It was, in fact, a threat to every dissenting opinion and to every non-Nazi's life.

The persecution policy against the Jews commenced with non-violent measures such as disfranchisement and discriminations against their religion, and the placing of impediments in the way of success in economic life. It moved rapidly to organized mass violence against them, physical isolation in ghettos, deportation, forced labor, mass starvation, and extermination. The Government, the Party formation indicted before you as criminal organizations, the Secret State Police, the Army, private and semi-public associations, and "spontaneous" mobs that were carefully inspired from official sources, were all agencies concerned in this persecution. Nor was it directed against individual Jews for personal bad citizenship or unpopularity. The avowed purpose was the destruction of the Jewish people as a whole, as an end in itself, as a measure of preparation for war, and as a discipline of conquered peoples.

The conspiracy or common plan to exterminate the Jew was so methodically and thoroughly pursued, that despite the German defeat and Nazi prostration this Nazi aim largely has succeeded. Only remnants of the European Jewish population remain in Germany, in the countries which Germany occupied, and in those which were her satellites or collaborators. Of the 9,600,000 Jews who lived in Nazi-dominated Europe, 60 percent are authoritatively estimated to have perished. 5,700,000 Jews are missing from the countries in which they formerly lived, and over 4,500,000 cannot be accounted for by the normal death rate nor by immigration; nor are they included among displaced persons. History does not record a crime ever perpetrated against so many victims or one ever carried out with such calculated cruelty.

... THE LAW OF THE CASE

The end of the war and capture of these prisoners presented the victorious Allies with the question whether there is any legal responsibility on high-ranking men for acts which I have described. Must such wrongs either be ignored or redressed in hot blood? Is there no standard in the law for a deliberate and reasoned judgment on such conduct?

The Charter of this Tribunal evidences a faith that the law is not only to govern the conduct of little men, but that even rulers are, as Lord Chief Justice Coke put it to King James, "under God and the law." The United States believed that the law has long afforded standards by which a juridical hearing could be conducted to make sure that we punish only the right men and for the right reasons. Following the instructions of the late President Roosevelt and the decision of the Yalta conference, President Truman directed representatives of the United States to formulate a proposed International Agreement, which was submitted during the San Francisco Conference to Foreign Ministers of the United Kingdom, the Soviet Union, and the Provisional Government of France. With many modifications, that proposal has become the Charter of this Tribunal. ...

The Third Count of the Indictment is based on the definition of war crimes contained in the Charter. I have outlined to you the systematic course of conduct toward civilian populations and combat forces which violates international conventions to which Germany was a party. Of the criminal nature of these acts at least, the defendants had, as we shall show, clear knowledge. Accordingly they took pains to conceal their violations. It will appear that the defendants Keitel and Jodl were informed by official legal advisors that the orders to brand Russian prisoners of war, to shackle British prisoners of war, and to execute commando prisoners were clear violations of International Law. Nevertheless, these orders were put into effect. The same is true of orders issued for the assassination of General Giraud and General Weygand, which failed to be executed only because of a ruse on the part of Admiral Canaris, who was himself later executed for his part in the plot to take Hitler's life on July 20, 1944. ...

The Fourth Count of the Indictment is based on crimes against humanity. Chief among these are mass killings of countless human beings in cold blood. Does it take these men by surprise that murder is treated as a crime?

The First and Second Counts of the Indictment add to these crimes the crime of plotting and waging wars of aggression and wars in violation of nine treaties to which Germany was a party. There was a time, in fact I think the time of the first World War, when it could not have been said that war-inciting or war-making was a crime in law, however reprehensible in morals.

Of course, it was under the law of all civilized peoples a crime for one man with his bare knuckles to assault another. How did it come that multiplying this crime by a million, and adding fire arms to bare knuckles, made a legally innocent act? The doctrine was that one could not be regarded as criminal for committing the usual violent acts in the conduct of legitimate warfare. The age of imperialistic expansion during the Eighteenth and Nineteenth centuries added the foul doctrine, contrary to the teachings of early Christian and international law scholars such as Grotius, that all wars are to be regarded as legitimate wars. The sum of these two doctrines was to give warmaking a complete immunity from accountability to law.

This was intolerable for an age that called itself civilized. Plain people, with their earthy common sense, revolted at such fictions and legalisms so contrary to ethical principles and demanded checks on war immunity. Statesmen and international lawyers at first cautiously responded by adopting rules of warfare designed to make the conduct of war more civilized. The effort was to set legal limits to the violence that could be done to civilian populations and to combatants as well.

The common sense of men after the First World War demanded, however, that the law's condemnation of war reach deeper, and that the law condemn not merely uncivilized ways of waging war, but also the waging in any way of uncivilized wars—wars of aggression. The world's statesmen again went only as far as they were forced to go. Their efforts were timid and cautious and often less explicit than we might have hoped. But the 1920's did outlaw aggressive war.

The re-establishment of the principle that there are unjust wars and that unjust wars are illegal is traceable in many steps. One of the most significant is the Briand-Kellogg Pact of 1928, by which Germany, Italy, and Japan, in common with practically all nations of the world, renounced war as an instrument of national policy, bound themselves to seek the settlement of disputes only by pacific means, and condemned recourse to war for the solution of international controversies. This pact altered the legal status of a war of aggression. ...

THE RESPONSIBILITY OF THIS TRIBUNAL

To apply the sanctions of the law to those whose conduct is found criminal by the standards I have outlined, is the responsibility committed to this Tribunal. It is the first court ever to undertake the difficult task of overcoming the confusion of many tongues and the conflicting concepts of just procedure among divers systems of law, so as to reach a common judgment. The tasks of all of us are such as to make heavy demands on patience and good will. Although the need for prompt action has admittedly resulted in imperfect work on the part of the prosecution, four great nations bring you their hurriedly assembled contributions of evidence. What remains undiscovered we can only guess. We could, with witnesses' testimony, prolong the recitals of crime for years—but to what avail? We shall rest the case when we have offered what seems convincing and adequate proof of the crimes charged without unnecessary cumulation of evidence. We doubt very much whether it will be seriously denied that the crimes I have outlined took place. The effort will undoubtedly be to mitigate or escape personal responsibility. ...

The American dream of a peace and plenty economy, as well as the hopes of other nations, can never be fulfilled if those nations are involved in a war every generation so vast and devastating as to crush the generation that fights and burden the generation that follows. But experience has shown that wars are no longer local. All modern wars become world wars eventually. And none of the big nations at least can stay out. If we cannot stay out of wars, our only hope is to prevent wars.

I am too well aware of the weaknesses of juridical action alone to contend that in itself your decision under this Charter can prevent future wars. Judicial action always comes after the event. Wars are started only on the theory and in the confidence that they can be won. Personal punishment, to be suffered only in the event the war is lost, will probably not be a sufficient deterrent to prevent a war where the warmakers feel the chances of defeat to be negligible.

But the ultimate step in avoiding periodic wars, which are inevitable in a system of international lawlessness, is to make statesmen responsible to law. And let me make clear that while this law is first applied against German aggressors, the law includes, and if it is to serve a useful purpose it must condemn aggression by any other nations, including those which sit here now in judgment. We are able to do away with domestic tyranny and violence and aggression by those in power against the rights of their own people only when we make all men answerable to the law. This trial represents mankind's desperate effort to apply the discipline of the law to statesmen who have used their powers of state to attack the foundations of the world's peace and to commit aggressions against the rights of their neighbors. ...

The real complaining party at your bar is Civilization. In all our countries it is still a struggling and imperfect thing. It does not plead that the United States, or any other country, has been blameless of the conditions which made the German people easy victims to the blandishments and intimidations of the Nazi conspirators.

But it points to the dreadful sequence of aggressions and crimes I have recited, it points to the weariness of flesh, the exhaustion of resources, and the destruction of all that was beautiful or useful in so much of the world, and to greater potentialities for destruction in the days to come. It is not necessary among the ruins of this ancient and beautiful city, with untold members of its civilian inhabitants still buried in its rubble, to argue the proposition that to start or wage an aggressive war has the moral qualities of the worst of crimes. The refuge of the defendants can be only their hope that International Law will lag so far behind the moral sense of mankind that conduct which is crime in the moral sense must be regarded as innocent in law.

Civilization asks whether law is so laggard as to be utterly helpless to deal with crimes of this magnitude by criminals of this order of importance. It does not expect that you can make war impossible. It does expect that your juridical action will put the forces of International Law, its precepts, its prohibitions and, most of all, its sanctions, on the side of peace, so that men and women of good will, in all countries, may have "leave to live by no man's leave, underneath the law."

Source: Office of United States Chief of Counsel for Prosecution of Axis Criminality, *Nazi Conspiracy and Aggression* (Washington, DC: Government Printing Office, 1946), Vol. 1, pp. 114–115, 119–120, 134–135, 160–163, 170–173.

Study Questions

1   Compare and contrast the visions that Henry Luce and Wendell Willkie expressed for the postwar future.
2   How did Yalta redraw the map of Europe politically? What compromises do you think were made by all three leaders? For instance, do you think Stalin was sincere in signing an agreement that called for free elections in Poland and elsewhere in Europe? Why were Roosevelt's actions at Yalta so controversial?
3   What were the goals of the United Nations? Were the founders overly optimistic? To what degree did the United Nations Security Council enshrine the dominant role of the Great Alliance in the postwar era?
4   What crimes were German leaders charged with at Nuremberg? Do you think Justice Jackson makes a convincing case for the culpability of those facing trial? How convincing is Jackson that victor's justice is not being applied to those charged at Nuremberg?

Chapter 11   Legacies of War

1 John J. Toffey IV, Excerpt from *Jack Toffey's War*, 2008

*John Toffey III left for the war in 1942 and was never to return. He was
a National Guardsman who had been mobilized into federal service in 1940
and rose to the rank of lieutenant colonel. Before his overseas deployment,
his family followed him for two years to army bases in New Jersey, Georgia,
Louisiana, Washington, and North Carolina before returning to their home
in Cincinnati. In his memoir published in 2008, his son Jack recalls how, at
age 13, he learned of his father's death at the Anzio beachhead in 1944. He
also describes the way his mother, sister, grandmother, and other relatives
coped with the loss and went on with their lives.*

I was still keeping quiet in my room on the third floor on Sunday morning,
June 25. I happened to be looking out my window when I saw Homer drive
up and park his Oldsmobile in front of the house. It was unusual for Homer
to appear on a Sunday morning. He was usually at church. I watched him
get out of the car, come around, and open the door for Granny. They stood
together for a minute before Homer turned and started up the walk to our
front door with Granny a step or two behind. Something about this scene
didn't seem right. When I got to the living room, I saw Mom and Granny

The United States in World War II: A Documentary Reader, First Edition.
Edited by G. Kurt Piehler. Editorial material and organization © 2013 Blackwell Publishing Ltd.
Published 2013 by Blackwell Publishing Ltd.

and Homer standing there. No one was saying anything, Mom handed me the telegram Homer had given her, and as I started to read it, she put both arms around me.

THE SECRETARY OF WAR DESIRES ME TO EXPRESS HIS DEEP REGRET THAT YOUR HUSBAND LIEUTENANT COLONEL JOHN J TOFFEY JR WAS KILLED IN ACTION ON THREE JUNE IN ITALY LETTER FOLLOWS.

ULIO THE ADJUTANT GENERAL

That was it. No pair of officers wearing Class A uniforms and appropriately somber faces expressing the thanks of a grateful nation. Instead there was Homer, bearing to our house the burden of the terrible telegram as he had brought word of Dad's having been wounded fourteen months earlier. Homer because, when Dad left us in Fayetteville [North Carolina], we didn't have a house of our own, and Homer's address was as close as we could come to permanence. ...

Mom and Granny and Homer had to attend to the grim logistical matters of their own. Sometime that Sunday they started making the phone calls to all the relatives and friends too close to learn of Dad's death in the papers. Mom, of course, called Deo to break the news that her son was dead. Deo in turn would tell her sisters and brothers and their spouses. Then she would begin to notify all her army friends. Mom would call our Cincinnati friends, while Granny and Homer took care of all their relatives in Columbus and beyond. ...

... Along with letters of condolence came citations posthumously awarding Dad a Purple Heart (his third) and an Oak Leaf Cluster to his Silver Star (his second). Then came what the Army Services Force called his "personal effects," the first of which was in the form of a check for $14.17. Then in Dad's metal footlocker came his Combat Infantry Badge and other decorations, a magnifying glass, a pen and pencil set, a Hermann Goering Division armband, a pair of civilian shoes, a souvenir map of Sicily, some photos in a folder, scarves, his OD blouse and "pink" trousers, and a trench coat. And finally there came a glasses case "damaged, apparently by bloodstain." Before sending the case, a lieutenant wrote to ask if Mom wanted it, saying, "It is our desire to refrain from sending any article which would be distressing; at the same time, we do not feel justified in removing the item without your consent."

And there were other matters to attend to as well. There were pensions due to Mom, Anne, and me as surviving next of kin. From the Social Security Administration Mom learned that she would receive $21.91 a month as Dad's widow, Anne would get $14.61, and I would get $14.60. I didn't understand why Anne was entitled to a penny more than I was, unless it was because I might be able to get a job sooner. The Veterans Administration added another $78.00 for Mom, $22.80 for me, $22.00 for Anne. Though these amounts would change in time, the three of us would begin our new husbandless, fatherless life compensated with $174.72 a month. To receive his money Mom had to fill out countless forms and provide documentation of Dad's military service and his death. Even a little bank near Fort Dix [New Jersey] where Mom and Dad kept a joint account required similar documentation before it could drop Dad's name from the account.

But Mom wanted and perhaps needed something to do. What might she do with her love of the written and spoken word, her sense of humor, her flare for the dramatic? Teach. She wrote to Dr. Samuel Shellabarger, headmaster of the Columbus School for Girls, seeking a position teaching English. Dr. Shellabarger had nothing at the time, he said, but thought something might open later in the summer. It did, and in September Mom found herself employed for the first time in her life, teaching freshman and sophomore girls in the school that she had attended and Anne was attending.

As the aftermath wore on, there was the matter of "Disposition of World War II Armed Forces Dead," as a pamphlet from the War Department put it. The pamphlet explained that there were four options, three of which applied to us: "The remains be interred in a permanent American military cemetery overseas; The remains be returned to the United States, or any possession or territory thereof, for interment by next of kin in a private cemetery; The remains be returned to the United States for interment in a national cemetery." If none of these was satisfactory, next of kin could submit a specific desire to the Quartermaster General.

Though the decision was technically Mom's, she felt strongly that Deo should have a say in the matter. Probably the decision came down to a choice between the first and third options. When Jack Senior died in 1936, he was buried at Arlington National Cemetery with honors befitting his rank. Deo would join him there when her time came. To bring Dad's body back and have it buried there with the same honors must have been a compelling option. However, back then, the quick return of flag-draped, ice-packed caskets by plane to Dover Air Force Base was many years in the future; it might be years before bodies would be coming home. To have Dad's body brought home for eventual burial at Arlington would have meant for all the family a revival of all the grief that had attended the War Department telegram.

Meanwhile, there was some question whether the temporary cemetery would become a permanent facility under the jurisdiction and supervision of the United States government. If so, then Deo and Mom would leave Dad's remains there. If not, he would come back to Arlington. At last assurance came, and the two women who loved him agreed that Dad would lie near where he first had been buried—in the military cemetery at Nettuno, once part of the Anzio beachhead. ...

All these years later, it seems as though life in the summer of 1944 was a lot like life before Dad's death, only without the letters. It was still Mom, Anne, and I, just as it had been for the almost twenty months that Dad was overseas. While he was away, I hadn't thought seriously about Dad's not coming home. Mom, on the other hand, must have been unable to put from her mind for very long the image of the dreadful telegram. Still, she kept her fear from Anne and me, just as she and Dad had kept us from their prewar worries about making it through the Depression.

After a trip east to be with Dad's family, we returned to Columbus to start the new school year. In her new teaching job, Mom was teaching girls whom I was seeing socially. How I hoped that she would not entertain her pupils with cute anecdotes or snapshots of my infancy. Between Mom's salary and the government pensions, we were getting along. Mom began to have gentlemen callers.

One of these was a distant cousin of Dad's. Learned and witty, with an explosive laugh, he owned and directed a small boarding school in Connecticut. Though he was some seventeen years older than Mom, she saw in him, I think, a secure world of ideas and books. When they married in 1946, we said good-bye to Columbus.

That fall I went to Exeter, as Dad had. As the train began to carry me away, Mom trotted along the platform and called out her parting words. "If you have a stomach ache, don't let them give you a laxative!"

In Exeter's butt rooms I learned to smoke and play bridge. In her classrooms I sat in awe and occasional trepidation before the men who taught me the stuff of secondary education. Later I realized how much I admired them. Many men on the Exeter faculty had been there when Dad was, but I don't recall any of them ever saying, "I knew your father when he was here."

One master, however, did have a story about Dad. In early June 1944, Robert Bates arrived on the beach at Nettuno and was in the Third Division's rear area when Dad's body was brought back. The mood at the division headquarters was somber enough that Bates asked why and who. An Exeter graduate, Bates left the army a lieutenant colonel and returned to Exeter to teach in 1946, the year I arrived. While looking over a student list one day, he saw my name. It sounded familiar. Then he recalled the scene two years earlier. While I was at Exeter, he never told me, though he did tell one of my classmates. Not until we met at a reunion many years later did the story come out. ...

Source: Jack J. Toffey IV, *Jack Toffey's War: A Son's Memoir* (New York: Fordham University Press, 2008), pp. 214–215, 225–227, 229–230.

2 US War Department, Excerpt from Pamphlet, "Going Back to Civilian Life: A Supplement Explaining the Provisions of the 'GI Bill of Rights,'" 1944

The United States has a long tradition of aiding veterans. Disabled veterans and war orphans have received pensions since the American Revolution. During the Revolutionary War and into the nineteenth century, veterans often received land grants from the national government in compensation for their service. To ensure that aged veterans stayed out of the poorhouse, the federal government bestowed old age pensions on veterans of the Revolutionary War and successive nineteenth-century conflicts. With a great deal of reluctance, US Congress granted World War I veterans a deferred bonus for their war-time service. The Service Adjustment Act of 1944, more widely known as the GI Bill of Rights, marks a departure from previous policies toward returning veterans. By design, the GI Bill sought to aid the transition not only of disabled servicemen and servicewomen, but also of able-bodied personnel, with unprecedented provisions for unemployment insurance, loans to purchase a home, business or farm, and money for education. The GI Bill set important precedents in terms of both aiding veterans and providing federal support for higher education. In reading the provisions, keep in mind that the tuition reimbursements were generous enough to pay the cost of attending Ivy League schools and elite institutions in the United States and around the world.

War Department Pamphlet No. 21-4A, *Additional Information for Soldiers Going Back to Civilian Life: A Supplement Explaining the Provisions of the "GI Bill of Rights" (Public Law 346-78ᵗʰ Congress)*, War Department 10 August 1944

...

Education. Educational aid for veterans is available from the Veterans' Administration provided: (1) you were discharged under conditions other than dishonorable; (2) you were not over 25 at the time you entered service, or can demonstrate that your education or training was interrupted or interfered with by service; or you desire a refresher or retraining course; (3) you served 90 days or more (not counting the time in Army Specialized Training Program or Navy College Training Program, which course was a continuation of a civilian course and was pursued to completion, or as a Cadet or Midshipman in a Service Academy) or were discharged or released from actual service because of an actual service related injury or disability; and (4) you start such education not later than two years after discharge or end of war (whichever date is later).

Length of training. One year (or its equivalent in part-time study). If you complete these courses satisfactorily, you will be entitled to additional education or training not to exceed the length of time you spent in active service after 16 September 1940 and before the end of the present war (not including ASTP or Navy College program). No course of education or training shall exceed 4 years.

Expenses paid. The Veterans' Administration will pay to the educational or training institution the customary cost of tuition, and such laboratory, library, infirmary, and similar payments as are customarily charged, and may pay for books, supplies, equipment and such other necessary expenses (exclusive of board, lodging, other living expenses and travel) as are required. Such payments shall not exceed $500 for an ordinary school-year.

Where to apply. Make application to the nearest regional office (or facility having regional offices activities) of the Veterans' Administration, or directly to the educational institution you wish to attend. Proper application forms will be available at either of those places.

Types of educational institution. Public or private, elementary, secondary, and other schools furnishing education for adults; business schools and colleges, vocational schools, junior colleges, teachers' colleges, normal schools, professional schools, universities, and other educational and training institutions, including industrial establishments.

If Unemployed. To cover temporary periods of unemployment following, discharge, financial help is available to you, either through State or Federal sources. ...

Federal Provisions. Weekly allowances of unemployment compensation are available through a Federal program if you are not eligible under a State program. If you qualify under both, money received under a State plan is subtracted from the Federal allowance. Under the Federal plan, you may receive four weeks of allowance for each calendar month of active service after 16 September 1940 and before the end of the present war, up to a total limit of 52 weeks.

If you are completely unemployed, your allowance is $20 a week. If you are partially unemployed, you receive the difference between your wage and the weekly allowance plus $3. If you are self-employed, you may still be eligible if your net earnings in the previous calendar month were less than $100. Allowances remaining unpaid at your death do not become part of your estate. ...

Loans for Homes, Farms, Business. These three types of loans are available to veterans who served on or after 16 September 1940 and before the end of the present war, and who are discharged or released under conditions other than dishonorable, after active service of 90 days or more, or because of service-incurred injury or disability. Applications must be made within two years after discharge or separation, or two years after the end of the war (whichever is later), but in no event more than five years after the end of the war.

The Administrator of Veterans' Affairs will guarantee up to 50% of any such loan or loans, provided that the amount guaranteed shall not exceed a total of $2,000. The Administrator will pay the interest on the guaranteed amount for the first year. Loans guaranteed by the Administrator bear interest of not more than 4 % per year and must be paid up within twenty years ...

Source: *Additional Information for Soldiers Going Back to Civilian Life: A Supplement explaining the Provisions of the "GI Bill of Rights" (Public Law 346-78th Congress)*. War Department Pamphlet No. 21-4A (Washington, DC: Government Printing Office, 1944), pp. 2–5, 7–8.

3 *Harvard Crimson*, "Wistful Vista II," 1946; "The Counsellor and the Dean," 1947

During the war, many elite colleges that only enrolled men struggled as the draft siphoned off much of their student body for the war effort. In some cases colleges opened their doors to women for the first time, while others made up the shortfall by hosting military training programs. For instance, the Army through the Army Specialized Training Program (ASTP) and the Navy through the V-12 sent scores of young draftees to college. The end of the war combined with the educational opportunities afforded by the GI Bill of Rights sent many returning male GIs to trade schools, high school, college, graduate school, law school, and medical school. All institutions of higher education struggled to accommodate these returning GIs, including Harvard. In the following two articles from the Harvard Crimson, *the student newspaper describes how most institutions of higher education experienced problems finding housing for new students, especially those with families.*

The shortage of housing for GIs was part of a wider shortage of suitable
dwellings for Americans. Little new construction had taken place in the
Great Depression and World War II, and as marriage and birth rates soared,
many young GI families struggled to find a house to purchase or apartment
to rent. The GI Bill fostered some other changes at Harvard and in the wider
American society. The anonymous writer in the Crimson *wonders if the*
changes brought by GIs to Harvard were positive.

"Wistful Vista II," *Harvard Crimson*, June 21, 1946

It begins to look as if there will be no place in Cambridge for G.I. Joe
College and his family next fall. Each week the number of unfilled housing
applications at the office in Straus Hall jumps closer to the estimated 2500
that will confront University officials by September. The bottleneck has been
predicted for many months; the Housing office has scoured a Cambridge
already crowded to the saturation point; the Alumni have been asked to
help, and the University has achieved near miracles on a shoe-string invest-
ment. But the fact remains that unless the University administration matches
talk with cash, unless emergency units of almost any sort are set up within
the next three months, close to 20 percent of the student body must forego
either their families or their education.

Unlike many colleges throughout the country, Harvard entered the housing
free-for-all late in the game. Six months after M.I.T. broke ground for their
college-financed West gate project, Harvard was still tied down in complex
arrangements with the city and federal government aimed at importing sec-
ond-hand, defense plant dwellings for use on Cambridge sites. The negotiations paid off—200 families now live in the Jarvis Field and Business School
developments—while 100 more will find lodging, though definitely not low-
cost, in the recently acquired Brunswick Hotel. More than anything else,
University Hall has counted on its allotment of facilities at Fort Devens to
satisfy the demand at its pack [*sic*] next fall. But all of these projects combined can house but 900 families. The remaining 1600 applicants will form
the ranks of Cambridge's own Displaced Persons, shuttling between boarding house and hotels until either patience or health gives out.

It is too late to talk about a boat missed a year ago. An examination of
Tech's project, college planned, constructed and owned, is ample proof of
what can be done by getting in on the ground floor and devoting large scale
funds and talent toward the solution of a large-scale problem. A project of
the same type at Harvard could not be completed in time to ease the
September squeeze. Now University Hall must scramble to avert tragedy

with all the means it can beg, ... [borrow] or steal over the summer. It is also too late to fret over the eyesore quality of a colony of Quonset huts. The alternative picture of a family of three living in one room is not pretty either.

Quonset huts seem to be the only solution to a crisis that has been allowed to reach its eleventh hour. The University has contracted for forty of these structures. If the administration plans to use this as a model for other developments, forty are sufficient. But if the University means to drop the job there, it will be a clear demonstration that Harvard is still economizing as usual while colleges with much smaller endowments rally to meet this crisis in education. No less than ten times that number of emergency units, placed on Soldiers Field, along the River, in the Dunster tennis court, and in every nook, and cranny that is not in current use, will fill the gap.

Harvard has contracted to educate some 6000 veterans. It must realize that part of this responsibility includes expenditures that will insure the married veteran even a small part of the care lavished on his unmarried colleague.

"The Counsellor and the Dean," *Harvard Crimson*, March 12, 1947

Today, with its biggest enrollment in history successfully swallowed and with a gradual return to normal expected to start next fall, the University stands astride the conquered problems of the immediate postwar veteran influx and contemplates the coming problems of readjustment. Pausing only for a quick glance backward on a nearly finished job, Wilbur J. Bender's "Report On The Veteran" in the current Alumni Bulletin throws a penetrating searchlight onto the matter of Harvard, the veteran, and the future. As Counsellor for Veterans, Mr. Bender has pointed clearly to the problems which, as the next Dean of the College, he will have a major share in solving.

First among these stands tuition. Today Harvard has the lowest rates of any major college in the East. Yale, Dartmouth, and M.I.T. have succumbed to the onslaught of higher costs by raising their tuition, and there is no guarantee that Harvard will not be forced to follow suit in the future. But, as Mr. Bender points out, a raise in tuition may "price Harvard out of the market" when it comes to maintaining its standings as a democratic institution on a national basis. Students from the Mid and Far West would be unlikely to shell out increased tuition, and another hundred or so for the Pullman people twice a year, while meeting high metropolitan living expenses, when they could go to increasingly good state colleges almost for nothing.

More immediately and not much less potently than a rise in tuition, the attitude of the veteran threatens to change the nature of the College. "The lights are burning very late," Mr. Bender writes, "and there is not much leisurely talk or fellowship or group spirit. In the College, particularly, there is an unhealthy emphasis on grades." Here is a problem that Bender will inherit in all its complexity from Dean Hanford next July: how to relax the veteran and Keep Harvard from becoming a round-the-clock grind factory. This is no easy task, with graduate schools expecting their peak demand for admission to last longer than in the College. Nonetheless, a greater emphasis on activities, more efficiently run activities, a Student Activities Center—in general, more official interest in the extra-curriculum, might help to alleviate what it [sic] known, in quotes, as "student apathy."

Other, less concrete issues fall into the beam of Mr. Bender's searchlight. The fact, for instance, that students "are not very hopeful of the good times coming and tend to concentrate on digging individual foxholes in the shape of training for careers" stands opposed to the non-professionalized aims of the general education plan. This conflict and the issues of tuition and extra-curricular life are the biggest but by no means the only questions raised by Mr. Bender's "Report," which covers everything from the problems of the married veteran to those of the engineer who has forgotten his mathematics during the war. The new dean has cut out his work for himself.

Source: "Wistful Vista II," *Harvard Crimson*, June 21, 1946, http://www.thecrimson. com/article.aspx?ref=469700; "The Counsellor and the Dean," *Harvard Crimson*, March 12, 1947, http://www.thecrimson.com/article.aspx?ref=471121.

4 Eli Ginzberg, Excerpt from *Breakdown and Recovery*, 1959

The war took a toll on many American service personnel long after the fighting stopped. For some of the most severely wounded, debilitating brain injuries or the loss of limbs meant they would spend the rest of their lives in Veterans' Administration hospitals. Others were psychologically scarred. The following account describes the efforts of one returning veteran to cope with the aftermath of combat and the tremendous guilt he felt over a split-second decision. Enemy bullets, aerial bombardments, and artillery fire killed the majority of those who died in combat, but the friendly fire incident recounted below was not uncommon. This is an excerpt from a study commissioned by Dwight Eisenhower while he served as Columbia University President. It was conducted by a team of social scientists who sought to better "uncover the causes of the major deficiencies in the nation's human resources that World War II revealed." The team had access to the Veterans' Administration files, with the provision they did not reveal the names of individual cases like the one below.

D. L. M. spent his early life in a small Midwestern town. His father was a farmer with a comfortable income. When D.L.M. was thirteen, however, his father died and shortly thereafter the family lost its savings because the local bank failed. Although he wanted to continue in high school D.L.M. had to devote all his time to working on the farm. For the next eighteen years he lived at home with his mother, who became quite nervous after her husband's death. At the age of twenty-eight he gave up farming and took a job as a sheet-metal worker in a factory. Three years later, and several months before he was drafted, he married a local school teacher. They continued to live with his mother on the farm.

After he was drafted, D. L. M. was assigned to a newly activated infantry division which had just started training on the West Coast. For six months he went through intensive training including desert maneuvers. Then the division went to Hawaii where he spent another ten months in training and guard duty. During this time he had two operations for a chronic eye disorder, but otherwise he was in good health. He went with his outfit to New Guinea where, as a newly promoted private first class, he first saw combat in the summer of 1944. The fighting, mostly patrol action against isolated Japanese units, lasted until early 1945, when the entire division was sent to the Philippines. Relieving one of the invasion units, D.L.M.'s regiment was immediately thrown into heavy fighting. The advance was slow both because of the mountainous terrain and the stubborn Japanese resistance. In thirty days they had advanced only 13 miles. Casualties were heavy.

On one occasion D.L.M.'s battalion was instructed to take a small mountain that had been the site of fanatical enemy resistance for several days. One attack failed and a second advance was ordered under the cover of darkness. As a member of a squad which had been reduced to seven men, D.L.M. advanced through the underbrush and emerged close to the Japanese lines just as the sun was rising. The fighting was continuous and fierce for two days. Enemy mortar fire was heavy and accurate. By the end of the first day D.L.M. and a buddy were the only ones in his squad still alive. Pinned down in a dugout, he did not notice when this buddy crawled off to the side in an attempt to circle around and advance a few yards closer to the enemy position. Then he suddenly saw a figure stooped over and running directly at him. Automatically he opened fire and with some satisfaction saw the figure crumple. Only when the figure began to shout at him in English did he realize that he had wounded his own buddy. Completely shattered by this experience, D.L.M. broke down completely. Although the mountain was soon captured, he felt no sense of elation. His thoughts centered constantly on what he felt was his unforgivable sin. Depressed and afraid, he was evacuated to the hospital.

There he was constantly upset; he jumped at the slightest noise and swore that he would never pick up a rifle again. Although the doctor tried to convince him that he had done the right thing and that if the oncoming figure had been Japanese he would have been killed, he refused to believe him. Again and again he mulled over the events of that day and always came to the conclusion that he was guilty of a terrible crime. To shoot an enemy was bad enough, but necessary. To shoot a friend was not only bad, it was unforgivable. He trembled all over when he thought of it, and there was a constant ache in his back. By the time he reached the States he was suffering from malaria as well and had lost 20 pounds, because he often refused to eat. Discharged in the fall of 1945, he was somewhat less anxious, but far from recovered.

Nevertheless, on returning home, he refused psychiatric treatment from the Veterans Administration because he was afraid that his friends and neighbors would condemn him for and laugh at his weakness. During the first year after his discharge, D.L.M. was unable to work at all. His back hurt; he was nervous and depressed. Then he took a part-time job with a roofing company. His income was small, largely because he found it very difficult to do much work. His family were supported by his pension and his wife's teaching. However, by 1951 he was working steadily for the roofing company and had been put in charge of several branch offices. The prospect of his actually supporting his family proved stimulating. Then the company went out of business and about the same time his wife became pregnant and had to stop work. D.L.M. started his own roofing business, but to date he has been able to realize only a very small profit. He spends much of his time moping around the house and still is preoccupied with what he considers to be his guilt. The events of that day in April 1945 are etched on his mind in bold-face type. Not a day goes by but what he thinks of them and shudders imperceptibly.

Source: Eli Ginzberg et al., *Breakdown and Recovery* (New York: Columbia University Press, 1959), pp. 115–117.

5 Mira Ryczke Kimmelman, Excerpt from *Life Beyond the Holocaust*, 2005

Mira Kimmelman, a native of Danzig, Germany, survived the Auschwitz death camp and the Bergen Belsen concentration camp before being liberated by British forces in April 1945. Her entire family, except for her father, was killed during the Holocaust. Although Mira's father remained in Germany

after the war and tried to reestablish himself in business, she decided along
with her husband to emigrate to the United States. Sponsored by relatives
in Ohio, they journeyed by ocean liner to New York City, taking charge of
a group of Holocaust orphans who were also resettled in the United States.
In this memoir, she refers to her husband as Dad and mentions the assistance
offered by the Hebrew Immigrant Aid Society (HIAS), which aided her
resettlement in America.

After one week in New York City, Dad and I had to depart for Cincinnati.
The weather in New York was steaming hot on Sunday, August 1, 1948,
when we left the Hotel Marseilles in Manhattan for Penn Station. A taxi
took us plus our two suitcases and one canvas bag (these were all our material possessions) to catch the evening train to Cincinnati. Our family there
had been alerted about the time of our arrival. All our travel expenses had
been paid by HIAS, for which we were most grateful. ...

Once we arrived in Cincinnati, my cousin Rose told us the true story
about sponsoring us. Financially, nobody in the family had enough assets to
bring us over and to guarantee that they could support us. They turned to
the people who owned the tailor shop where Uncle Max and Sam Roth
worked and asked for their help. We knew the names of our sponsors and
told Rose that Dad and I would like to meet them and thank them in person.
Cousin Rose told us: "You cannot meet them, they do not want to meet you.
We had a gentlemen's agreement that they would only sponsor you under
the condition that they would never have to meet you. They did us a favor
by sponsoring you." We were shocked but we had to accept this fact. We
never met them, we never had to ask them for help, and we could never say
thank you.

Our first meal in the home of our relatives was a lavish lunch. We felt so
welcome and admired how warm a relationship there was between the three
generations that lived under one roof, in one apartment. Uncle Max asked
me many questions about his family. He remembered life in Poland at the
end of the nineteenth century and remembered many details from his early
years in Slupca. Over and over he asked me if I was sure that only my father
and I had survived. He knew that he had one nephew, Heniek Jakubowski,
who went to Palestine. But all relatives that lived in Poland during World
War II perished. Then came the strangest question: "What happened to all
the money and jewelry that belonged to my parents?" His mother died in
1910, and his father remarried, had another child, and died in 1920. All
I could tell him was that if there was money or jewelry, his parents must
have given it to their children and that I had no knowledge about this. Dad

told him that the Nazis stripped the Jews of all their material possessions before they killed them. This Uncle Max did not know.

Both Dad and I were anxious to find work. We did not want to be a burden to our family and wanted to earn money as soon as possible. Rose told us that the Jewish Federation in Cincinnati had been notified of our arrival and they had already begun looking for jobs for us. "Once we find work, we shall also look for a place to live," I assured my family. They had opened their modest home to us and had been so warm and kind. We did not want to impose on their hospitality. While waiting to hear from the Jewish Federation, Rose and Uncle Max took us on a tour of their city. We traveled by streetcar from their neighborhood in Avondale to downtown. Rose told us that Cincinnati had about half a million inhabitants, twenty thousand of whom were Jews. She also told us that there were neighborhoods in Cincinnati where Jews could not rent an apartment or buy a house. These were the "restricted" neighborhoods. We also found out that some companies did not employ Jews. This came as a shock to us. We never thought that we would have to experience discrimination and anti-Semitism in the United States. How can this be true in such a free country, a country that welcomes refugees? Nobody ever mentioned this to us in Europe. This was truly an eye-opener. ...

While we were exploring Cincinnati, the Family Service of the Jewish Federation called and told Aunt Yetta that they had found a job for Dad. He was to report to the place that offered the job for an interview. Dad put down on his job application his profession in textiles, and the federation found a place for him with the Adler Company, a factory that produced hosiery for men. Uncle Max got up early the next morning to take ... [Dad] to his interview. The Adler Company was located on Queen City and Harrison Avenue. They had to take two streetcars and one bus to get there. The interview took place on Thursday, August 5. With Uncle Max as an interpreter, Dad's interview did not last long. Fortunately, one of the vice presidents of the Adler Company, Harry Groban, was present, and he asked Dad if he spoke Yiddish. Mr. Groban took a liking to Dad right away and hired him. Dad's background was as a textile engineer. He worked before the war in a large textile factory in Piotrkow, Poland. Here he was hired to work as a laborer in the shipping department. His pay would be sixty-three cents per hour, with the opportunity to work overtime. Dad was to report for work the following Monday. ...

It was September and the High Holy Days were upon us. Shortly before our holidays, we were visited by two ladies from the Jewish Family Service. They came to offer us financial help so that we could purchase new clothing and food for the holidays. We thanked them politely and declined their offer.

258   The United States in World War II

"We are both working. We earn enough and do not need money." We never accepted charity and never would. Both of us felt offended. We understood that their intentions were good. They wanted to help us. We told them how glad we were to be in this country, that we appreciated the fact that the federation helped in securing jobs for us, but we would never accept any money. Then they asked if they could help with medical expenses, should they occur. Again, we declined their offer. What troubled us was the fact that the Family Service was solely interested in material help. Not once did they ask about our spiritual and social needs. We were so lonely. No one ever invited us into their homes. The only homes we had been to were the homes of my relatives. As newcomers, as refugees, and as Holocaust survivors, we were not accepted by the American Jewish community. This was painful and many times we felt like outcasts. Only many years later did we understand that people were apprehensive about getting close to us, did not know how to talk to us—maybe were afraid to offend us.

Source: Mira Ryczke Kimmelman, *Life Beyond the Holocaust: Memories and Realities* (Knoxville: University of Tennessee Press, 2005), pp. 71, 73–75, 79.

Study Questions

1   How was John Toffey's life changed by the death of his father? Why do you think so few of his teachers at Exeter wanted to talk to him about his late father?
2   How generous were the GI Bill of Rights benefits for veterans who wanted to go to school?
3   How was Harvard University changed by the arrival of veterans on the GI Bill of Rights? Were all these changes positive?
4   Do you think "D.L.M." ever recovered from the guilt described in Eli Ginzberg's account? Does the case history of "D.L.M." offer an optimistic prognosis? What has prevented "D.L.M.'s" situation from getting worse?
5   Why do you think so many Americans were reluctant to talk with Mira Kimmelman about her experiences during the Holocaust? How welcoming were Americans to the Kimmelmans?

Chapter 12 Commemoration and Memory

1 Archibald MacLeish, "Memorials Are For Remembrance," *The Architectural Forum*, 1944

Efforts to commemorate World War I had divided Americans. They debated where the war dead would be buried and whether the United States should maintain overseas cemeteries in Europe. Fierce differences emerged over what type of memorials should be built, with many Progressives arguing in favor of such living memorials as hospitals, schools, parks, highways, community centers, and playgrounds. Others, especially artists and sculptors, insisted that only traditional monuments such as statues would be suitable to honor those who had served and died for their country. Even before victory had been achieved in World War II, Americans again considered how to mark this global conflict. In this article, the poet and Librarian of Congress Archibald MacLeish adopts a middle position, arguing that both living memorials and traditional ones were appropriate ways to memorialize this war.

There was an argument after the last war about war memorials. Some people thought we should build memorial hospitals or memorial schools instead of memorial statues. They argued that the hospitals would be useful whereas

The United States in World War II: A Documentary Reader, First Edition.
Edited by G. Kurt Piehler. Editorial material and organization © 2013 Blackwell Publishing Ltd.
Published 2013 by Blackwell Publishing Ltd.

the statues would merely be statues. It was a question of mathematics. A hospital would be a memorial plus a service to the community. A statue would be a memorial and nothing more. Therefore, a hospital was superior to a statue.

I hope that debate will not be renewed after this war—or that, if it is renewed, it will be renewed on a sensible issue. The question is not whether a useful memorial would be more useful than another. The question is whether a useful memorial would be better.

Which means, better *as* a memorial. No one doubts that structures can be built and called memorials which will be of use to the community. What some people question, and question seriously, is whether the added usefulness of a hospital or a library or a school or an auditorium is an advantage when the object is to construct, not a library or a hospital, but a memorial to young men killed in war.

They have a right, I think, to an answer—and to an answer on their own terms. They have a right to an answer even when they use the debate to beat dead donkeys, demanding to know whether we are now so dependent on functions to create forms that, where there are no functions, we are obliged to invent them. The real question in issue, whether we like it or not, is precisely the question they raise. The real question in issue is whether a memorial structure which serves a utilitarian purpose will be better or worse *as a memorial* than a structure which has no purpose but the purpose of commemoration.

But what, then, is a memorial? What is it for? What is it supposed to do?

I should say, for myself, that the purpose of a memorial is to make the minds of men remember. It is a structure built by the living not only to honor the dead but to keep the names of the dead, and of their deeds, alive. Which means, of course, to keep them alive in the minds of generations which had not been born when these battles were fought and these dead died.

I say "for myself" because there are intelligent men who take a different position, arguing against the traditional war memorials on the ground that the people of America do not think of the dead when they build, but of the living. They argue that American civilization is free of the regard for the dead, the regard for the past, which has occupied the minds of earlier civilizations, and that American architecture is an architecture indifferent to the monumental and memorial forms which have characterized the architecture of other peoples. I do not believe them, and I do not think the position can be supported on these grounds. A great people, now as before, is a people in which the sense of the past has become the sense of the future: a people in which the sense of history has turned its face about to become the sense of destiny. And the architecture of a great people is an architecture which not only works but speaks—an architecture able, in its supreme expressions, to turn the people's past into their purpose.

But whether or not they are right in theory and aesthetic, those who take this view are wrong in fact. The American people *will* be thinking of their dead in this war when they raise their memorials, and the structures they build will be commemorative structures: or will be so intended. One may quarrel with the intention, but one can hardly deny that it exists. And neither, I think, can one deny its sincerity. I have seen arguments for "useful" memorials which came close to scepticism on that point, and even to open cynicism. I have seen it broadly hinted that the desire of the citizens of American communities to remember their dead should be so molded and managed that it would become a desire for something which would be "better" for them than a mere memorial would be. Find out what the town needs most, and get the people to make a memorial of that! Make this sentimental monument-building serve a useful purpose—something the town will be glad to have fifty years from now when the war is forgotten—and the dead are forgotten!

But, of course, it is precisely to keep the people of the town from forgetting the dead and forgetting the war that the memorial is to be built. To turn it into something else which cannot keep the memory of the dead alive is to cheat the town of its dearest hope. And the cheat will be no more excusable because a bronze plaque to the left of the front door, or a marble panel by the drinking fountain, calls the building a memorial. Unless it is in fact and in truth a memorial, affecting the minds of men as a memorial should affect them, the structure will fail to do what it pretends to do. There is a word for failures of that kind whether in business or in art.

But to say all this does not mean that there is no proper relation between the usefulness of a structure and its adequacy as a memorial. Of all categories of art, the art of the people's memorial to their dead is, or should be, the most democratic, the most general. It exists for, and it should speak to, every man and woman and understanding child. It should be seen even by those who do not wish to see it—even by those who would like to forget that men have suffered for belief before and may again. It should be a part of the consciousness of the people, a part of their recognition of themselves, a presence in the minds of all those who lived in the town or loved it or remembered it, as the smell of the wild carrots is part of the common memory in one place, or the smell of the salt marshes in another, or of coal smoke, or sweet grass, or the sprinkling cart on the asphalt. No child should grow up in the town without knowing it and knowing what it means—not by a plaque or a preachment but by the thing itself.

The usefulness of a structure—or, more precisely, its useful relation to the life of the community in which it stands—may relate directly and helpfully to its accomplishment of these ends. In an ideal world—a world in which every town and village could find an artist of genius and, what's more, could recognize him when it found him—the commemorative purpose might be achieved without resort to utility. A great monument is, next to a great poem, the most enduring means to make the minds of men remember. But great monuments demand great artists and great artists are not numerous to begin with, nor when they do exist, select. The practical choice facing most American communities after this war will not be a choice between great monuments and useful buildings. It will be a choice between monuments of a kind which are already far too familiar, and structures which may, by their usefulness, or through their usefulness, make up in part their lacks as works of art.

In that choice utility is entitled to consideration, not as utility, but as an aid in accomplishing what the memorial was intended to accomplish. A second-rate monument is, of all substantial objects, the least visible and the least affective. A monstrosity may be visible in its ugliness, but a mediocre piece is merely not there—as the soldier statues in so many towns are merely not there. A building, on the other hand, which relates to the life of the town—which is part of the life of the town—may survive other and more permanent things and may speak as well as it knows how to speak when they are silent.

It is this relation to the life of the town which counts. But relation to the life of the town, let it be said again, is not the same thing as relation to the town's needs. A town may need a hospital without centering its life in the hospital when it is built. It may need a number of buildings and services. To provide them, no matter how necessary they may be, will not produce a memorial unless the life of the town is in the structure.

The first labor, therefore, and the most important labor, in the building of a memorial which is to find its commemorative power in its use, is the town's labor and not its artist's or its architect's. The town must choose for itself, and out of its knowledge of itself the kind of memorial which will touch its daily life—touch it in such a way that the memorial will become part of its life and part of its consciousness. There is hardly an American community in which some characteristic of the town, some relation of the town to a hill or a river or a harbor, some square or street or corner, has not become by use, by custom, a center of the town's life. These preferences, unconsciously made by generations of men and boys, are the true elections. And they last, with luck for generations. What must be done first is to consider what these places are and which of them is nearest to the town's sense of its own identity, and how best this street or building or bridge or park can be used to hold the past in its continuing present.

It is useless, in anything as particular and intimate as this, to talk of types of buildings—libraries, schools, community centers. What may have meaning for one city will be meaningless to another. In one village I know, the best memorial to the boys it has lost in this war could probably be made in the playing field they used. In another, a library room looking down the street that makes the town's center would hold many memories and for years to come. But there are no generalities. The question in each case is a question for the community, and a question only the community can answer.

If the men and women of the American villages and towns would ask themselves: What is there in this town which is most like it? What is there here that speaks of the town most movingly to those who think back to it? What is there here *they* must have thought of when they thought of home? And what could be done with that corner, that square, that grove, that brook, to make it hold the image of their longing for it so that other later men would feel it also? If the men and women of the American towns would find these answers for themselves, they would build memorials, with the aid of artists or without it, which would "prevail on the hearts of unborn men to remember" for many years to come.

Source: Archibald MacLeish, "Memorials Are For Remembrance," *The Architectural Forum*, September 1944, pp. 111–112, 170.

2 Elie Wiesel, Introduction to President's Commission on the Holocaust, *Report to the President*, 1979

After the initial wave of monument building in the late 1940s and early 1950s, further concerted efforts to memorialize World War II were made in the 1970s and 1980s to commemorate the Holocaust. In 1978, in an effort to aid the Middle East peace process as well as court favor with the American Jewish community, Jimmy Carter created a commission to study the commemoration of the Holocaust. Headed by the writer and later Nobel Laureate Elie Wiesel, the commission called for a living memorial to ensure the lessons of the Holocaust were remembered. The commission's report led to the establishment of a permanent US Holocaust Memorial Council that oversaw the construction of the United States Holocaust Memorial Museum in Washington, DC. Although federal land for the Museum was provided to the Holocaust Commission at no charge, private donations paid the cost of the building and exhibitions.

President's Commission on the Holocaust
Office of the Chairman
September 27, 1979

Dear Mr. President:

It is with a deep sense of privilege that I submit to you, in accordance with your request, the report of your Commission on the Holocaust. Never before have its members, individually and collectively, given so much of themselves to a task that is both awesome and forbidding, a task which required reaching far back into the past as well as taking a hard look into the future.

Our central focus was memory—our own and that of the victims during a time of unprecedented evil and suffering. That was the Holocaust, an era we must remember not only because of the dead; it is too late for them. Not only because of the survivors; it may even be late for them. Our remembering is an act of generosity, aimed at saving men and women from apathy to evil, if not from evil itself.

We wish, through the work of this Commission, to reach and transform as many human beings as possible. We hope to share our conviction that when war and genocide unleash hatred against any one people or peoples, all are ultimately engulfed in the fire.

With this conviction and mindful of your mandate, Mr. President, we have explored during the past several months of our existence the various ways and means of remembering—and of moving others to remember—the Holocaust and its victims, an event that was intended to erase memory.

Our first question may sound rhetorical: Why remember, why remember at all? Is not human nature opposed to keeping alive memories that hurt and disturb? The more cruel the wound, the greater the effort to cover it, to hide it beneath other wounds, other scars. Why then cling to unbearable memories that may forever rob us of our sleep? Why not forget, turn the page, and proclaim: let it remain buried beneath the dark nightmares of our subconscious. Why not spare our children the weight of our collective burden and allow them to start their lives free of nocturnal obsessions and complexes, free of Auschwitz and its shadows?

These questions, Mr. President, would not perhaps be devoid of merit if it were possible to extirpate the Holocaust from history and make believe we can forget. But it is not possible and we cannot. Like it or not, the Event must and will dominate future events. Its centrality in the creative endeavors of our contemporaries remains undisputed. Philosophers and social scientists, psychologists and moralists, theologians and artists: all have termed it a watershed in the annals of mankind. What was comprehensible before Treblinka is comprehensible no longer. After Treblinka, man's ability to cope with his condition was shattered; he was pushed to his limits and beyond. Whatever has happened since must therefore be judged in the light of Treblinka. Forgetfulness is no solution.

Treblinka and Auschwitz, Majdanek and Belzec, Buchenwald and Ponar, these and other capitals of the Holocaust kingdom must therefore be remembered, and for several reasons.

First, we cannot grant the killers a posthumous victory. Not only did they humiliate and assassinate their victims, they wanted also to destroy their memory. They killed them twice, reducing them to ashes and then; denying their deed. Not to remember the dead now would mean to become accomplices to their murderers.

Second, we cannot deny the victims the fulfillment of their last wish; their idée fixe to bear witness. What the merchant from Saloniki, the child from Lodz, the rabbi from Radzimin, the carpenter from Warsaw and the scribe from Vilna had in common was the passion, the compulsion to tell the tale—or to enable someone else to do so. Every ghetto had its historians, every deathcamp its chroniclers. Young and old, learned and unlearned, everybody kept diaries, wrote journals, composed poems and prayers. They wanted to remember and to be remembered. They wanted to defeat the enemy's conspiracy of silence, to communicate a spark of the fire that nearly consumed their generation, and, above all, to serve as warning to future generations. Instead of looking with contempt upon mankind that betrayed them, the victims dreamed of redeeming it with their own charred souls. Instead of despairing of man and his possible salvation, they put their faith in him. Defying all logic, all reason, they opted for humanity and chose to try, by means of their testimony, to save it from indifference that might result in the ultimate catastrophe, the nuclear one.

Third, we must remember for our own sake, for the sake of our own humanity. Indifference to the victims would result, inevitably, in indifference to ourselves, an indifference that would ultimately no longer be sin but, in the words of our Commissioner Bayard Rustin, "a terrifying curse" and its own punishment.

The most vital lesson to be drawn from the Holocaust era is that Auschwitz was possible because the enemy of the Jewish people and of mankind—and it is always the same enemy—succeeded in dividing, in separating, in splitting human society, nation against nation, Christian against Jew, young against old. And not enough people cared. In Germany and other occupied countries, most spectators chose not to interfere with the killers; in other lands, too, many persons chose to remain neutral. As a result, the killers killed, the victims died, and the world remained world.

Still, the killers could not be sure. In the beginning they made one move and waited. Only when there was no reaction did they make another move and still another. From racial laws to medieval decrees, from illegal expulsions to the establishment of ghettos and then to the invention of death-camps, the killers carried out their plans only when they realized that the outside world simply did not care about the Jewish victims. Soon after, they decided they could do the same thing, with equal impunity, to other peoples as well. As always, they began with Jews. As always, they did not stop with Jews alone.

Granted that we must remember, Mr. President, the next question your Commission had to examine was whom are we to remember? It is vital that the American people come to understand the distinctive reality of the Holocaust: millions of innocent civilians were tragically killed by the Nazis. They must be remembered. However, there exists a moral imperative for special emphasis on the six million Jews. While not all victims were Jews, *all* Jews were victims, destined for annihilation solely because they were born Jewish. They were doomed not because of something they had done or proclaimed or acquired but because of who they were: sons and daughters of the Jewish people. As such they were sentenced to death collectively and individually as part of an official and "legal" plan unprecedented in the annals of history.

During our journey to Eastern Europe—a full description of which is attached (Appendix B)—the Commission observed that while Jews are sometimes mentioned on public monuments in Poland, they were not referred to in Russia at all. In Kiev's Babi Yar, for instance, where nearly 80,000 Jews were murdered in September 1941, the word Jew is totally absent from the memorial inscriptions.

Our Commission believes that because they were the principal target of Hitler's Final Solution, we must remember the six million Jews and, through them and beyond them, but never without them, rescue from oblivion all the men, women and children, Jewish and non-Jewish, who perished in those years in the forests and camps of the kingdom of night.

The universality of the Holocaust lies in its uniqueness: the Event is essentially Jewish, yet its interpretation is universal. It involved even distant nations and persons who lived far away from Birkenau's flames or who were born afterward.

Our own country was also involved, Mr. President. The valiant American nation fought Hitler and Fascism and paid for its bravery and idealism with the lives of hundreds and thousands of its sons; their sacrifices shall not be forgotten. And yet, and yet, away from the battlefield, the judgment of history will be harsh. Sadly but realistically, our great government was not without blemish. One cannot but wonder what might have happened had the then American President and his advisors demonstrated concern and compassion by appointing in 1942 or 1943 a President's Commission to prevent the Holocaust. How many victims, Jews and non-Jews, could have been saved had we changed our immigration laws, opened our gates more widely, protested more forcefully. We did not. Why not? This aspect of the Event must and will be explored thoroughly and honestly within the framework of the Commission's work. The decision to face the issue constitutes an act of moral courage worthy of our nation.

The question of how to remember makes up the bulk of the Commission's report. Memorial, museum, education, research, commemoration, action to prevent a recurrence: these are our areas of concern. I hope that these recommendations will be acceptable to you, Mr. President, reflecting as they do the joint thinking of the members of the Commission and its advisors over a period of 7 months.

During that time, we held meetings and hearings and studied known and hitherto undisclosed material. Our hope was to reach a consensus among our diverse membership, which includes academicians and civic leaders, Christians and Jews, native Americans and survivors from the deathcamps who found a welcome and a refuge here and who now, as American citizens, enjoy the privileges of our democracy.

Special attention was paid to the opinions, views, and feelings of the survivors, men and women who know the problems from the inside and who ask for nothing more than the opportunity to show their gratitude. "Our adopted country was kind to us," says Commissioner Sigmund Strochlitz, "and we wish to repay in some way by helping to build a strong and human society based on equality and justice for all." Their willingness to share their knowledge, their pain, their anguish, even their agony, is motivated solely by their conviction that their survival was for a purpose. A survivor sees himself or herself as a messenger and guardian of secrets entrusted by the dead. A survivor fears he or she may be the last to remember, the last to warn, the last to tell the tale that cannot be told, the tale that must be told in its totality, before it is too late, before the last witness leaves the stage and takes his awesome testimony back to the dead.

In the hope that you will enable this testimony to be brought to the attention of the American people, and the world, I submit the attached report to you, Mr. President.

Respectfully yours,
Elie Wiesel
Chairman

Source: President's Commission on the Holocaust, *Report to the President*, by Elie Wiesel, Chairman (Washington: Government Printing Office, 1979), pp. i–iv.

3 Ronald Reagan, Remarks on Signing the Bill Providing Restitution for the Wartime Internment of Japanese-American Civilians, 1988

The internment of Japanese Americans was quickly recognized as a grievous error, especially after the war ended. By the 1950s many high school and college textbooks condemned the internment camps as concentration camps. In the 1950s Hollywood movies such as Go For Broke *and* Bad Day at Black Rock *portrayed the* Nisei *who fought in the US Army as patriotic Americans who served their country bravely despite the injustices visited on them. By the 1960s, Japanese civil rights organizations started lobbying Congress both to apologize for the internment of Japanese Americans and to offer compensation. In the closing months of his presidency, Ronald Reagan signed legislation enjoying bipartisan support that issued a formal apology for the injustices against Japanese Americans during the war, and provided limited compensation to living survivors of the internment camps.*

August 10, 1988

The Members of Congress and distinguished guests, my fellow Americans, we gather here today to right a grave wrong. More than 40 years ago, shortly after the bombing of Pearl Harbor, 120,000 persons of Japanese ancestry living in the United States were forcibly removed from their homes and placed in makeshift internment camps. This action was taken without trial, without jury. It was based solely on race, for these 120,000 were Americans of Japanese descent.

Yes, the Nation was then at war, struggling for its survival, and it's not for us today to pass judgment upon those who may have made mistakes while engaged in that great struggle. Yet we must recognize that the internment of Japanese-Americans was just that: a mistake. For throughout the war, Japanese-Americans in the tens of thousands remained utterly loyal to the United States. Indeed, scores of Japanese-Americans volunteered for our Armed Forces, many stepping forward in the internment camps themselves. The 442d Regimental Combat Team, made up entirely of Japanese-Americans, served with immense distinction to defend this nation, their nation. Yet back at home, the soldiers' families were being denied the very freedom for which so many of the soldiers themselves were laying down their lives.

Congressman Norman Mineta, with us today, was 10 years old when his family was interned. In the Congressman's words: "My own family was sent first to Santa Anita Racetrack. We showered in the horse paddocks. Some families lived in converted stables, others in hastily thrown together barracks. We were then moved to Heart Mountain, Wyoming, where our entire family lived in one small room of a rude tar paper barrack." Like so many tens of thousands of others, the members of the Mineta family lived in those conditions not for a matter of weeks or months but for 3 long years.

The legislation that I am about to sign provides for a restitution payment to each of the 60,000 surviving Japanese-Americans of the 120,000 who were relocated or detained. Yet no payment can make up for those lost years. So, what is most important in this bill has less to do with property than with honor. For here we admit a wrong; here we reaffirm our commitment as a nation to equal justice under the law.

I'd like to note that the bill I'm about to sign also provides funds for members of the Aleut community who were evacuated from the Aleutian and Pribilof Islands after a Japanese attack in 1942. This action was taken for the Aleuts' own protection, but property was lost or damaged that has never been replaced.

And now in closing, I wonder whether you'd permit me one personal reminiscence, one prompted by an old newspaper report sent to me by Rose Ochi, a former internee. The clipping comes from the *Pacific Citizen* and is dated December 1945.

"Arriving by plane from Washington," the article begins, "General Joseph W. Stilwell pinned the Distinguished Service Cross on Mary Masuda in a simple ceremony on the porch of her small frame shack near Talbert, Orange County. She was one of the first Americans of Japanese ancestry to return from relocation centers to California's farmlands." "Vinegar Joe" Stilwell was there that day to honor Kazuo Masuda, Mary's brother. You see, while Mary and her parents were in an internment camp, Kazuo served as staff sergeant to the 442d Regimental Combat Team. In one action, Kazuo ordered his men back and advanced through heavy fire, hauling a mortar. For 12 hours, he engaged in a singlehanded barrage of Nazi positions. Several weeks later at Cassino, Kazuo staged another lone advance. This time it cost him his life.

The newspaper clipping notes that her two surviving brothers were with Mary and her parents on the little porch that morning. These two brothers, like the heroic Kazuo, had served in the United States Army. After General Stilwell made the award, the motion picture actress Louise Allbritton, a Texas girl, told how a Texas battalion had been saved by the 442d. Other show business personalities paid tribute — Robert Young, Will Rogers, Jr.

And one young actor said: "Blood that has soaked into the sands of a beach is all of one color. America stands unique in the world: the only country not founded on race but on a way, an ideal. Not in spite of but because of our polyglot background, we have had all the strength in the world. That is the American way." The name of that young actor — I hope I pronounce this right — was Ronald Reagan. And, yes, the ideal of liberty and justice for all — that is still the American way.

Thank you, and God bless you. And now let me sign H.R. 442, so fittingly named in honor of the 442d.

Thank you all again, and God bless you all. I think this is a fine day.

Source: Remarks on Signing the Bill Providing Restitution for the Wartime Internment of Japanese-American Civilians, August 10, 1988, *The Public Papers of President Ronald W. Reagan*. Ronald Reagan Presidential Library, http://www.reagan.utexas.edu/archives/speeches/1988/081088d.htm.

4 Tom Brokaw, Remarks at the Dedication of the National World War II Memorial, 2004

The World War II generation dominated American society for nearly 50 years after the end of the war in 1945. Every president elected after 1952 until the election of William Jefferson Clinton in 1992 had served in uniform during World War II. Dwight D. Eisenhower and Ronald Reagan had served in the Army and John F. Kennedy, Lyndon B. Johnson, Richard Nixon, Gerald R. Ford, and George Bush in the Navy. Jimmy Carter attended the US Naval Academy during World War II. In many ways, there were two "greatest generations" as most of the senior military leadership – Eisenhower, Marshall, King – were veterans of World War I. As the World War II generation entered their sixties and seventies in the 1980s and 1990s, they became increasingly interested in recalling their war-time experiences and sharing them with family and wider audiences through oral histories and memoirs. They also sparked an interest in building a national World War II memorial in Washington, DC, which would be dedicated in 2004. Tom Brokaw, a television journalist, coined the term "greatest generation" and used it as the title for his book of interviews with members of the World War II generation, published in 1998.

It goes without saying that this for me is a special privilege here today, because we gather to pay tribute to sacrifice and valor, to common cause and compassion, to triumph and determination. It has taken too long to erect this monument to symbolize the gratitude of our nation now and forever more to those of you who answered the call at home and abroad in what General Kelley rightly called the greatest war the world has ever known. A war in which more than 50 million people perished in their homes and on the battlefields a long way from home; in infernos at sea and beneath the sea and planes falling from the sky; in gas ovens and in slave labor camps. A war for all of its cruelties and terrible cost was a just war and a great victory that will be remembered for as long as history is recorded.

So it is fitting that we gather today around this handsome and evocative monument to such a noble undertaking. But no monument, however well positioned or polished, can take the place of the enduring legacy of all of you, the people that we honor here today. Your lives and how you lived them, the country you defended and loved and cared for the rest of your days, that is the undeniable legacy of you, the men and women I call "The Greatest Generation." Now my declaration that this is the greatest generation has occasionally been challenged even by members of that generation. My short answer is, that's my story and I'm sticking to it.

My longer answer, however, can be found in the trials and triumphs of your generation. At an early age this generation learned the harsh reality of deprivation and common cause during the great depression. They quit school not to indulge their selfish interest but to put food on the family table or shoes on their brothers and sisters. They just didn't double date, they went six and eight to a car to a dance or a movie where admission was maybe a dime. They learned to live without more than with. And as their children learned later, they never took a dollar for granted, or spent one without thinking about it first.

Veterans here today will tell you that the first thing they noticed about basic training was breakfast. You could eat all that you wanted. Many got their first new pair of boots or trousers in basic training after a young life of hand-me-downs. Many will also tell you that before war came to America at Pearl Harbor they were opposed to this country getting involved. But when the Japanese attacked and the Germans declared war they converted overnight and transformed America into a mighty military machine and uniform and factories and laboratories and shipyards and coal mines and farm fields and shops and offices.

Men, women, young and old, everyone had a role. Farm boys who had never been in an airplane were soon flying new bombers with four engines. Surgical nurses were in mash units on front lines operating while they were being shelled. Teenagers were wearing sergeant stripes and fighting from North Africa to Rome. Guys from the city streets were in close quarter combat in dense jungles. Women were building ships and whatever were needed and driving trucks. Kids went without gum and new toys and in too many cases they went the rest of their lives without fathers they never knew.

In the halls of Congress and at the White House they bet the future of this country on the absolute necessity of unconditional victory while simultaneously creating new international, political, financial, and military institutions and alliances that protected and enhanced America's national interests through cooperation and common goals, through not just shared strength, but also a shared commitment to diplomacy.

And when victory was complete, this generation, all of you, returned to this country and married in record numbers and went to college in record numbers thanks to the G.I. Bill. You gave us new industries and new art, new science, and unparalleled prosperity. But you also understood the real meaning of victory. You did not take revenge. Instead, you embarked on your next mission. Unprecedented for military victors, you rebuilt the shattered countries and confidence of your enemies.

Wherever you settled, you brought with them a discipline and maturity beyond your years, shaped by the hardships of depression, the training and the horrors and the deprivations of war. Those of you who returned with unshakable nightmares of war were held through long nights by your uncomplaining wives, and when daybreak came you went off together to resume your lives without whining or whimpering.

You were conditioned to serve so you became members of the school board or elders in your church, you ran for mayor and governor and Congress, the Senate and the White House. You were the join-up generation. You had given so much, but you didn't hesitate to give more. Because too many of your friends had died defending the way of life and system of government that is renewed only by good people willing to do the right thing. Some of you became rich, famous and powerful. But the tell-tale strength of this generation came from the ordinary men and women who awoke every morning to tend to the needs of their families, their communities, their nation, and mankind without expectation of recognition or reward. Not every member had a common point of view. There were ferocious political battles by day, and one shared concern by night fall, what is best for the country?

On some issues it took a little longer than others. While this was a great generation, it was not perfect. When the men came home, it took them a while to fully appreciate the right of women to take their place at their side whatever the endeavor. And despite the patriotism and the courage of black Americans and Hispanic-Americans, Japanese-Americans, Native Americans and other people of color during the war, it took too long, much too long, to legally and morally confront the cancer of racism.

When America was divided by another war and a cultural upheaval, "The Greatest Generation" was bewildered and divided, as well. It didn't give up on the generation that came after, their kids. Even though you wanted them to cut their hair, to get married before they lived together, and for God's sake turn down the music. Moreover, as the men and women of "The Greatest Generation" know not everyone in their own generation was up to the standard. There were the slackers and the cowards; the profiteers and the blowhards; the bullies and the boneheads. But they've been forgotten now. They have been lost in the pettiness of their own behavior, overwhelmed by the sweeping and indisputable achievement of the authentic members of your generation, "The Greatest Generation."

On a personal note, I want to thank all of you for the privilege of sharing your stories and your lives. I am humbled by our relationship. Those of us in succeeding generations are deeply indebted to you for first giving so much of your youth, your families and your friends to war, and then so much of the rest of your days to your country, and to the world. As I know personally, so many of you have been reluctant to talk about those difficult days because the painful memories have not faded. And because, as so many of you have said, you were the lucky ones. You came back. You survived. So many of your friends did not.

So you have felt an enduring obligation, a duty to them. To live your life in a way that honors them. Your lives have led the way in war and peace. And now it falls to the succeeding generations, to the rest of us to honor your lives, the greatest legacy of "the Greatest Generation," not with words or memorials or ceremonies or tributes. We are honored and obligated to honor you with our lives by fulfilling our duty, the duty to carry on your noble mission. I salute each and every one of you. Thank you all very much.

It's now my pleasure to introduce a man who embodied the best of the greatest generation in his portrayal of Captain John Miller, Charlie Company, Fifth Rangers in *Saving Private Ryan* with his friend and collaborator, Steven Spielberg. He also gave the nation a *Band of Brothers*, that memorable account of heroism, loyalty and humility in combat. And when the need was greatest for this memorial, this remarkable American answered the call without hesitation. He is a movie star. But as I have come to know from personal experience, he is first a husband, a father, and a citizen. Ladies and gentlemen, the youngest member of "The Greatest Generation," the school-teacher from Pennsylvania, Ranger Captain John Miller, my friend Tom Hanks.

Source: American Battle Monuments Commission, Washington, DC. Text available online at http://www.wwiimemorial.com/.

5   Geoffrey Wheatcroft, "Munich Shouldn't be Such a Dirty Word," *Washington Post*, 2008

In the aftermath of World War II, many argued one of the great lessons of this conflict was the failure of the West to stand up to Hitler in 1938 and instead sign the Munich Pact, ceding him control of Czechoslovakia's Sudetenland. During the Cold War many insisted that this lesson should be applied in dealing with the Soviet Union. Even after the Cold War, the lessons of Munich continued to be evoked in urging courses of action in Yugoslavia, Iraq, Afghanistan, and Darfur. In a column written for the Washington Post, *Geoffrey Wheatcroft, an English author, argued care should be taken in heeding what he considered the more ambiguous lessons of Munich.*

Seventy years ago this month, British Prime Minister Neville Chamberlain flew to Germany to meet Adolf Hitler once, twice and then a third time. On Sept. 30, 1938, they agreed that the German-speaking "Sudetenland" of Czechoslovakia should be ceded to Germany. Ever since, the name of this Munich agreement has been used as the ultimate political curse.

In truth, the story of the agreement is far from what is usually supposed. Over and again, "Munich" has been wilfully misunderstood and misinterpreted, with repeatedly disastrous consequences.

The Georgian crisis has just brought more cries of "appeasement" and "Munich." One writer in the Times of London described French President Nicolas Sarkozy as coming back from Moscow "waving a piece of paper and acclaiming peace in our time," the ill-fated words Chamberlain used on his return to London. Washington Post columnist Robert Kagan compared the Russian attack on Georgia to the 1938 "Sudeten Crisis that led to Nazi Germany's invasion of Czechoslovakia." These are only the latest in a long line of mischievous claims that any compromise is "another Munich" — and they run alongside a line of sorry military adventures for more than 50 years conditioned by the fear of emulating Chamberlain.

When Egyptian President Gamal Abdel Nasser seized the Suez Canal in 1956, one London politician after another recalled the 1930s. "It is exactly the same that we encountered from Mussolini and Hitler in those years before the war," said Labor Party leader Hugh Gaitskell. Prime Minister Anthony Eden, who had resigned as foreign secretary in 1938 to protest appeasement even before Munich, was driven by the dread of being seen as another Chamberlain. Eden mounted a foolish military expedition that turned into a national humiliation and ended his career.

Although the Suez plot was thwarted by President Dwight D. Eisenhower (who asked Eden, "Anthony, have you gone out of your mind?"), not all Americans agreed with Ike. The Senate majority leader told him he should let the British know that "they have our moral support to go in." Ten years later, that senator — Lyndon B. Johnson, by now the president — learned the hard way that going in could be easier than getting out, and became another victim of the "Munich complex."

One of his top military advisers was Gen. Curtis LeMay, who had angrily told President John F. Kennedy to his face that refusing to take military action against Cuba during the October 1962 missile crisis was "almost as bad as the appeasement at Munich." Still spooked by the shadow of Munich, LBJ would escalate the Indochina war to show that he "wasn't any Chamberlain umbrella man."

Nor did President Bill Clinton want to be another Chamberlain. He bombed Serbia in 1999 and mused, "What if someone had listened to Winston Churchill and stood up to Adolf Hitler earlier?"

And of course, the present administration has endlessly exploited the rhetoric of Munich. Former defense secretary Donald H. Rumsfeld compared opponents of the Iraq war with the earlier appeasers, and last May, President Bush derided the idea of negotiating with terrorists: "We have heard this foolish delusion before. As Nazi tanks crossed into Poland in 1939, an American senator declared: 'Lord, if I could only have talked to Hitler, all this might have been avoided.'" So Saddam Hussein was another Hitler, Bush is another Churchill (at any rate, he keeps a bust of Churchill in the White House), and there must be no more Munichs. We see the outcome today.

Quite apart from their unhappy consequences, all these invocations of Munich begin by rewriting history. Chamberlain was a democratic leader who knew that most of his people understandably did not want to go to war in 1938, only 20 years after another terrible war in which about three-quarters of a million British men had been killed.

Besides which, Chamberlain was far from alone in thinking that he was addressing a real grievance. The one accurate thing about Kagan's quaint comparison is that the residents of the breakaway Georgian region of South Ossetia no more want to be ruled by Georgia today than the Sudeten Germans wanted to be ruled by the Czechs 70 years ago.

While it's lamentably true that German resentment at "the slave treaty of Versailles" following World War I helped bring Hitler to power, there is another inconvenient truth: Between the wars, British and American liberals almost universally believed that the post-1918 settlement had been unjust. H.N. Brailsford, the leading leftist English commentator on foreign affairs, had written in 1920 that, of all the Versailles treaty's redrawing of borders, "the worst offence was the subjection of over three million Germans to Czech rule." Experience seemed to show that nationalism was the great force of the age and that it needed to be assuaged — or appeased, a word first used, it should be remembered, by those who advocated doing so.

To be sure, Churchill denounced the Munich agreement in a resonant speech: "This is only the first sip, the first bitter foretaste of a bitter cup which will be proffered to us year by year unless by a supreme recovery of moral health and martial vigour, we arise again and take our stand for freedom as in olden time." But he was speaking as someone untroubled by any sympathy for national self-determination.

As the blogger Andrew Sullivan has said, every Republican nowadays wants to be Churchill. But they should look at his record more closely. A few years earlier, Churchill had broken with the Conservatives (and all enlightened opinion) over his opposition to any form of self-government for India: He had no time for Indians (or later Egyptians) taking their own "stand for freedom." Churchill was a realpolitiker who believed in imperialism and spheres of influence — the very things that Bush and the neoconservatives now profess to abhor.

And Americans most of all should pause before invoking Munich. After 1918, the United States had withdrawn from the world, with Congress slamming the door on immigrants (even desperate Jews fleeing Nazi Europe) and refusing to join the new League of Nations (a fact of which Bush seems unaware whenever he refers scornfully to the League). In 1932, when Franklin D. Roosevelt was elected president, the Democrats were at least as isolationist as the Republicans, and as late as the fall of 1940, FDR was still campaigning for a third term on the unambiguous promise to keep the United States out of any foreign wars. That helps explain why he sent a telegram reading "Good man" to Chamberlain when his British counterpart returned from meeting Hitler, and subsequently told the U.S. ambassador in Rome, "I am not a bit upset over the final result."

No American of any significance advocated military resistance to Hitler in the 1930s, and no such intervention would have been possible anyway. In September 1939, the U.S. Army was smaller than the Belgian army, and as the first grave setbacks in North Africa in 1942–43 would show, it was scarcely ready for serious fighting even after the United States entered the fray.

Some other words of Churchill's are too rarely quoted. They are from one of the finest and most moving, though least known, speeches he ever gave, paying tribute to Chamberlain after his death from cancer in November 1940. It had been Chamberlain's fate "to be disappointed in his hopes, and to be deceived and cheated by a wicked man," Churchill said. "But what were these hopes in which he was disappointed? ... They were surely among the most noble and benevolent instincts of the human heart — the love of peace, the toil for peace, the strife for peace, the pursuit of peace, even at great peril, and certainly to the utter disdain of popularity or clamour."

In his bow to Chamberlain's memory, Churchill showed a magnanimity and wisdom that others have lacked. "Long and hard, hazardous years lie before us," he continued, "but at least we entered upon them united and with clean hearts."

Never once did Churchill advocate preemptive war, and he always recognized that democracies should use arms only as a last resort. Maybe the presidential candidates should be asked whether the United States entered the Iraq war "united and with clean hearts." That could be the real "lesson of Munich."

Source: *Washington Post*, September 28, 2008.

Study Questions

1   What are living memorials? What are their virtues? Why did it take so long to build a national World War II memorial in Washington, DC?
2   What were the lessons of history that were important to remember in the eyes of Elie Wiesel?
3   Why did Ronald Reagan sign legislation offering compensation to Japanese Americans interned by the United States? What are the reasons he gave for compensating Japanese Americans?
4   What are the unique virtues of World War II in the eyes of Tom Brokaw? Do you think he has overstated this generation's virtues? In what possible ways?
5   Do you agree with the argument put forth by Geoffrey Wheatcroft that appeasement and the quest for peace should not always be dismissed as a foreign policy option?

Bibliography

Introduction

Adams, Michael C. C. *The Best War Ever: Americans and World War II*. Baltimore: Johns Hopkins University Press, 1994.

Kennedy, David M. *Freedom from Fear: The American People in Depression and War, 1929–1945*. New York: Oxford University Press, 1999.

Kindsvatter, Peter S. *American Soldiers: Ground Combat in the World Wars, Korea and Vietnam*. Lawrence: University Press of Kansas, 2003.

Linderman, Gerald F. *The World Within War: America's Combat Experience in World War II*. New York: Free Press, 1997.

Murray, Williamson and Allan R. Millett. *A War to Be Won: Fighting the Second World War*. Cambridge, MA: Harvard University Press, 2000.

O'Neill, William L. *A Democracy at War: America's Fight at Home and Abroad in World War II*. New York: Free Press, 1993.

Overy, Richard. *Why the Allies Won*. New York: Norton, 1995.

Piehler, G. Kurt and Sidney Pash. *The United States and the Second World War: New Perspectives on Diplomacy, War, and the Home Front*. New York: Fordham University Press, 2010.

Polenberg, Richard. *War and Society: The United States, 1941–1945*. Philadelphia: Lippincott, 1972.

Roeder, George H., Jr. *The Censored War: American Visual Experience During World War II*. New Haven: Yale University Press, 1993.

The United States in World War II: A Documentary Reader, First Edition.
Edited by G. Kurt Piehler. Editorial material and organization © 2013 Blackwell Publishing Ltd.
Published 2013 by Blackwell Publishing Ltd.

Terkel, Studs. *"The Good War": An Oral History of World War Two*. New York: Pantheon, 1984.

Weinberg, Gerhard L. *A World at Arms: A Global History of World War II*. New York: Cambridge University Press, 1994.

Chapter 1 The Controversial War

Birdwell, Michael E. *Celluloid Soldiers: Warner Bros.'s Campaign Against Nazism*. New York: New York University Press, 1999.

Clifford, J. Garry. *The First Peacetime Draft*. Lawrence: University Press of Kansas, 1986.

Dallek, Robert. *Franklin D. Roosevelt and American Foreign Policy*. New York: Oxford University Press, 1979.

Doenecke, Justus. *Storm on the Horizon: The Challenge to American Intervention, 1939–1941*. Lanham, MD: Rowman and Littlefield, 2000.

Heinrichs, Waldo. *Threshold of War: Franklin D. Roosevelt and American Entry Into World War II*. New York: Oxford University Press, 1988.

Marks, Frederick W. III. *Wind Over Sand: The Diplomacy of Franklin D. Roosevelt*. Athens: University of Georgia Press, 1988.

Chapter 2 Pearl Harbor and Meeting the Fight

Borg, Dorothy and Shumpei Okamoto (eds.). *Pearl Harbor as History*. New York: Columbia University Press, 1973.

Larrabee, Eric. *Commander in Chief: Franklin Delano Roosevelt, His Lieutenants, and Their War*. New York: Harper and Row, 1987.

Prange, Gordon. *At Dawn We Slept: The Untold Story of Pearl Harbor*. New York: Penguin, 1982.

Stoler, Mark A. *Allies and Adversaries: The Joint Chiefs of Staff, the Grand Alliance, and U.S. Strategy in World War II*. Chapel Hill: University of North Carolina Press, 2000.

Utley, Jonathan. *Going to War With Japan, 1937–1941*. New York: Fordham University Press; reprint ed., 2005.

Wohlstetter, Roberta. *Pearl Harbor, Warning and Decision*. Stanford, CA: Stanford University Press, 1962.

Chapter 3 The Pacific War

Bailey, Beth and David Farber. *The First Strange Place: The Alchemy of Race and Sex in World War II Hawaii*. New York: Free Press, 1992.

Bartholomew-Feis, Dixee R. *The OSS and Ho Chi Minh: Unexpected Allies in the War Against Japan*. Lawrence: University Press of Kansas, 2006.

Bradley, James, with Ron Powers. *Flags of our Fathers*. New York: Bantam Books, 2000.

Cameron, Craig M. *American Samurai: Myth, Imagination, and the Conduct of Battle in the First Marine Division, 1941–1951*. Cambridge: Cambridge University Press, 1994.

Dower, John W. *War Without Mercy: Race and Power in the Pacific War*. New York: Pantheon Books, 1986.

Gailey, Harry. *Bougainville, 1943–1945: The Forgotten Campaign*. Lexington: University Press of Kentucky, 1991.

Kaminski, Theresa. *Citizen of Empire*. Knoxville: University of Tennessee Press, 2011.

Spector, Ronald. *The Eagle Against the Sun: The American War with Japan*. New York: Random House/Vintage, 1985.

Werrell, Kenneth P. *Blankets of Fire: U.S. Bombers Over Japan During World War II*. Washington, DC: Smithsonian Institution Press, 1996.

Chapter 4   The War in North Africa and Europe

Ambrose, Stephen E. *Citizen Soldiers: The U.S. Army from the Normandy Beaches to the Bulge to the Surrender of Germany*. New York: Simon and Schuster, 1997.

Ambrose, Stephen E. *D-Day, June 6, 1944: The Climatic Battle of World War II*. New York: Simon and Schuster, 1994.

Atkinson, Rick. *An Army at Dawn: The War in North Africa, 1942–1943*. New York: Holt, 2002.

Brown, John Sloan. *Draftee Division*. Lexington: University Press of Kentucky, 1986.

Doubler, Michael D. *Closing with the Enemy: How GIs Fought the War in Europe, 1944–1945*. Lawrence: University Press of Kansas, 1994.

Mansoor, Peter. *The GI Offensive in Europe: The Triumph of American Infantry Divisions, 1941–1945*. Lawrence: University Press of Kansas, 1999.

Moore, Brenda. *To Serve My Country, To Serve My Race: The Story of the Only African-American WACs Stationed Overseas During World War II*. New York: New York University Press, 1997.

Schrijvers, Peter. *The Crash of Ruin: American Combat Soldiers in Europe during World War II*. New York: New York University Press, 1998.

Tomblin, Barbara. *With Utmost Spirit: Allied Naval Operations in the Mediterranean, 1942–45*. Lexington: University Press of Kentucky, 2004.

Weigley, Russell F. *Eisenhower's Lieutenants: The Campaign in France and Germany, 1944–1945*. Bloomington: Indiana University Press, 1981.

Wells, Mark K. *Courage and Air Warfare: The Allied Aircrew Experience in the Second World War*. London: Frank Cass, 1995.

Chapter 5 Mobilizing the Home Front

Blum, John Morton. *V Was for Victory: Politics and American Culture During World War II*. San Francisco: Harcourt Brace, 1986.

Campbell, D'Ann. *Women at War with America: Private Lives in a Patriotic Era*. Cambridge, MA: Harvard University Press, 1984.

Cohen, Lizabeth. *A Consumers' Republic: The Politics of Mass Consumption in Postwar America*. New York: Knopf, 2003.

Erenberg, Lewis A. and Susan E. Hirsch. *The War in American Culture: Society and Consciousness During World War II*. Chicago: University of Chicago Press, 1996.

Hegarty, Marilyn. *Victory Girls, Khaki-Wackies, and Patriotutes: The Regulation of Female Sexuality during World War II*. New York: New York University Press, 2007.

Sittser, Gerald L. *A Cautious Patriotism: The American Churches and the Second World War*. Chapel Hill: University of North Carolina Press, 1997.

Tuttle, William M. *"Daddy's Gone to War": The Second World War in the Lives of America's Children*. New York: Oxford University Press, 1993.

Winchell, Meghan K. *Good Girls, Good Food, Good Fun: The Story of USO Hostesses During World War II*. Chapel Hill: University of North Carolina Press, 2008.

Chapter 6 The Arsenal of Democracy

Fraser, Steve. *Labor Will Rule: Sidney Hillman and the Rise of American Labor*. New York: Free Press, 1991.

Gluck, Sherna *Berger*. Rosie the Riveter Revisited. New York: Meridian, 1987.

Johnson, Charles W. and Charles O. Jackson. *City Behind a Fence*. Knoxville: University of Tennessee Press, 1981.

Koistinen, Paul. *Arsenal of World War II: The Political Economy of American Warfare, 1940–1945*. Lawrence: University Press of Kansas, 2004.

Lichtenstein, Nelson. *Labor's War at Home: The CIO in World War II*. New York: Cambridge University Press, 1982.

Milkman, Ruth. *Gender at Work: The Dynamics of Job Segregation During World War II*. Urbana: University of Illinois, 1987.

Ohly, John H. *Industrialists in Olive Drab: The Emergency Operation of Private Industries During World War II*. Washington, DC: Government Printing Office, 1999.

Chapter 7 The Quest for Freedom

Allen, Robert. *The Port Chicago Mutiny*. New York: Amistad, 1993.

Bernstein, Alison R. *American Indians and World War II: Toward a New Era in Indian Affairs*. Norman: University of Oklahoma Press, 1991.

Bruscino, Thomas. *A Nation Forged in War: How World War II Taught Americans to Get Along*. Knoxville: University of Tennessee Press, 2010.
Daniels, Roger. *Prisoners Without Trial: Japanese Americans in World War II*. New York: Hill and Wang, 2004.
Kryder, Daniel. *Divided Arsenal: Race and the American State during World War II*. New York: Cambridge University Press, 2000.
Meyer, Leisa D. *Creating GI Jane: Sexuality and Power in the Women's Army Corps during World War II*. New York: Columbia University Press, 1996.
Moore, Deborah Dash. *GI Jews: How World War II Changed a Generation*. Cambridge, MA: Harvard University Press, 2004.
Nalty, Bernard C. *Strength for the Fight: A History of Black Americans in the Military*. New York: Free Press, 1986.
Peters, Shawn Francis. *Judging Jehovah's Witnesses: Religious Persecution and the Dawn of the Rights Revolution*. Lawrence: University Press of Kansas, 2000.
Takaki, Ronald T. *Double Victory: A Multicultural History of America in World War II*. Boston: Little, Brown, 2000.

Chapter 8 The American Response to the Holocaust

Breitman, Richard and Allen Kraut. *American Refugee Policy and European Jewry, 1933–45*. Bloomington: Indiana University Press, 1987.
Feingold, Henry L. *Bearing Witness: How America and Its Jews Responded to the Holocaust*. New York: Syracuse University Press, 1995.
Grobman, Alex. *Rekindling the Flame: American Jewish Chaplains and the Survivors of European Jewry, 1944–1948*. Detroit: Wayne State University Press, 1993.
Ross, Robert W. *So It Was True: The American Protestant Press and the Nazi Persecution of the Jews*. Minneapolis: University of Minnesota Press, 1980.
Rubinstein, William D. *The Myth of Rescue: Why the Democracies Could Not Have Saved More Jews from the Nazis*. London: Routledge, 1997.
Woolner, David B. and Richard G. Kurial (eds.). *FDR, the Vatican, and the Roman Catholic Church in America, 1933–1945*. New York: Palgrave Macmillan, 2003.
Wyman, David S. *The Abandonment of the Jews: America and the Holocaust, 1941–1945*. New York: Pantheon Books, 1984.

Chapter 9 From Strategic Bombing to the Atomic Bomb

Alperovitz, Gar. *The Decision to Use the Atomic Bomb and the Architecture of an American Myth*. New York: Knopf, 1995.
Biddle, Tami Davis. *Rhetoric and Reality: The Evolution of British and American Ideas about Strategic Bombing, 1914–1945*. Princeton: Princeton University Press, 2002.
Chappell, John D. *Before the Bomb: How America Approached the End of the Pacific War*. Lexington: University Press of Kentucky, 1997.

Crane, Conrad. *Bombs, Cities, and Civilians: American Airpower Strategy in World War II*. Lawrence: University Press of Kansas, 1992.

Hogan, Michael J. (ed.). *Hiroshima in History and Memory*. Cambridge: Cambridge University Press, 1996.

Maddox, Robert James. *Weapons for Victory: The Hiroshima Decision Fifty Years Later*. Columbia: University of Missouri Press, 1995.

Sherry, Michael S. *The Rise of American Air Power: The Creation of Armageddon*. New Haven: Yale University Press, 1987.

Sherwin, Martin. *A World Destroyed: The Atomic Bomb and the Grand Alliance*. New York: Knopf, 1975.

Chapter 10 Visions of a Postwar World

Anderson, Carol. *Eyes Off the Prize: The United Nations and the African-American Struggle for Human Rights, 1944–55*. Cambridge: Cambridge University Press, 2003.

Bloxham, Donald. *Genocide on Trial: War Crimes Trials and the Formation of Holocaust History and Memory*. New York: Oxford University, 2001.

Harbutt, Fraser J. *Yalta 1945: Europe and America at the Crossroads*. Cambridge: Cambridge University Press, 2010.

Hoopes, Townsend and Douglas Brinkley. *FDR and the Creation of the U.N.* New Haven: Yale University Press, 1997.

Louis, William Roger. *Imperialism at Bay: The United States and the Decolonization of the British Empire, 1941–1945*. New York: Oxford University Press, 1978.

Maguire, Peter. *Law and War: An American Story*. New York: Columbia University Press, 2001.

Schild, Georg. *Bretton Woods and Dumbarton Oaks: American Economic and Political Postwar Planning in the Summer of 1944*. New York: Palgrave MacMillan, 1995.

Totani, Yuma. *The Tokyo War Crimes Trial: The Pursuit of Justice in the Wake of World War II*. Cambridge, MA: Harvard University Asia Center/Harvard University Press, 2008.

Weinberg, Gerhard L. *Visions of Victory: The Hopes of Eight World War II Leaders*. New York: Cambridge University Press, 2005.

Chapter 11 Legacies of War

Brooks, Jennifer E. *Defining the Peace: World War II Veterans, Race, and the Remaking of the Southern Political Tradition*. Chapel Hill: University of North Carolina Press, 2004.

Coyne, Kevin. *Marching Home: To War and Back with Men of One American Town*. New York: Penguin Books, 2003.

Gambone, Michael D. *The Greatest Generation Comes Home: The Veteran in American Society*. College Station: Texas A & M University Press, 2005.
Gerber, David (ed.). *Disabled Veterans in History*. Ann Arbor: University of Michigan Press, 2000.
Van Ells, Mark D. *To Hear Only Thunder Again: America's World War II Veterans Come Home*. Lanham, MD: Lexington Books, 2001.

Chapter 12 Commemoration and Memory

Bodnar, John. *The "Good" War in American Memory*. Baltimore: Johns Hopkins University Press, 2010.
Brinkley, Douglas. *The Boys of Pointe du Hoc: Ronald Reagan, D-Day and the U.S. Army 2nd Ranger Battalion*. New York: William Morrow, 2005.
Fussell, Paul. *Wartime: Understanding and Behavior in the Second World War*. New York: Oxford University Press, 1989.
Linenthal, Edward Tabor. *Sacred Ground: Americans and their Battlefields*. Urbana: University University of Illinois Press, 2003.
Novick, Peter. *The Holocaust in American Life*. Boston: Houghton Mifflin, 1999.
Piehler, G. Kurt. *Remembering War the American Way*. Washington, DC: Smithsonian Institution Press, 1995.
Rosenberg, Emily S. *A Date Which Will Live: Pearl Harbor in American Memory*. Durham, NC: Duke University Press, 2003.

Index

The United States in World War II: A Documentary Reader, First Edition.
Edited by G. Kurt Piehler. Editorial material and organization © 2013 Blackwell Publishing Ltd.
Published 2013 by Blackwell Publishing Ltd.